D0884452

JOURNEY
INWARD

JOURNEY INWARD

Jean Craighead George

E. P. DUTTON • NEW YORK

Grateful acknowledgment is made for permission to quote from "Fourth Meditation" copyright © 1958 by Theodore Roethke from The Collected Poems of Theodore Roethke. Reprinted by permission of Doubleday & Co.

Grateful acknowledgment is made for permission to quote from "Groping" appearing in Frequencies by R. S. Thomas. Reprinted with permission from Macmillan, London and Basingstoke.

For information contact:
E.P. Dutton Inc., 2 Park Avenue, New York, N.Y. 10016

Library of Congress Cataloging Number 82–71028
ISBN: 0-525-24108-6

Published simultaneously in Canada by
Clarke, Irwin & Company Limited, Toronto and Vancouver

Designed by Nancy Scarino

10   9   8   7   6   5   4   3   2   1

First Edition

To

Gretchen and Kathy and Sis

Good Friends

Moving away is only to the boundaries of the self.

Better to stay here, I said, leaving the horizons clear.

The best journey to make is inward.

R.S. THOMAS

Contents

JOURNEY
INWARD

1

A Tent
in the Wilderness

I dropped a last freshwater mussel into a bucket to feed Lotor, my pet raccoon, and turned from the stream that flowed tannic-black through the forest.

Lotor was the mother of two suckling kittens. All morning she had been harassing one kit unmercifully, dunking it in the water pan and carrying it around in circles, while she swung it violently by the scruff of the neck. I feared for the crying kit and, hoping to divert the mother from her strange behavior, had come to the stream to dig her favorite delicacy, freshwater mussels.

Swinging my load, I walked slowly in the June sunshine as I crossed the woodland meadow that bordered Mink Stream. At the edge of the raspberry patch that made a transition between the bright meadow grasses and the dim forest, I paused to listen to a male song sparrow. He was singing as if his heart would burst, throat feathers above the tan spotted breast plunking like piano keys.

I knew this bird well—in fact, I knew him by name. My husband, John, called him Able. He was among the first of more than three hundred birds that John would eventually band during a four-year study, as part of his work toward a Ph.D. in ecology at the University of Michigan. Since my father was an entomologist-naturalist and my mother had been an assistant entomologist, I came to the project with an enthusiasm of my own. What I did not know, as I put down my bucket and raised my binoculars to focus on the song sparrow, was the nature of the long odyssey I was beginning. For years I would be encountering wild birds and beasts, living with them, seeing myself in them, and all the while trying to understand what the experience meant to me.

The song sparrow came into focus. On his right foot glinted a numbered aluminum band from the Fish and Wildlife Service; on his left was a ring of blue plastic. These bands distinguished him from all other birds. He was a known entity.

We knew, for example, that Able was at least three years old. For two of those years he'd had the same mate, who was also banded. I had dubbed her Peggy. Each spring they would return to this same bit of woodland meadow and set up housekeeping. Able arrived first, and began to mark out his own invisible property lines from numerous "singing posts." Peggy arrived a few days later. They usually built two nests a season—sometimes more if one was destroyed by a predator—and averaged about three fledglings a year.

This year Peggy had not returned, and John presumed (though he could not be sure, since her bands had not been found and returned) that she had fallen prey to a hawk or a snake, or else collided with the side of a building during migration. So Able had taken another mate. John had caught her in his live trap, a rectangular, four-chambered box with doors that closed when a bird stepped on the treadle. He had banded her, holding her gently on her back, with her foot between his thumb and forefinger, and released her again. In early May she had disappeared, and now Able was with Peggy the Third.

Their nest in the raspberry thicket, a tidy structure of grass lined with rootlets and feathers, held four huddled, naked babies. I dared not walk over to look at them, since snakes and other predators had somehow learned that our trails led to birds' nests. Consequently John approached a study nest only when it was essential for data on egg-laying and hatching, and then he did so by devious leaps and circuitous bounds—foxlike behavior that had me laughing. Sometimes John was a clown in the cloak of a scientist.

Able, he taught me, had five different songs—an unusually large repertory even for a song sparrow. He began it with "chip, chip, chee,

2

yer, zig, zig, zig,'' and went on to variations on the same theme. Now, as I stood at the edge of the meadow, he bubbled from one song to the next and back to the first, over and over again. Such a burst told me that he was upset, but why? I looked around for answers. Was there another male on his property? That would be one reason for continuous song—a territorial battle. Or was he telling Peggy the Third to come out and hunt food for the nestlings? Some broody females needed prodding. After jotting down a note about Able's conspicuous behavior, I walked up the hill under the translucent leaves of the beech trees. The mayapples and trilliums that had flowered a month ago were bearing seed capsules whose green and brown matched the dead leaves on the forest floor. I wondered at the intelligence of brainless flowering plants, whose colors called in the bees to pollinate them and then camouflaged their fruits against fruit-eating creatures.

The open end of that thought found me at home—in a nine-by-nine-foot Army surplus tent pitched on the top of the highest knoll in an ancient beech-maple forest. Situated at the northern end of the Strang farm near Ypsilanti, Michigan, the knoll was near the center of a mile-square section, around which lay the tilled fields of several other farms. The land pattern formed by the forest and fields attracted just about every species of wildlife to be found in southern Michigan. This was one reason why we were camped at its center. The other reason was esthetic: the view down through huge gleaming beeches and swarthy-trunked maples to the meadow and stream. By praising it, John had gotten permission to camp here from its owner, Mrs. Cora Strang. He was an expert charmer.

We had been married while John was a Navy lieutenant assigned to duty on a destroyer escort, the S.S. *Mervine*. I was living at home and working as a reporter for the *Washington Post*. Although I had heard much about John—he'd been a roommate of my twin brothers, John and Frank, at the University of Michigan—I did not actually meet him until September 1943. I married him the following January.

"That young man has come to marry you," my ninety-year-old grandmother said the night he arrived at our home in Washington. Later, when he slipped his arms around me and pressed me to him, I knew she was right. I was ready to marry—all of me except for that spark in the far right-hand corner that makes each one of us different from everyone else. In that far corner, my own belief in myself as a writer still held out. My

3

solution would be to open up that corner and include John in it.

I moved to New York, where I took an apartment in Brooklyn Heights, so as to be near the Brooklyn Navy Yard, John's home port, and went to work as an artist for *Pageant* magazine and later as a reporter for Newspaper Enterprise Association. In the evenings and on weekends I sat down at the typewriter with some of John's notes obtained from interviews with Buck Queen, a dog trainer and fox hunter who lived down the road from my family's weekend cabin along the Potomac River in Maryland. When John was on leave he and I spent hours talking to Buck Queen about dogs and foxes. We finally obtained a young fox pup who denned in our fireplace and draped herself around my shoulders when I typed. John brought to the book his observations of birds and animals and occasionally tapped out a paragraph. The collaboration to me was a sorely needed bond between two people who were more or less strangers and were separated most of the time by the war. With the fox book finished and accepted by a publisher, we bought two little minks from a ranch and began the second of what would be six animal biographies.

It was while I was working on that first book that I heard about the Newbery Medal, which is awarded each year by the Association for Library Service to Children, part of the American Library Association, for the outstanding contribution to children's literature. It became my objective, and I thought about it a great deal. Meanwhile, though, John had taken a deep breath and announced that he had had enough of New York, that what he wanted to do was to go back to the University of Michigan and get a Ph.D. with the help of the G.I. Bill of Rights and a teaching fellowship. To this blunt masculine decision I gave my whole-hearted support. I liked a man who knew his own mind. But also, as I looked back from the Pulaski Skyway in New Jersey at the skyline of the city, I realized how sorry I was to be leaving behind the artists, writers, editors, theater directors and publishers who had come into my life and opened up so many possibilities. Though I wanted to tell John all this, I remained silent. I did not want him to think I was criticizing him, since that might mean losing his love. I somehow believed that a woman did not put her own needs above her husband's. Even though we had been married for more than two years, we had had only two months of living together, and I still thought like a bride. By the time we drove into Ann

Arbor, Michigan, I was already adjusting to the idea of life in a university town.

That autumn of 1946 we rented a small apartment in town and set up the tent in the woods the next spring. I now entered John's world with enthusiasm. I finished the mink book, John checked it out between his classes and his research. The following spring Lotor came into my life—a thumbellina of a creature, no more than three inches long, whom a farmer had found crying and alone in the loft of his barn. Her mother had been killed on the road. As I cradled her in my palm, I thought about her life in the treetops. "I'll have a whole new world to write about up there," I said, "where the limbs are avenues and the holes are apartments." I started a book about her that same afternoon—with John's blessing and his teachings. The natural history of the Strang woods, the book's stage, rolled out before me as I sat at my typewriter table.

I fed Lotor first with an eyedropper, then from a baby bottle, and watched her grow. From the day her eyes opened, she followed me everywhere: down steps, into the car, to the tent and up onto the seat beside me. Free to roam the forest, she spent most of the day at my heels—a living demonstration of how important the one who feeds and cares for a young mammal is. I was her mother.

On the more and more frequent occasions when she felt the need to explore, I was at her heels, rather than the other way round. Following her to the meadow and the stream, I learned how a raccoon pulls mussels ashore with its hands, not cracking them but leaving them out in the air to open. I learned how raccoons fish, by chasing minnows into shallow water and flipping them ashore; how they find grubs in logs with their sensitive fingers, and how they sleep draped in the crotch of a tree on hot summer days.

Now I was about to learn something else, which appeared to be some kind of maternal wisdom.

I picked up the bucket and walked toward the empty cider barrel where Lotor was resting with her kits. She heard my steps and came to greet me. I picked her up, smelling the fresh sweetness of her fur. Not caged, free to come and go, she was kept clean by the sunlight and forest air. She purred loudly and contentedly as I scratched behind her ears; for like all mammals, she responded to touch.

Lotor was a petite raccoon, her face well marked with an unusually black mask in which her eyes were two glints of light. Her small hands, furred to the claws on the back and bare on the palms, were constantly moving. One was in my pocket, the other under my collar, both searching like eyes; in a real sense, the hands of the raccoon can see.

At the end of February John had bred her to a pet raccoon that belonged to a high school boy. Sixty-three days later she gave birth to two kits in her cider-barrel den. The newborns had black skin and yellowish fur, and each weighed about two and a half ounces. I briefly saw them clinging to her mammae when I rolled Lotor on her side. After she turned her back and huddled over them, I did not get a look at them again until they were about a week old. She was more relaxed by then, propped like a teddy bear with a youngster on each arm. The whole family had purred in unison, their breathing a windy song.

A couple of days before, for reasons I could not fathom, Lotor had begun her harassment of the smaller of the two kits. Blaming this behavior on her captivity, I had gone off to the stream to collect a more natural food for her. Now, our greetings completed, I put her down and she cavorted affectionately about my feet. Then she rushed into the barrel and came out again with the smaller kit held by the scruff of the neck, once more running in circles with it in what appeared to be great distress. When I held out a mussel, she sniffed and returned the kit to the den. Coming out again, she first snatched a mussel and then discarded it on finding that the shell was tightly closed. Quickly she toppled the bucket, ran her hands over its contents, and came up with a mussel that was open. She lapped it out of its shell and felt for more. I put several on the ground and filled the bucket from the spring to keep the others alive.

Sensing a presence, I glanced up to see Cora Strang walking down the lane toward the tent, and called out a hello.

"I just took some bread out of the oven," she said. "I thought you might like a loaf."

"I sure would. I'll put on some tea and we'll cut it right now."

Sitting down in the rocking chair she had given me, Cora gazed contentedly about her while I pumped the Coleman gas stove, opened the bung on the big cider barrel in which we kept the water we hauled from the farmhouse, and filled the teakettle. "I don't know why you stay out here," she said. Her eyes moved from the ancient beech trees to the tent,

6

with its bedsprings and mattress, the sheepherder's wood stove, the long worktable that was simply a door on sawhorses, and the old dresser that was both kitchen table and food box.

In the stillness I could hear Able the song sparrow, singing and singing.

Cora studied the ravine and spring where we kept the butter and milk cool, then the hemlock grove where the outhouse stood. "I thought you might like to move into the west wing of the house," she persisted. "It stands empty since Lois married and Mr. Strang died."

"Oh, thank you," I answered, "but I'm very happy here. I like to camp. My father was a naturalist. He took my brothers and me camping almost every weekend when we were kids."

"But you'll lose this baby, too, if you stay out here in the woods." She firmed the bottom lip of her small, pursed mouth.

"No," I said, slowly touching my hard stomach. "This one's for keeps. I can tell." I glanced at Lotor. "For the first time I'm wondering what kind of mother I'll be. I never asked myself that when I was pregnant before."

Cora rocked, her wispy hair falling across her brown eyes and around her pouchy little cheeks. A graduate of Ypsilanti Normal School, Cora had taught school before marrying Olin Strang and taking up the work of a farm wife. After his death she had continued with the chores, preparing the meals, doing the laundry, raising chickens, gardening, canning and baking for her bachelor son.

I sliced the still warm bread and poured the tea.

Lotor, having devoured her feast, touched my shoe and sat down on my foot. A baby called from the darkness of the barrel. Her whiskers straightened, she turned, dove into the den and came out a moment later with the smaller kit in her mouth. Swinging it back and forth, she dunked it into the mussel bucket and held it under.

"She's trying to kill it!" I gasped. I snatched the baby from her and held it under my shirt, against my bare stomach, to warm and dry it. "Now, why would she do that?"

Cora Strang rocked forward. "Must be something wrong with the baby. Once I had a cat that ate its kitten. The kitten had three legs."

"How did she know it needed four legs? Animals can't count. And they don't know good from bad."

"That may be what the books say, but I've seen different. They know."

Holding up the kit, I turned it over in my hands, then took another look at its face.

"There *is* something odd about it," I said. "You're right. It's a little cockeyed. It's not perfect." The forehead of the little raccoon was steeply sloped, the eyes angled inward. Dropping to my knees, I reached into the barrel and brought out the other. She looked like a well-stuffed teddy bear, with big eyes set straight into her head.

I sat holding the rejected kit against me until Cora Strang had gone. I had already given it a name: Cross Eyes. Then I walked to the spring where we kept the milk, heated some of it, and began bottle-feeding it, wondering meanwhile what to do with the kit next.

John came home late in the afternoon. Wearing his old Navy gob hat, his binocs strung around his neck, his clipboard with field notes dangling from his belt, he was my image of a field naturalist—the information-gatherer who saw order in the forest. Six feet tall, handsome, graceful and strong, he swung up the lane, the light striking his Roman profile, and I jumped to my feet to greet him.

"Able's been singing and singing," I said.

"He's lost Peggy the Third." John wiped his binocs and put them into the case.

"Oh, that's terrible. What happened?"

"Must have been the black snake."

"I'll kill it. I really will. I know where it suns."

"You can't. The snake is part of the ecology. You can't interfere." John slipped his arm around me. "What've you got there?"

"The smallest of the kits." I explained what had happened.

"I'll be damned," John said.

"She wanted to drown it," I went on. "Nature's not perfect, the way I thought it was."

"Nature is always experimenting. Some of the experiments work and some don't. That's how evolution proceeds." John was giving one of his occasional lectures on evolution. I listened in silence as we walked to the tent, where I had a lamb stew simmering on the gasoline stove. Soon the coffee was perking rhythmically. A leaf left its twig in the canopy and

8

spiraled down to the dining table. Tent life at this hour was magical. The wind brought the scent of hay in from the fields, and the wood pewees that nested overhead began their pensive evening song. I sat down on a log stool beside John and stared with him into the twilight.

"Some day we'll remember these years at the tent as the most beautiful of our lives," he said, pulling his stump seat closer to mine.

"This I do know," I said, "we'll never have a more glorious dining room." Above me the beech leaves glowed in the backlight and the huge green branches of the maples bowed and pranced in the wind. A red-eyed vireo dodged through the maze of twigs and leaves without hitting one. Such a dining room. Such an incredible dining room.

As I washed the dishes the child within me stirred. I patted it, conscious of a twinge of fear as I thought of Cross Eyes, and of how much could go wrong with one little life. Shaking off the fear, I wondered what to do with the little raccoon. I recalled hearing John say how all living things tick along at their own rate of development, which moves on again after missing a beat. For example, a bird that does not hear its own species' song at a certain age does not sing. Was there a time for a mother raccoon to react to a deformity by instinctively trying to get rid of it? Having passed that moment, would she then accept the offspring? I would find out.

I took care of the little animal for a few days while Lotor and the other kit—whom I now called Fingers—went on growing and changing. One morning, holding Cross Eyes in my palm, his head tucked into his groin, his arms covering his mismatched eyes, I pushed him into the dark of the barrel. Lotor's cool paws touched my hand lightly, hesitating while she investigated my rings. Then, finding the kit, she clasped him down against the fur of her belly.

I waited for her to fling him out. She didn't. Rocking back to a sitting position to relieve the pressure of the baby inside me, I once again puzzled over the rules: in a scientific wildlife study, there was to be no interference. In the years to come, would there be cross-eyed raccoons to mess up John's or somebody else's data? I felt a bit guilty about what I had done, but I had been feeling that way about many things lately.

"What will we do if we have a cross-eyed baby?" I asked John when he came to bed. I don't remember his answer, if he even gave one.

9

2

Nature's Uneven Hand

I opened my eyes when the pewee sang his predawn song, one of the poignant sounds of the deep woods. The tent flaps were tied up and my eyes were level with the hawkweed and daisies that grew in the forest opening behind the tent. I lay still as the light came up, cherishing the illusion that I was adrift on a sea of blossoms. As a child I'd been told by my grandmother that I had my head in the clouds. Now, as a young married woman, I could tell myself that I had my head in a sea of daisies. For several days lately, now and then I had felt the child in my womb pulling hard on my guts. I ignored the sensation, for I was strong and came from a long line of women who gave birth easily. I watched the flowers bob and leap until the upheaval in my belly subsided.

Species by species, the birds were breaking into song. Each species has a light cue, an internal schedule, to which it awakens and begins to sing. In the dimness of that forest the singing began with the wood pewee; then came the robin, the vireos and then the song sparrow.

"I don't hear Able." John was on his elbows listening; in this community of forest birds, he knew almost every individual personally. I watched as he dressed in the early light, picked up his clipboard and hurried off into the woods. I dressed quickly too, but held off from going out to learn what had become of Able. A cross-eyed raccoon was enough for one week. I walked to the commode under the sugar-maple tree to which we had nailed a mirror, and combed my hair, put on mascara and lipstick. Then I filled the washpan with water from the cider barrel for John. Finally I made the bed. When there were no more chores, I headed down the hill.

I heard John call out, "Jean! Come here." The ring in his voice was one of wonder, not dismay, and I ran down into the meadow to join him. His binoculars were directed at the top of the hawthorn.

"Meet Peggy the Fourth," he said. "Able's not singing because he's stopped advertising for a mate. He's got one."

I lifted my own field glasses and saw the new Peggy flicking some obscure signals to Able with her wings.

"Will she start a new nest?"

"She's been feeding these nestlings ever since I arrived." That, according to our reading, was not supposed to happen.

Fascinated by the foster mother who fed another female's young, I went back to the tent that morning pleased that there was a bit of humanity in the birds—or perhaps more precisely, since they had been around longer, a bit of the birds in humanity.

About three days later I was making a watercolor of Lotor and her kits to illustrate the book in progress, when John strode up the hill from the meadow.

"Able's dead," he said. "He's nowhere around. I've been watching for over two hours."

Stunned, I put down my brush. "Maybe he's at the stream."

"Can't be. That's another song sparrow's territory. He can't move; he's surrounded by other territories. That's the law of the birds: set up boundaries and stay with them; and when challenged, sing, don't make war."

"We're a million years behind," I said.

"Maybe one hundred and seventy million."

"I'm really upset about Able," I told John. "He was a personal friend."

"Well, he's given me a lot of good data." Placing his clipboard on the dining table, John took out Able's data sheet, opened it to the last page, and wrote "Deceased," followed by the date and hour.

11

"The four nestlings are fine," he said, closing Able's file. "But they're hungry. All opened their mouths when I jiggled the bush—they think the motion means a parent."

"Now what's going to happen? Will the foster mother keep on feeding them?"

"We'll have to wait and see." We walked to the meadow, where we concentrated on the behavior of Peggy the Fourth. She fed the nestlings at a terrific pace, pausing only to call softly—one note, the note to the male. As the sun dipped low, I went to make dinner.

From halfway up the knoll I heard pots and pans clanging. With a shout I broke into a run, knowing full well what was up. I had left open the bottom drawer of the chest in which I stored the pots and pans. Lotor and her kits would be at their favorite pastime—rolling pots. Recalling that I had left the cornmeal out, I sprinted. Too late. The pans were scattered across the tent floor and Lotor was sitting in the roasting pan, the cornmeal box held to her chest with one hand while the other dipped into the meal and scattered it for yards.

Snatching both handles of the roaster, I picked it up and dumped Lotor under the biggest beech. Fingers and Cross Eyes scampered at my feet until I turned to go back to the tent. Then they set off on a race against me to the pans, pounced on them and clattered them all over the floor again.

"I'll never learn," I said, jamming the pots back into the drawer. I was grateful that at least I'd had the foresight to close the door to the canned food cabinet. Lotor had already decimated that department by removing most of the labels from the tin cans with her adroit little hands. To eat from the cabinet was a game of chance. I would open what I thought to be a can of beans only to find that what I had was soup or cherries.

With the pots in place, I heard a chuttering purr. Tracing this soft, endearing music, I saw a ripple move from the foot of the bed toward the top. A raccoon head came out, then another and another, and while I stood staring, all three put their heads on my pillow and lay still, with their chins just above the top of the cover.

My friend Gerrie Quick, a veterinarian's daughter, once said as she watched me with the raccoons, "People raise their kids the way they raise

12

their pets.'' I pictured my children rolling pots, ripping labels off cans, dangling car keys in the toilet bowl and romping through bedclothes; and I sighed.

The following morning, John dressed for an appointment with his thesis chairman, Dr. Harry Hann. I walked with him as far as our old Buick, parked at the edge of the forest, then hurried back to my work. As I approached the tent I was met by an ''erraking'' sound, the expletive of the raccoons. Lotor accosted me, pawed at my pants, ran off, came back and erraked again. She wanted help, I decided, and I followed her to a medium-sized maple behind the tent. One leap, and she was climbing the trunk. I followed her gaze as she stopped and stared up among the leaves. There, silently looking down while they clung precariously to the trunk, were Fingers and Cross Eyes. I ran to get John, who was still trying to start the car. He came quickly, and stood stroking his chin.

''That's interesting,'' he said. ''I don't think they can climb down.''

''Now there's a subject for a graduate thesis,'' I told him. ''Why is it that four-week-old raccoons can climb up a tree but not down? What does that do for the survival of their species?''

''Keeps them up in the trees, far from the marauding fox, until they're big enough to defend themselves.''

John went to the tent, strapped on his climbing spurs, and started up, grabbing the tree trunk with both hands. Lotor climbed the other side, passing him on the way up. For a wild thing, to be pursued is a cue to start running. As the little raccoons scrambled up the tree, Lotor saw the problem, raced ahead of them and blocked their ascent, holding them at bay until John could grab them. He stuffed them into his shirt, needing both hands to climb down. As he descended, the kits began running inside his shirt, scratching and nipping, and he could only set his jaw, growl and hang on until he got to the ground.

When he opened his shirt to let them out, they grabbed at his belt and clawed his stomach. With a Wagnerian bellow John pulled them off and put them on the ground. Lotor picked up Fingers by the scruff of the neck and carried her into the barrel, then returned for Cross Eyes, sinking her teeth into his flesh as she carried him. He squealed in pain.

''She's punishing them,'' I said. ''Wild babies should simply grow. There is no right or wrong for them. Why is she doing this?''

13

While John dusted off his shirt and pants and put on his jacket, I sat down in front of the raccoon barrel, perplexed by what seemed to be some universal rules of rearing offspring. Or was I misinterpreting what I had seen?

That afternoon, with John still away, I headed down the hill to check on the song sparrows, as he had asked me to do. I heard the pressure of Lotor's feet on the dry leaves, and thrilled once again to the idea that a wild creature chose to follow me. Lotor stopped; her ears went back, and the fur on her back rose like a cat's. A black snake was sliding through the grass in the direction of Able's nest. I picked up a rock and lifted it over my head, ready to slam it down on the snake, when I realized what I was doing. No, I could not interfere with John's thesis—his key to jobs and promotions and respect in the scientific community. That very black snake might be responsible for the fascinating situation at Able's nest and might be a key element in a bigger picture of life in the region.

I was about to go on to Mink Stream when I realized that John was back. In a minute he was jogging down the hill to meet me. Before our lips could touch in greeting, a sudden burst of song sent John's field glasses to his eyes.

"Another male at Able's nest," he said, and my glasses went up too. After a long watch John lifted the clipboard on his belt and jotted down a note.

"A foster mother," he said, "and now a foster father. Able's nestlings are being raised by a whole new set of parents."

"A whole new set of parents. That's incredible!" I was sure now that John's research would make ornithological history. Excited for him, I was suddenly content to be here. I had really not been very comfortable with this pregnancy but had not dared to say so. It was June; every bird was nesting or feeding young, and the fieldwork was prodigiously tiring. I did not want to be responsible for the least pause in the work. Sometimes I wished John would ask how I felt, so that I could share my concern; but he never did. It did not matter, I told myself finally, since if he had, I would have simply looked out across the ocean of flowers and said, "I'm fine, just fine." With the data John was getting, the future looked good. A tent in the wilderness would not be home for long. A sturdy house would enclose us soon, and the tent would be merely a pleasant adjunct.

At dawn the next day the bedsprings popped as John crawled out of

14

bed. As he pumped the stove, the child in my belly tore at my left side. I turned over and was staring out through the flowers when a cool paw on my toe announced the arrival of a friend.

"Lotor!" I said, and pulled back the sheet to find her snuggled at my side, but with a hint of distress in her voice. The springs squeaked and popped as I peered under the bed. Cross Eyes and Fingers were climbing among the coils.

"I can see my own kids now. They will crawl in the bedsprings." Laughing at the thought, I looked up at John, who had the coffee perking.

"If they do I'll whack them."

"Whack them?" I sat up. "You wouldn't whack a child?"

"Yes, I would. That's how *I* was raised."

"I don't believe you'd do that." I turned and rolled up in the sheet. John and I had not discussed child-rearing before. I had very definite ideas about it and so, apparently, did he. We should talk about it now, I thought—right now. But afraid to make a scene or argue with my husband, I simply stared at the tent ceiling until the urge to challenge what he had said had passed.

Several days later, when I set out for Mink Stream with a sheet of watercolor paper, Lotor and her kits were at my heels. I paused at the raspberry patch, where Able the Second and Peggy the Fourth were flitting about the bush, feeding their foster fledglings.

"The wonders go on and on," I told myself, watching the couple.

Cardinal flowers were in bloom by the stream, and a wood thrush was singing—only a partial song, now that the breeding season was ending and his young were on their own.

I had just sat down to paint when Lotor erraked with such intensity that I got up, expecting to see both kits in the clutches of some predator. Instead, they were jumping onto the trunk of a maple and she was cursing and pulling them down. When I realized we were in for another episode, I lunged for Fingers, who flattened her ears in the excitement of a chase and ran up the tree, while Cross Eyes followed her to a limb about fifteen feet above the ground.

Lotor took a nose-focus on the kits, honed in on them and charged up the tree like a squirrel. Like a squirrel she ran out on a limb, and there all similarity to squirrel behavior ceased.

Grabbing Cross Eyes by the scruff of the neck, she dislodged him from his perch and dangled him over the ground. With an "errak" she hurled him to earth, then grabbed Fingers and threw her down. Both kits hit with a thud. Not finished with her lesson, Lotor ran down the tree, jumped on them and pummeled them until their eyes rolled in their heads.

Satisfied, she turned and walked calmly down the path, the kits following demurely at her heels. This time I knew I had not misinterpreted what Lotor was doing. As though to prove John right, she had clearly been punishing them.

3

A Song Sparrow
Named Charlie

I lost the baby. For three days and three nights I wept; then gradually the hormones that had been triggering maternal emotions began to slow down. Dr. Helen Price, my redheaded obstetrician, said, "You're in good health. Go home and get pregnant again, right away. There are good eggs and bad eggs, good sperm and bad sperm. Let's get the good ones together."

John and I drove back to the farm talking about the completion of his research, the German exam I was helping him with and our own prospects.

John and Frank, my brothers, had both completed the fieldwork for their Ph.D.s, and together with their wives, Margaret and Esther, had recently left Ann Arbor for the Grand Tetons in Wyoming, where they had built themselves cabins. Each of the couples now had a golden-headed child. As we wound down Cherry Hill Road toward the Strang farm and our tent, I thought of them all with envy.

"When will we have a home?" I asked. My nesting hormones had not quite been turned off, after all.

"Soon," John said.

"I like that kind of talk. Let's talk some more."

But we didn't.

At the farm we parked the car at the tractor barn and walked to the tent; we drove only when we had something to unload. The cows were coming in from the meadow and an entire killdeer family was wheeling through the sky, keeping in touch with each other by calling. The air smelled of the sweet grasses and warm animal bodies and once more I felt the importance of John's research. Locked to his elbow, I walked happily down the lane.

"I have a surprise for you," he said as we rounded the last fence and approached the tent. He flung out his hand. There, singing loudly and conspicuously on one of the front tent stakes, was a male song sparrow.

"Meet Charlie," he said.

The bird completed a phrase, then spilled over into another and then another.

"Our own virtuoso," I exclaimed happily. "How come?"

"He's a bachelor. He's singing for a wife."

"In the woods? I thought song sparrows needed field edges and fields."

"That's why he's a bachelor. He's got a lousy piece of property and no self-respecting female song sparrow will have him."

Charlie was so involved in singing for a wife that our arrival went virtually unnoticed. Instead of flying off to some remote corner of his property as we opened the tent flaps, he simply moved to a rear tent stake and sang again.

And so, with Charlie's song ringing in my ears, I once more began life in the woods—a life where a thousand doors were being opened on the natural world by the likes of Charlie.

"A bachelor bird," I chuckled as we rolled up the flaps and let the sun in. "John, do you suppose there are homosexuals and old maids in nature, too?"

"Even transsexuals. There's a fish called the swordtail. The female lays eggs when she's young; then, in her later years, she switches over to cast milt on the eggs of other females. Success in nature is offspring."

"Yes," I whispered, feeling guilty and angry all over again at my own failure.

Crazy Charlie warbled on as I jumped from the tent platform and walked to the barrel to greet Lotor and her two kittens. For the first time, a light shone in the eyes of Fingers and Cross Eyes. I knew it meant they would not be with us long. Soon the wild state would take possession and they would go back to the woods.

"Hello!" Cora Strang's son Gilbert was coming down the lane carrying something that squirmed.

"Here's a puppy," he said, holding out a furry, soft-nosed creature with black eyes, a spotted face and body, and the long ears of a hound. Gib's bluetick hound, Fanny, had given birth to pups about a month ago. I took the pup and held it close.

"You need a pet," he said. "Heals the loss."

I studied Gib's face. A wistful, wiry man, he was a bachelor. How could he know what I felt? But, of course he did. I remembered seeing him put a kitten with a cow who was bawling for the calf he had sent to market. He knew a lot about life.

"The puppy's name is Gunner," he said. "She came right over to me when I picked up my 'coon rifle."

"Gunner," I said, holding the round, wobbly pup. "Gunner George. Sounds good." I snuggled her against my cheek. She smelled like milk and hay, and my heart stopped bawling. Gib was right.

The whimper from the pup brought Lotor on the run. She rose on her hind legs and searched for the creature whose presence her nose and ears had reported. I was about to lean down and let her touch the puppy when she climbed me like a tree. With one foot in my pants pocket, the other on my belt, she hung there sniffing.

Dog! The signal went off inside the raccoon. Her ears pulled back in hostility. But all infants, from bird to man, and perhaps even further down the scale, have a built-in protective mechanism—a "cute," appealing look of helplessness. The large head and big eyes, the wobbly, jerky movements are releasers. They set off parental love. Lotor now got the wobbly signals that read *baby*. As she put up her ears again, she touched Gunner gently, then began to lick and groom her. Just as she had taken her kits from me, she now grabbed Gunner by the scruff of the neck and backed down my leg. I leaned over and put them both on the ground. Gunner sniffed at the strange mother, wobbled and sat down. Purring loudly, Lotor once more licked the young thing.

Then Cross Eyes appeared in the doorway of the barrel, and a stronger message reached his mother—the need to protect her own offspring from a dog. Erraking nervously, she ran to the barrel, pushed

19

Cross Eyes into the darkness and followed him inside. Except for that transient nervousness, Gunner and the raccoons were off to a peaceable start.

After feeding Gunner that evening, John and I lined a cardboard box with old rags and she clambered in, somehow knowing it was for her. Sitting on her haunches, she looked up with wide, trusting eyes, wagged her tail and accepted us unconditionally as friends.

"She's one huge ego trip," I said with delight. "Lotor is nice but she always maintains a distance. This animal just out-and-out loves us."

As I came home the next day Andy Berger, another Ph.D. candidate, walked into view carrying something that wiggled.

"I'm sorry about your miscarriage," he said, "so I brought you this little fellow." He held out a snub-nosed baby skunk. He lifted his head and sniffed, his black-and-white cap bristling like a scrub brush, his plumed tail held tensely over his back.

As I took him, the wide skunk mouth opened, the red tongue coiled around my thumb and he sucked heartily.

"He's from a late litter, I guess," Andy said.

"Can he spray yet?"

"Not yet. Too young."

Andy sat down on a stump stool while I pumped up the stove to heat milk. Having found no food in my thumb, the little skunk had tucked his head into the crook of my elbow and was crying.

"Denny's pregnant." Andy's eyes sparkled and a smile lit up his face. I paused, petted the little skunk and swallowed before I could say, "That's great news." Quickly, I filled a baby bottle and stuck the nipple into the pink mouth. "Congratulations," I finally said, more steadily. Then I concentrated on the skunk, holding his little skunk's paw as he fed.

John came home looking discouraged and hot. He had been up since dawn collecting data in the field.

"And who is it we have here?" he asked.

"*Mephitis mephitis,* the North American striped skunk," I answered. "To me he is Meph, the pet skunk, and that is the title of the next book we do."

I put down the bottle and stroked the fat, glistening animal. Lotor stood up on her hind legs and touched my knee, seeking out the skunk with her nose. I lowered him; his tail went up, and although Andy had assured me Meph could not spray, I quickly put him down. He turned himself into a U, his eyes and anus aimed at Lotor. She took care of him by jumping onto his tail. For a moment I thought I smelled the essence of skunk musk.

"How do you suppose she knows a skunk can't spray when its tail's down?" I asked incredulously.

"I smell him," said John. "He did spray."

"He's too young," said Andy.

"What shall we do about his glands?" John asked.

"Do about them? Nothing. He'll never be able to go back to the woods if we descent him. He needs his weapon."

"That's my feeling, too." John sniffed the air again. "Funny, I can't smell him anymore," he said.

"It's like garlic eaters," said Andy. "Neither can I."

And so Meph joined our ark, a fearless little creature with more self-confidence than all of us put together. Within two days he was tame as a kitten. He pummeled the floor with his front feet when he wanted his bottle, ran the raccoon kits up the tree, intimidated Gunner with a tail flash, and took over my paint box for a bed. He had been designed by nature to get across the message that for him there were no enemies under the sun.

As the summer days ran out Charlie went on singing from tent post to tent post. One morning while John and I were lying in bed I saw him fly to the ground, alight under the seeding hawkweeds and begin pecking. Creeping out of the tent on hands and knees, I frightened him off and studied the spot. Pushing back the leaves, I found that the floor of the clearing was thick with seeds.

"There's so much bird food around," I said coming back into bed. "So how come this is poor song-sparrow land?"

John answered, again as an expert, "An animal's land is more than food; it's a niche. For birds this is nesting sites, roosts, cover from the weather, singing posts, leaf density, open spaces. The modern-day song sparrow just can't fill all his needs in this shrubless tent area.

"By the way," John said thoughtfully, and I pushed up onto my elbows. He and I had not talked about how we felt about the miscarriage and I hoped he was going to say something at last. The sun was barely up, the woods were tinged pink, the cicadas were singing. In this peaceful

21

atmosphere could we express ourselves so that I could be rid of my guilt about losing his child? Apparently we couldn't. What he had been about to say was "Dr. Hann's coming out here Sunday to go over the study area with me. I invited him to dinner."

"Oh." I bit my lips. I had been crazy to think that a lost baby was important when you were working on a comprehensive scientific study. I finally said, "Then I'll buy a ham. And I'll make a rock oven and cook potatoes, squash and corn." My voice rose higher as I covered my disappointment, overcooperating as I had learned to do as a child.

"That'll be great. And maybe make a cake, too."

"I will," I said. And I did.

For John's sake I wished to entertain him well.

Charlie sang no more.

"He's either dead or married," I said to John on a warm autumn morning. The area around the tent where Charlie had sung trillingly was so still as to seem funereal.

John was bent over his maps of bobolink territories, one next to the other all across the alfalfa field. Each line was a boundary over which the owner did not fly unless pressed by extraordinary circumstances. As I looked at him going over and over the details, I suddenly wanted to tell him to get on with the writing of his thesis so we could move out of the university and into real life. But the words would not come out. I could adjust to living in the tent for many more years, so there was no point in upsetting him at this stage of his work. Rather than show anger that we weren't moving forward, I turned my thoughts to Charlie. Insignificant though he seemed to be, he was up against some weighty problems: property, wealth, status and the possible extinction of his genetic code, unless by now he had found a mate.

"Maybe Charlie's migrated," I said.

"I don't think so." John put down his pencil and stretched. Pushing aside his work, he walked to the front of the tent, which was wide open to the forest. "It's too warm for the song sparrows to migrate," he went on. "It takes a temperature of nearly four degrees centigrade to send them on their way."

"I thought it was the shortening of the day that started them off, like the swallows of Capistrano that depart around the twenty-third of October and arrive every March nineteenth, precisely. That has to be light, because the light would be the same every year.''

''Probably it is, but each species is somewhat different. Temperature seems to be the starting gun for the song sparrows. Their departure dates vary.''

John went on to discuss migration. Although I was eager to learn, he had a way of talking down to me that made me feel ill-informed and second-rate—a feeling which drove me outside to look for Charlie.

Charlie was a loser too, I thought. Although he appeared to be a handsome and vigorous bird, his predicament in life was not hopeful. Nature seemed to be selecting him out for removal; but I loved him for trying to survive, locked as he was onto a lousy piece of land to which no female would come.

As an undergraduate at Penn State I had studied animal behavior with Ray Carpenter, who had been the first scientist to investigate the naturalistic behavior of New World primates, the howling and red spider monkeys. When I sat down in his class on the first day of my sophomore year, he was completing his paper on the behavior of free-ranging rhesus monkeys he had imported to Puerto Rico from India. During the next three years he often invited me to view his movies of these interacting animals. As dramas unrolled he interpreted, never anthropomorphizing. He did, however, speak of leadership, dominance, mother-infant and father-infant relationships as well as clan and interclan relations—matters that sounded just as human as Charlie's territorial poverty syndrome.

Lotor followed me down the hill to the spring, where I had last seen the bachelor bird. I would begin looking for him there. Unlike the area around the tent, this one had ferns and viburnums that made a cover for Charlie, serving to fulfill his need to be in a bush—a need as strong in a song sparrow as a turtle's need to bask in the sun.

After searching the ferns I sat down near the spring, cupped my hands behind my ears and tried to pick up the thin ''seeee-see'' call of the song sparrow in autumn. I could faintly hear Able II down in the meadow. His voice was wistful, as if, or so I dared to speculate, he were preoccupied with the angle of the sun's rays, the tilt of the earth, the bite of the wind, all of which signaled that it was time to fly south for the winter. How does a bird sense these elements, I asked myself, tilting my own face to the sun in an effort to tune in on the season. Presently I had an overwhelming desire to light a fire in an open fireplace, with sturdy walls around me. I hugged my knees, all but smelling the wood smoke from the fireplace as the migratory instinct pulled my own imagination indoors. A beechnut fell from a twig like a background note; the last trace of green had faded from the leaves, revealing the autumn colors. It was as though all the stress and frustration of living in the tent, of the miscarriages and of waiting for the thesis to be done, had blown off on the wind. As I sat quietly merging my senses with the autumn scene, I was aware of my own interior voice, which nothing could silence.

"Since the third grade you've wanted to be a writer and you spent hours secretly writing poems and stories. You never quite believed you would ever be one, and so far you really aren't." It was true that I would soon be finishing another book—the one on the raccoon. But once again, because I could not tell John that I thought I should now be author or at least senior author, I had let the byline stand as John and Jean George.

I concentrated on finding Charlie.

Beside me, Lotor picked up a beechnut. Leaning against the trunk of a tree to free her forepaws, she rolled the prickly burr until it burst open and three triangular nuts fell out. She ate them with loud cracking sounds.

"So that's how you open beechnuts!" I said, wondering if the knowledge was inherited. It must be, since she would never have seen one before now, and yet she knew how to open it. I, on the other hand, tried to crack those same nuts with a hammer and ruined them. I took out my notebook to make a quick sketch of Lotor opening shells, all the while listening for Charlie.

Silence. He was not even scratching for food under the leaves. And no sign of a mate. I could hear John's distant footsteps on the ridge but not a wing rustle from Charlie. I concluded that he was dead.

Lotor got up and walked toward the stream. Cross Eyes and Fingers had not been with her for several weeks. This was the dispersal season, that period of the year when the young of most wild species leave home to seek their fortunes. I smiled as I watched Lotor go, for her stride was open and free and she tossed her head with an abandon she had not shown since she had given birth to the kits. The dispersal season, I noted, was a good time for adults.

After a long wait, I imitated the call note of the song sparrow—one

24

way of attracting birds in the wild. A good imitator like John would bring a bird winging his way to see who was trespassing on his property. I did not arouse even a worried click from Able II, who was not far away, and so I gave up and started home.

"No Charlie," I said when I met John on the trail.

"He may very well be dead," he mused. "He was very conspicuous and vulnerable, singing so much in the open woods. Owls and hawks and foxes take prey that show themselves."

A wind kicked up a shower of red, yellow and orange leaves and sent them spiraling around us like falling flames. They covered the ground, the tent roof and the dining table. At dinnertime I did not brush them off the table, but put the plates and cups upon them, so that we sat down to a wild autumn tablecloth. Later, while doing the dishes, another wind loosed a thousand more leaves, some of which fell into the dishpan. When I lifted the frying pan it was plastered with color.

"Where else," I said to John, "will I ever again wash in a dishpan full of autumn leaves and have pots that look like this?"

John looked at me thoughtfully. I was standing at the outdoor table, my blond hair tied up high with a blue scarf so that long curls fell down the back of my head, my shirt wet with splashes, my arms and face browned. I am a moderately good-looking woman; but at that moment, with arms plastered with leaves, and with my husband gazing affectionately at me, I felt downright beautiful.

"What are you thinking?" I asked, waiting eagerly for what I hoped he would say.

"That I'm married to a high-powered Cadillac," he answered.

I was devastated. With all the love that must have been shining out of my eyes at that moment, I was simply a souped-up power machine! I wanted to cry; instead, leaning on a childhood survival technique, I brushed his remark from my mind and went deeper inside myself, a migrant along with the birds.

A rustle sounded under the tent floor and Meph came out to greet the twilight. As soon as I had weaned him from the bottle he had switched from our diurnal rhythm to a schedule of his own. As a nocturnal beast, he was up for the night.

John picked him up and scratched his head while I went to the pantry

25

for a can of dog food. Although Meph preferred chili con carne to all other foods, and would stamp on the floor and demand a share when I cooked it, dog food was better for him. Suddenly a whir of wings startled me. A bird flew out from under the tent.

"Charlie!" I exclaimed. "John, he's right here, living under the tent. What does that mean?"

"I don't know for sure."

"That he's the lowest of the low men on the song-sparrow totem pole? A minus ten?" I shook my head as Charlie flew to a tent stake, where he chirped softly and fluttered his wings at Meph.

"He's courting Meph," I said. Putting the skunk food down, I leaned forward in the rocker.

"Maybe Charlie has stopped singing because he thinks he has a mate, Meph, the pet skunk."

John ignored me while he studied the bird. "One thing *is* known," he said thoughtfully. "That Charlie did come out from under the tent floor. We'll start from there to find out why."

When night fell and the stars were out, John lit the lamp and took out his field notes. I opened my paint pots. I had a job illustrating a story for a filmstrip company. A children's book illustrator had approached me after seeing my illustrations for *Vulpes, the Red Fox,* and asked me if I wanted some work on the side. I had said yes promptly, for John's income as a graduate student was no more than survival-pence.

Dipping my brush in paint, I laid down a pink wash and leaned back to let it dry. Then I felt a warm pressure against my foot and looked down to see Meph's distinctive head against my shoe. I reached down to scratch his ears, and he clattered his teeth in skunk language.

"Charlie's under the tent; Lotor's in her barrel; Meph's on my shoe," I said.

"And Gunner's got her nose against my boot," added John. "The ark is safe."

Hardly had he spoken than the tent began to flap like the canvas of a sailboat coming about. After glancing up at the center pole to make certain it was not going to collapse, John went outside and squinted up with a sailor's professional eye.

"Here comes winter!" He picked up an armload of wood, opened the door of the sheepherder's stove and laid a fire. The flames roared and the stove danced, while outside a cold wind ripped the leaves from the trees. The tent was magical at moments like this, and I felt guilty for wanting John to move faster on his thesis. Later, under the feather quilt, I found myself thinking of Charlie again.

"I'm so glad Charlie's alive," I said.

"By dawn he'll be off to Alabama." John shivered and drew me close.

"I'll miss him. I think he's trying to tell me something."

But Charlie did not go. He greeted us at around ten the next morning when we set off into the woods to make notes on vacated bird territories. The robins had departed some time ago, along with the vireos and buntings. The field birds were gone and so were all the other song sparrows.

"Why didn't Charlie go?" I asked.

John did not know.

That night Charlie came out from under the tent, preened on a stake and went back underneath.

"The weather report says tonight the temperature will go below freezing," John said. "That will surely send him off."

Lotor showed up at the door, sped across the tent floor and vanished into the darkness. We worked for a while by the heat of the stove, then gave up and went to bed. I rolled into a ball, uncurling slowly as I warmed.

"Hey," I said. "My feet just touched something furry."

"I've got a fur for each foot," said John.

"So much for the young-going-off-to-seek-their-fortunes," I said. "Out here, there seem to be more exceptions to rules than there are rules."

The following morning I lifted the tent flap to see a heavy frost on the dry yarrow and hawkweed. At breakfast we could hear the warblers coming through on migration, and we could see the hawks peel off at the top of a wind spiral as they sped southward. I looked under the tent.

"He's gone at last," I said.

The cold lingered for a few days; then the air warmed and the remainder of October was quite mild and pleasant. Once more we slept with the tent flaps rolled up.

One morning, walking down the trail on my way to visit Cora, I saw

27

a song sparrow on the fence post. Lifting my field glasses, I noted the bands.

"Charlie!" I said. "Well, now you've really blown it. Everyone's gone." After watching him as he flew from the post to a weed in the alfalfa field, then over the lane to the next field, I turned back to find John.

"Charlie's still here," I said with a grin. "And he has taken over some mighty fine property."

For the next week we enjoyed the presence of the upwardly mobile song sparrow who was now growing sleek and fat on cold crickets and grasshoppers. No more undersides of tent floors for him. He roosted in the best song-sparrow cover and flitted over his land with the assurance of a man of means.

"I think he's the beginning of a new breed of song sparrow," I said to John one morning when he was flying past. "The Kingdom Snatchers."

"Except for one thing. He has no wife."

When Charlie was still around a week later I turned for information to the authority on song sparrows, Margaret Norse Nice. Mrs. Nice—a "housewife," as professors of ornithology always added—had written one of the classic bird monographs, *Studies in the Life History of the Song Sparrow,* a report on an eight-year project involving 533 banded adult song sparrows in the yard and fields around her home at Interpont, Ohio. I admired this woman greatly. From her monograph I knew that the migration of the song sparrow occurs between mid-September and the end of October. A cold snap triggers the flight south. If, however, the cold is not deep enough to trip the internal mechanism of a particular individual—and each bird has a slightly different threshold of tolerance—that bird will not go. After the migration period is past, before the beginning of November, the urge to migrate fades and the bird remains in the north. It is then a "winter bird."

So we had a winter bird—that inspiring spark of life that lingers to warm the spirits of mankind in the dark hours of the year.

I closed the book and went outside to find Charlie.

If October had been warm, a cold November soon made up for it and, before Thanksgiving, we were forced to move back to our apartment in Ann Arbor. Left behind were Lotor, Cross Eyes and Fingers; Gunner and Meph went with us. As we drove away I got a last glimpse of Charlie flitting toward the woods.

"Now," I said, "he's got our territory too."

Meph adjusted to town life by learning to use a box of Kitty Litter. Skunks, like many other wild animals, are so scrupulously clean that they assign themselves latrines in the wild. I capitalized on that habit and was grateful for it.

As for me, I was quite happy to get back to town. Electricity, running water and flush toilets freed me to finish the filmstrip in a few weeks and begin writing the skunk book.

On weekends we returned to the tent, usually with some of our graduate friends in tow. Our tent became a kind of country home for the hardworking doctoral candidates. On Friday Denny called me to say she had made a big pot of chili con carne, and suggested that we all meet for dinner and sleep at the tent.

"We'll be late," she said. "So I'll have Andy drop off the chili in case you want to go ahead. I have a doctor's appointment."

For the first time since I'd miscarried, I was not envious of Denny's pregnancy. As I listened to her report of the flutters and movements of her baby, I wondered just what had healed me: the puppy, the skunk, the raccoons, the song sparrow or the whole forest? It did not matter which; what mattered was that I was happy for Andy and Denny and it felt fine to say so.

Hardly had we arrived at the tent, with Meph under one arm and the chili pot under the other, than Charlie made an appearance. I turned and watched him streak over the forest opening to the bushes and vines at the edge of the field, where he disappeared.

John fired up the stove and I was making salad when Gib came up the hill from the meadow. A cow had wandered off and he was looking for her.

"A big storm is coming," he said. "Been listening to the radio all morning. A real whiz of a blizzard." We stepped outside and studied the sky.

Gib did not linger. "I'll see you," he said and went off toward the maple-sugar house to search for the cow.

"Should we leave?" I asked John as we watched the clouds racing over the horizon. I could already smell the coming of snow.

"Let's stay. I'd love to be here in a blizzard."

I checked the canned food supply. Label-less though it was, the number of cans was enough to assure us three or four days of food, be it chicken soup or cherries.

The trees that had been swaying were now bending deeply and the excitement of the coming storm stirred my blood.

"I'll go to the farmhouse and phone Andy and Denny and tell them not to come," I said.

I started off into a scattering of snow crystals. By the time I got back the wind was carrying them horizontally, the ground was white, and John had wood piled inside and outside. We checked the flaps and side ropes of the tent and sat down before our cherry-red stove under the bright gas lamp, while Meph and Gunner curled up next to the indoor woodpile. I put the pot of chili on the fire, and in a few moments the essence of it had reached Meph's nose. When he got up, arched his tail and pummeled the floor with both front feet, there was no doubt about what he was saying.

"What a night for you," I said. "A pot of chili for four, with only two of us—and you—to eat it."

The tent shook, the storm intensified and John and I sat still as we became engulfed by a wind chorus, the wildest I had ever heard. When the fire died down we crawled into bed to feel the cold kiss of snow sifting down on us from the opening around the center pole. Around 2:00 A.M. I awoke. Feeling the crystallized moisture inside my nose, I knew the temperature was well below ten degrees Fahrenheit. I thought of Charlie. He could never get out of this one. Barefoot and small as he was, a warm-weather bird, he was not destined to be a survivor. Lying awake in the blizzard, I composed the first line of an elegy to a small bird.

We slept late in the darkness of the tent, and would have slept even later had not Gunner awakened us to be fed. When I sat up, not a sound came from the outside world. The storm was over, and judging from the sag of the roof and the tent's sides, we were buried in the forest.

After dressing by a snapping fire we pushed back the snow with shovel and broom and looked out over white on white. Every tree was sheathed in snow, each twig wrapped with it. No shadows fell. The excitement of the night was replaced by awe at being cocooned inside the blizzard into which the great forest had disappeared.

Mourning for Charlie, I pulled on my boots, then stepped out to help John clean the white pillows from the water barrel and dining-room table. Gunner rolled and dove like a weasel while Meph stayed curled up in a ball inside the tent. A wind came up and lifted the snow off the branches. It sifted down in an icy cloud, and when the air cleared, the forest was black and white, the trees around us restored to visibility. Presently the nuthatches yanked, the chickadees called and a troop of winter birds flew past. I followed them to the lane to note their bands and colors for John. Then I stopped still.

From out of the snow-covered bittersweet vine that twined the fence post flew Charlie.

"The snow," I gasped. "Of course, it's an insulation, not a freezing menace." I applauded the snow, and Charlie, as he flew down the fence line to find food in this hostile world.

"I hope you make it," I called, "because you're an inspiration."

A month later I awoke at Craigheads, Pennsylvania, where John and I were visiting my parents for Christmas, hopped out of bed and walked to the window.

"I'm pregnant," I said to John. He rolled to his elbow and looked at me sleepily.

"You are? When did that happen?"

"Last night."

"Oh, come on." He dropped back onto his side. "Don't tease me about that."

"I'm not teasing. I know. I know the way the winter bird knows things we don't."

4

The Ultimate Young Thing

To become pregnant at Craigheads, Pennsylvania, was fitting. The house stood on land that my ancestors had turned with the plow in 1742, when William Penn's son deeded a land grant to John Craighead. John was the youngest son of the Reverend Thomas Craighead, a Scottish physician turned Presbyterian minister, who had emigrated to New England in 1715.

Up and down the fertile Cumberland Valley, John's heirs built graceful limestone houses and spectacular barns. Most of them had since passed into other hands; but when I was growing up, the valley south of Carlisle still supported a number of his descendants.

My father had been born in a handsome Victorian house above the Yellow Breeches Creek, at the center of Craigheads. As a boy he explored the meadows and woods, discovering where the skunks lived and the copperheads denned. When he was sent to Harrisburg to go to high school, he awakened to new worlds with the discovery of the literary classics in the library of a great-aunt. During his high school years he read his way from the door around the room and back again. Years later he told me that the library had indeed inspired him to go to college and get his Ph.D. After eight generations, since increased to eleven, John Craighead's love of the land was still inherent, and Dad studied forestry and entomology.

Every summer while I was growing up, when Dad went west to supervise his field research stations, my mother, John, Frank and I moved to the Victorian house, which was up the road from Dad's and Mother's farm. During these summers we too learned to follow the skunks, the snakes and the birds; and in the old house, I read the classics myself. Grandmother Craighead's collection of literature was stored in the attic, and although not as extensive as the great-aunt's, it covered the major writers of the nineteenth century as well as Homer, Aeschylus, Sophocles and Euripides. It was here I learned about sex from *The Canterbury Tales,* a frankly titillating exposure compared to Mother's Victorian lectures on sex.

Each summer, aunts, uncles and cousins—as many as seventeen altogether—filled the house and sleeping porch and spilled over into the yard. Ours was a naïve existence. We fished, swam, rode the hay wagons and raised owls, falcons and guinea pigs. We really believed that if you were good, good would come back to you, and that work was salvation. Other virtues were sharing, being honest, minding your elders, and not having sex before marriage.

In the evenings we sang by the creek or played softball, with the parents joining in. When we were bored and likely to get into mischief, Mother would send us into the meadows to collect wild flowers, which we pressed and identified; she gave me lessons in sewing and canning fruit, both of which also bored me numb. I much preferred to be out with my brothers, catching frogs and jumping off the limbs of a tree into a deep pool of the creek.

Late in the afternoon of the day I woke knowing I was pregnant, I drove up the road to that nursery of my childhood hoping to get a sense of the past for my child of the future. I was not disappointed. The parlor was as dark and mysterious as it had been that day Dad gave me my first insect pet, a praying mantis. I thought of it as an enchanted creature, a stick come to life.

In the kitchen the walls still bore the drawings we had all painted and signed. This register of family and friends was initiated when I asked Uncle Gene, Dad's brother, if it would be all right if I drew a picture on the wall before he painted it that summer.

"Yes, if you wash six square feet of wall first," was his answer, and before the month was out, not only I, but everyone in the family and the neighborhood had added a drawing, and the kitchen walls were scrubbed clean. The results had never been painted over.

I climbed the back stairs to the small room that looked over the creek. Here, sitting in the window, I had written poetry and had confessed to my diary my love for the miller's son—then rubbed it out for fear of detection and teasing by my brothers. My fantasy loves were always poor boys from whom destiny kept separating me.

Walking through the living and dining rooms with windows that rose from floor to ceiling, I stopped to look at a photograph by my talented and energetic twin brothers. They dominated not only me but the entire family and community. Besides being A students, John and Frank were responsible for beginning the sport of falconry in the United States, and while in high school they wrote articles about it for the *Saturday Evening Post* and the *National Geographic*. They were athletes and artists as well. In the summer they initiated all the exciting endeavors, from climbing down the rainspouts during nap time to spelunking. The group of fans who continually followed them included grown men as well as boys and girls. Even in those early days at Craigheads, they had begun to build a way of life which in later years would be looked on with envy by job-locked people who saw their falconry, river running and grizzly-bear research as a kind of American wish fulfillment.

With two such brothers, a younger sister *had* to be a writer to find her niche and survive. The twins were sufficient unto themselves—although I lived in the same house with and followed them to rivers and cliffs, I was always an outsider—almost as much so as an only child. So I dreamed up an imaginary companion for whom I began writing stories.

On top of the bookcase by the fireplace I now found the family genealogy which had lain there through my childhood—skimmed now and then, but ignored by most of us. Curious about the ancestors of my just-conceived child, I turned to an account of the first of this family in America, the Reverend Thomas Craighead: "He is a man of singular piety, meekness, humility, and industry in the work of God," Cotton Mather wrote of him to a friend. "Should he be driven from you at a time when he was having some trouble with the parish it would be of such damage, yea, such a ruin, as is not without horror to be thought of."

But driven from them he was, and after months of searching for a new parish, he settled in Pequea, Pennsylvania. Then came this entry:

"While Mr. Craighead was pastor, the session of the Church complained because he debarred his wife, Margaret, from the communion table." He was dismissed, and it was many years and several parishes later before he resolved the matter and Margaret took communion. Eventually the man "who aroused his audiences to tears with his sermons" moved to North Carolina, where he died in 1766.

His son Alexander did better according to my standards. Not only did he likewise bring his parishioners to tears; he took up the cause of the American Revolution, was thrown out of his Philadelphia parish for liberalism and went to North Carolina himself, where he found a more sympathetic audience.

The descendants from those ancestors would become minister-farmers, teachers, professional people—and terrible businessmen.

My mother's family stories, by comparison, were full of humor. She was born into a second-generation Scottish family on her mother's side, and a seventh-generation American family on her father's side at Alexandria, Virginia. One story was of her sister my Aunt Polly, who dared to be bad because her mother had spanked her for something she had not done, and had then promised her that no spanking would be given the next time she deserved one. So on a rainy day, when Polly stuck her head out into the rain after being told not to, and was promptly called in for a spanking, her sisters trembled for her; but she reminded her mother of her promise and came skipping back unpunished. It was the genes of cousin Nannie, however, that I especially hoped would be passed on to my child. When her stern father told his children that anyone who picked the last pear on his favorite tree would be whipped, cousin Nannie put her fertile brain to work. She climbed a low fence near the tree, ate around the outside of the pear and left the core dangling on its twig.

A month later, Helen Price confirmed what I already knew. "One hundred percent pregnant," she said. "Now all you have to do is to be peaceful and calm as the wife of a Ph.D. candidate." Her cheeks tightened around a wicked smile. Then she said just what any good obstetrician should say: "This baby is going to be a knockout."

John's thesis was going slowly, and I fretted from time to time until we returned to the tent in March and the forest became a source of tranquillity. I would walk the trails with Gunner at my heels, amazed all over again by how different the forest looked now that I knew its birds and plants personally.

Meph had left us, taking off for a rendezvous with some female skunk in February, and Lotor and the kits had phased themselves back into the woods. We had not seen them since autumn.

On a March day I smelled in the air the dankness of growth and change that marks the arrival of spring. The last patches of snow were melting and bubbling into the brooks, the maple-sugaring was over, and the first bloodroots were poking above the ground. At the gate I met Joe, Gib's hired man, on his way to the sugar house to put away tools. We chatted a moment about spring and then he ran his fingers through his gray hair.

"By the way," he said, "ever see those raccoons of yours again?"

"No, I guess they finally dispersed and went off to their own hollows and trees."

"Well, I don't know about that," he said. "Fred Warner told me last fall that when he was short-cutting through these woods he found a mother raccoon and two young ones on the trail. They'd been shot."

"No!" I covered my ears, all the tragedies of keeping wild pets flooding over me. The falcon of my childhood had fallen before a boy with a .22 rifle, a dog had slaughtered my cottontail rabbit, the cat had killed a little screech owl. And now apparently Lotor and the kits were dead. My throat burned for I could see her romping down the trail, trusting and playful, to meet her murderer. I could not stand the picture and turned and ran back to the tent.

Every day I was helping John get his thesis in order and typed. The baby was growing and I felt again the need for a house with a fireplace and four sturdy walls.

It wasn't until just before twilight, when John took a break and checked a mist net to trap migrant birds, that I was at last able to tell him about Lotor. He did not say anything. What was there for him to say?

Suddenly a male woodcock, with his long beak and his eyes far back on the top of his head—the better to see the enemy—flew up almost at our feet. Like a skyrocket he shot up and up until he was almost out of sight. Then, high above the earth, he burst into a glorious melody and descended like a falling star. Wings whistling, he landed precisely where he had started.

I hugged my knees. The rites of spring were beginning, the woodcock was courting the female, the earthworms were turning toward the sun and I was part of the same seasonal celebration. My belly quivered and I felt life for the first time. ''Lotor and her kits are still part of the whole picture,'' I said to myself, feeling that I had understood something for the first time.

When we were ready to retire around midnight, John went outside to take down the net so that no birds would be entrapped while we slept. A few minutes later, he was back.

''Hey,'' he said, and when I looked up I saw perched on his finger a screech owl, seven inches tall, tidy, upright and smelling of the fresh spring night. His feathers, held loosely against his body, said that he was not frightened but at ease.

''He's wild,'' I said, ''and he's not afraid.''

''He never saw a person before,'' John surmised. ''So he's completely trusting.''

I extended my hand toward the owl, waiting for him to burst into flight. Instead, he stepped onto my finger. I drew him to me. We looked at each other. The wisdom of the owls was shining out of his eyes and I knew why people thought these birds intelligent. Their two eyes focus the way human eyes do, and they concentrate on what they see. He concentrated on me and said nothing.

Easing myself toward my watercolor pad with the owl on my finger, I sat down and began to paint. The hours rolled by; he still sat on my finger. When finally the painting was completed I arose and tiptoed to the tent door.

''I want him so badly,'' I said to John. ''But not after Lotor. No more pets for me.'' We stepped outside, and the owl held to my finger as he turned his head all the way around and looked at me from behind, then turned it all the way back. With a dip of his heels, he spread his wings and flew silently into the trees. From that moment on the forest was different, more functional and vivid because a small red screech owl lived there.

Late one afternoon in summer John came whistling down the lane, grinning, his binoculars swinging against his chest. Clearly something good had happened. Since he had been conferring with Dr. Hann, I immediately jumped to the conclusion that his committee had awarded him a Ph.D. without further ado because his thesis was so wonderful. Better still, would have been that John had bought a house.

"Looks like I've got a job," he called from the trail. "If I want it."

"Want it?" I said, thinking, That means we'll finish the thesis this month. "What is it?"

"Vassar College. The Zoology Department is looking for a lecturer in conservation and ecology. I was recommended by the dean of the School of Natural Resources. He told me to get down there for an interview, take the job and finish my thesis there. Then he added 'Move out!' " John's brows knitted as if puzzled. "Guess he thinks I'm getting to be a fixture."

I liked the idea of Vassar College: bright young women, less than a hundred miles from New York with its publishers, editors, artists and theaters, and only an hour from the Catskills, some of the most beautiful mountains I had ever seen. Happily I set the table and carried out a pot of chili.

"Vassar College. That sounds perfect."

"No," snapped John.

"Really? But it's a beautiful place."

"No," he said, "does not mean no to Vassar College, it means no to that stinker under the table." The ground trembled and a drumroll followed.

"Meph," I cried, and squatted on my heels to greet him.

"There must be some solution for this beggar." John smiled. "A person can't even eat his chili around here."

"Vassar College," I answered.

In July John was interviewed by Ralph Kempton and given the job and the morning I heard the news I strolled down the lane to visit Cora Strang. She was hovering over her egg basket like a mother hen.

"I've got a little bird for you," she said. "Fell out of the nest that belongs to those robins that hate John." She chuckled.

Ever since John had banded the robins that nested in the Strangs' apple tree three years ago, the adult birds—even though they flew south each winter—had had it in for him. They would scream, strike and dive-bomb him. Gib could approach them, and so could I, or Cora, or Joe, or even Fred the milk-truck driver, who resembled John a little, but not John. They knew him as clearly and precisely as a mother knows her child, and they treated him like an enemy.

Amazed at their ability to recognize him from year to year, John tried some experiments with disguises: Gib's hat, Cora Strang's big raincoat, one of my skirts, a cowboy hat. Nothing doing. The robins saw, screamed and struck—until the day John drove the tractor down the lane. That day they ignored him—until he parked and got off. Wham! The male robin struck him in the head. He got back on and the birds were quiet.

It is well documented that birds see only parts of creatures, a telltale eye, a red breast that says to a robin "male," a short neck that says "hawk." Yet the robins lost sight of the detail that was John when he got on the tractor. We could not understand what the detail was and probably never would, for birds' eyes are beyond human imagination; they record instantaneous movements, see seeds on the ground from the top of tall trees; see the fang that means danger, rather than the whole fox; yet John on a tractor was no longer John. Was it possible that they had not yet developed any instinctive reactions to the objects of the machine age and that John on the tractor had no identity? Would it take another hundred thousand years of evolution for robins to see a man on a machine?

I lifted the bright-eyed robin out of the basket and smelled his sweet feathers. He chirped and begged for food just as if I had pushed the button for "Here comes mother."

"I'd love to raise him," I said, "but no more tragedies, please. We'll put him in a bush near the apple tree and his parents will find him and feed him."

Cupping the perky, stubby-tailed bird in my hand, I carried him to the lawn and was balancing him on a twig in the forsythia bush when Gib approached.

"Cute, isn't he?" His eyes twinkled. "By the way, a friend of mine found a young horned owl that can't fly. I told him you might want it because you want to write a story about owls."

"A young horned owl?" I stopped myself from instantly saying "Yes." How could I take care of an owl and a baby? But then I thought of the book, the illustrations I could paint and of how my writing was richer when I lived with a wild thing. So even as I shook my head no I heard myself say, "Gib, I'd love to have an owl."

The owlet, which John named Bubo from *Bubo virginianus,* the scientific name for the species, was a sober-looking fellow, curious about all things that moved. Below his formidable beak and facial disk, dusty gold and brown feathers spoke of the night and the dark of the moon. Here, sitting on the tent floor, was the tiger of the woodland birds, the most powerful of all the owls. Although young, he was as big as an adult, about two feet high, with a wingspread of over three feet. He ran across the floor, snapped his beak and hid in a box.

In a few days we had Bubo calmed and somewhat tame by feeding him mice that I trapped around the tent. Within a week he showed the same awesome devotion to humans that the falcons and porpoises seem to feel, a kind of reverence for us, a sharing perhaps, of some kindred spirit. Since Bubo was about four weeks old and probably would not imprint on us, we decided to socialize him through the falconry techniques my brothers had taught me. John jessed him with leather straps and snapped on a leash. Next we let him get so hungry that he was savagely jumping on leaves for something to eat. Then we stood back, held out a mouse and whistled. After days and weeks of patiently waiting he finally flew to John's hand and we had an owl that would come home at our call, whether he was hopping around the knoll or sitting in a tree. Through food a bond was built between us and Bubo. This bond deepened when we stroked him or let him sit close to us on the edge of the table as we worked. We were, in his eyes, not exactly parents but certainly a friendly source of food.

To tame Bubo further I carried him on walks, happily anticipating Vassar and the baby developing quietly under my smock.

As August drew to a close it was apparent that my dream of having the thesis finished was totally unrealistic. When I worried aloud to John, he seemed calm, but it was a calm I had come to recognize as John's way of reacting to stress—a slowing down almost to a standstill.

"My teaching load at Vassar is light," he said. "I'll finish it on the job." Stretching, he rose and walked to the tent door. "Let's enjoy the woods."

The baby was due on September 18, 1950, and on that same day

John had to leave Ann Arbor in order to be at Vassar, with car and trailer in time for the first faculty meeting. As the days passed he became concerned about the timing.

"I hope you have the baby soon," he said. We were packing books. "I sure want to see him."

"Him? The baby will be here on September the eighteenth," I said reassuringly.

When the moment came to leave our forest, I was burdened with sadness. "Taking down tents makes me feel like a failure," I said, pulling up a stake. "It does something awful to me each time, and I've taken down a lot of tents in my day." As John loosened a rope, I was reminded of an incident years before, after John and Frank had gone off to college. Dad had turned for companionship to me and my cousins Ellen and Paula, Aunt Polly's oldest girls.

Once he took Paula and me camping at one of his favorite spots, near the Seneca Dam on the Potomac River. I told John now how Paula and I had tried to help him by pitching the tent, while he went off to fish for supper. When he returned, and I proudly showed him how smooth the tent was, he snapped, "This won't do. You've pitched the tent right on the path. The fishermen come down this trail all night and day. Take it down."

We shifted the tent to a better spot, and when I asked Dad what else we could do to help, he handed me a bait bucket and told us to go out on the Seneca Dam and collect hellgrammites, stone-fly larvae. This was a job I had done many times so, swinging the bucket, Paula and I waded into the water and climbed up on the long huge dam of loose rocks. The dam was more like a rapid than a barrier. It slowed down the water and diverted much of it into the old Chesapeake and Ohio Canal. After catching several dozen hellgrammites, Paula and I started back to camp. The rocks were slippery, the water fast. Suddenly I slipped, fell and knocked Paula down. Laughing hysterically, we bumped down the dam to the bottom. The bucket was gone.

My father's nostrils flared when he saw us approach empty-handed. "You lost the bucket because you were playing. I saw you out there laughing and having a big time." Unable to argue with my father I went back to camp in guilty silence.

That evening, to avoid more trouble, Paula went into the tent to read and I crept down to the river and sat in a water-filled rowboat. I kept my hands in my lap. Presently I noticed that a large catfish had somehow trapped itself in the boat. Feeling sorry for it I lifted it out and returned it to the water. Dad canoed into view, and I told him, smiling, "There was a poor fish in here. I let it go."

"That fish," he said calmly, "just happened to be tomorrow's breakfast." I covered my face. Nothing was going right.

The next day, I offered to pack the car and Paula and I did the job carefully and well. Dad slammed the trunk closed and took off. Halfway up the dirt road to the highway he slowed down.

"Did you get the tent?" he asked.

I stared at Paula, Paula stared at me.

"No," I whispered.

It was then, I told John, that I first became aware of a frustrated-achiever syndrome where men were concerned. "It seemed to me that I could never quite please them."

"You please me," he said. But September 17 found him pacing the apartment floor, looking anything but pleased.

"The baby will come tomorrow," I told him confidently. "You *will* see it."

We had finished packing our worldly goods into the trailer: bird traps, tent, camping stoves, an antique chest, a bed, two chairs and boxes and boxes of thesis data, books, manuscripts and illustrations.

At four o'clock, while I was tying a chair onto the trailer, I dropped the rope and bent over.

"Take me to the hospital," I said. "This is it." I hurried to tell my mother, who had arrived the day before.

Once I got to the hospital the contractions stopped. Dr. Price took soundings and put her hands on her hips.

"It's going to be a breech birth," she said. "Longer and more difficult."

"How long?" I was beginning to panic. "John is scheduled to leave at ten o'clock tomorrow morning."

"Long."

As if the child had heard and wished to please, it began turning around with great thumps and kicks. All night the baby and I worked at this maneuver until, at dawn, just as the sun shone through the hospital windows I stood up, kissed John, and called for transportation to the delivery room.

"This one is for keeps," I said as I got on the stretcher. "We can't phase this one back." He walked beside me to the door, leaned down and looked into my eyes.

"Give me a boy," he said, and again my heart sank. We were at long last, after six years of marriage, having a baby. What difference did it make what sex it was? But I looked up at him through that sea of flowers that made the world beautiful.

"I'll get you a boy," I said. But I cried.

I gave birth to an alert, blue-eyed, beautiful baby girl. When Dr. Price tucked her in my arms I kissed her until she wailed. John came in the room, pulled back the blanket and smiled at his daughter in awestruck wonder, for all his disappointment.

"She's so small," I said. "Five pounds. But look how perfect and gorgeous she is." I touched her hand and the pearly fingers gripped mine.

"We were going to call a girl Carolyn Laura, after her two grandmothers," I reminded him, "but she's so small she's not even a branch on the family tree. She's a twig."

"Hey, Twig Carolyn Laura George," John said. "I'll see you in Poughkeepsie."

I rocked Twig softly. Although I felt guilty over not giving him a son, my head was swimming with plans for a daughter.

5

The Women

By the time Twig, my mother and I arrived at Vassar, John was well known there. Bubo was flying in and out of the window of our assigned apartment and Gunner was in heat. We had planned to breed her eventually, but not just then.

Stepping out of the cab I had taken from the station, I saw a pack of dogs snarling and fighting their way down College Avenue with John and Gunner in their midst. As he pulled Gunner toward us, John passed a tall woman who, from her lean and authoritative look I was sure must be a professor, while another woman with the eyes of a deer hurried toward us from across the street. As I kissed John, glancing up along a cathedral arch of elms above the gingerbread houses, I saw the lean scholar pull her skirt around her to avoid the dogs. "Bitches ought to be spayed," she said.

"Why the bitches?" returned the other woman. "Owners of males have responsibilities, too. You don't impose our morals on dogs." Turning to me she said, "Hello, you must be Jean. I'm Evelyn Kivy. I'm with John in the Zoology Department and I came by to see if I could do anything." She was small and feminine with black curly hair cut close to her head. I introduced her to my mother, and together we made our way through the crowd of dogs to the porch of a college-owned Victorian house that had been converted into small apartments for young faculty members. John held off the dogs, and while we waited in the foyer he managed to pull Gunner from them and get her inside. Then he led us down a long dark corridor and opened a paneled door.

"This was once the sunporch," he said. The light flooded an enormous room where our meager pieces of furniture floated as though at sea. It seemed more like Charlie's property than the sturdy four walls and the open fireplace I had envisioned, though when I saw Cora Strang's rocking chair in front of a long bank of windows I felt somewhat reassured.

As I toured the one small dark bedroom, which had to be entered through the kitchen, and the closet with windows that was to be Twig's room, any expectations of a freshly painted apartment, with ivy framing the windows and a modern kitchen and bath, shriveled like hawkweed after a frost.

"No washing machine," said my mother. "And a baby in the house. Now, that's a problem."

"Flush toilets and a bathtub," I said quickly to cover my disappointment. When I saw Bubo perched by the tub, newspapers spread underneath to catch his droppings, his head turned upside down as he watched the water drip, I turned to John.

"I thought you were going to keep him at the lab?"

"One of the students who lives next to the lab has a bird phobia," he explained. "She all but fainted at the sight of him."

Bubo's feathered eyelids lowered and then slowly lifted as he focused on me. He snapped his beak three times. I heard the wind in the beech trees outside, and smelled the green scent of their leaves. The apartment would be just fine. John would be working long hours on his teaching and his thesis. I would have my daughter to play with, and while she slept I would watch Bubo and study his flights and wing-vaulted hops. I would have a chance to finish illustrating and writing the owl book with the old fuzzy fellow here at home.

Mother disapproved of the owl in the apartment and said so to Evelyn.

"I didn't bring up my children in this way," she said.

"But you *did*." I laughed. "We always had pets."

45

"I always stood for gracious living," she insisted. "It was the Craighead men who let the owls fly through the house and who would come to the table in their bare feet. Not I." Finishing her inspection of the apartment she said again, "You certainly ought to have a washing machine."

I waited for John to agree but he seemed to think I was perfectly capable of washing clothes in the bathtub.

"We need other things first," he said. "For instance, a dining table."

When Evelyn renewed her offer to shop and run errands for me, I suggested that she show Mother the campus before she went home the next day. "By the way," Evelyn said as she held the door for Mother, "there's a faculty meeting on Monday. The head of our department would like to introduce all three of you to the college faculty."

"Twig and me, too?"

"This is a woman's college. Of course, Twig and you."

On Monday I asked John what we should do with Gunner, for if we left her alone in the apartment she would wail like a banshee.

"We'll have to keep her in the car," he said. "She'll be quiet there."

So at four o'clock we put Gunner in our new-old Chevy and drove to the meeting which was to be held in the vaulted room of Aula, the faculty building. We took our seats near the podium. Twig slept through the business meeting, then awoke when Dr. Kempton began to introduce John. Her big eyes riveted on me, and her lower lip began to tremble. She whimpered at first and then screamed. Hugging, rocking, patting and jiggling her only sent her voice higher among the ceiling beams. Seated to my right and left were two Victorian-looking women—but women nonetheless. I unbuttoned my shift, held Twig close so as to cover my breast and pressed a nipple in her mouth. Kneading me, as all little nursing mammals do their mothers, she sucked quietly. The professors on both sides stared straight ahead with ladylike politeness. Their embarrassment was evident in the color of their faces. But Twig was quiet.

As I left the hall I heard someone say "nursing in public" in a tone of contempt, and my spine went hot with mortification. Immediately Evelyn was beside me, commenting on the joy of hearing a baby cry at a Vassar

46

faculty meeting. "This is a new trend here," she said, "bringing in young married couples. The college has been labeled a matriarchy in a Mellon financed study by Carl Binger and Nevitt Sanford of Stanford University. The president is trying to make it a more normal environment for young women by hiring men with families." I was standing with Evelyn on the porch, while John went for the car, when a small, round woman came trotting up the steps, smiling broadly. Evelyn introduced her as Mrs. Wolkonski, the head of the Russian Department.

"Your bitch is hung up with my dog," she said, and pointed to the petunia garden. "They're stuck end to end."

I wanted to sink out of sight. There was Gunner copulating on the Vassar quad, in full view of innocent young women whose parents had sent them off to this sequestered campus. But Mrs. Wolkonski went on smiling.

"Let me know when the puppies come," she said. "I'm curious to see what Lucky's pups will look like."

"Lucky?" I said.

"Yes, Lucky to be alive. I picked him up off the streets of Hell's Kitchen. He's ugly. Got whiskers on his chin and back. He is the color of a lion with the rear end of a dingo. What breed is your dog?"

"A bluetick hound." In answer to Mrs. Wolkonski's baffled look, I explained, "That's an American foxhound. It is bred especially to hunt the American red fox, who is faster, trickier and smarter than the English fox."

"How long is the gestation?" she asked.

"Sixty-three days," Evelyn answered as John, who had parked the car by the entrance, came up the steps. His face was white with anger. He had seen Gunner and Lucky.

"Who left the window down?" he snarled and I guessed I knew. After a moment or two he decided I should walk the three blocks home while he waited for Gunner and Lucky to uncouple. The congestion of blood around the male dog's baculum would keep the two linked for about another half-hour before they could separate.

That night, beginning right after supper, Twig screamed and cried until 3:00 A.M.—a pattern that was to go on for almost two months. I was beside myself over what to do for what someone had said was colic. John and I took turns walking with her in our arms until we all fell asleep from exhaustion. This routine was too much for John, so we worked out a schedule: he would carry her for a few hours after supper, while I slept, and then I would take over. I would rock her and sing to her, get mad, put her down to let her cry it out, and then pick her up again. The only thing that saved my sanity was Bubo. He flew to the back of the rocker when I whistled, pounced on wind-up toys in the dark and flew into the tub to bathe when I drew water. He was the spirit of the woods, whose presence somehow made the exhaustion endurable. At times I would envy him because he was a creature of instinct, whereas I was a mother whose baby was crying and for whom all the books and verbal advice on child care were no help at all.

Fortunately Twig was quiet during the day, and I found time then to do portraits of Bubo and to entertain the stimulating and lively faculty members John brought home. But I missed the woods and fields. One day I bought a piece of canvas and designed a baby sling, made with a tuck for the buttocks and holes for the feet. With Twig in it, nestled against my right hip, one afternoon, after a few try-out walks to the store, I stepped off the sidewalk and took the path under the dark rhododendrons that lined Vassar Lake. A tufted titmouse sang from a dead limb, a woodpecker called out his whereabouts and the sun shot lights over the water. I began to name the plants and birds for Twig, just as my father had begun my own lessons so long ago.

One day I climbed with Twig up a long slope, crossed Raymond Avenue and arrived on the Vassar campus. The college buildings were Ivy League Gothic and functional Richardson, and to me they were not particularly attractive. What made them so was the landscaping around them. Some genius had carefully planted the white pines, beeches, elms and other indigenous trees of the Hudson Valley so that they framed portions of brick walls, towers, spires and doorways. I would sit on the grass with Twig and pick out windows, chimneys and cornices in their leafy frames.

On Friday afternoons a senior named Kate would join us for an hour or so. She was fond of Twig and would bring her cookies and a ball to play with. Kate was the epitome of Vassar: slim, blond, fine-featured, intelligent and upper-class. She wore kilts, cashmere sweaters and the gold circle pin which at that time was the hallmark of good taste. At sixteen Kate had been given a debutante ball which she went through "for my parents' sake."

"It's degrading," she said. "Times are changing. Women don't have to be put up for sale anymore."

"I've had my four years of college," she told me one day. "I've traveled in Europe and Africa. I know what it is to win honors. In June, when I go home, I'll be expected to marry somebody from my own social background. I'm supposed to have babies, be on the school board and other worthy organizations. And if I am a really good Vassar graduate I'll become president of the local League of Women Voters."

I agreed that it all sounded pretty horrible, and said, "Then why don't you get a job on a freighter and go to Australia?"

"Well, I have one other choice. I could get my Ph.D. and come back and teach at Vassar."

"But why Vassar?"

"Most coed colleges and universities won't hire women. That's why women's colleges are so important, and they tend to hire their own grads. Of course your friend Dr. Kivy is an exception; but then she's famous."

It was true. Evelyn had run the first experiments to test the effects of radiation on the reproductive organs of male hamsters. When she bred them, the first generation were mostly deformed or stillborn. When she bred the survivors there had been no offspring. The second generation was completely sterile. It was all pretty scary.

When I asked Kate whether she had thought of going to a coed college, she said, "I've had more opportunities here than I ever would have had in a coed school. I've been editor of the newspaper and president of my class, both positions which traditionally go to men in coed schools. I may never be so lucky again."

On a bright day in December, when I had taken Bubo outside to exercise him, I turned around to see Kate and invited her in for coffee. As I opened the door Bubo swung his head low over his feet and then flew to his perch, alighting like thistledown.

Kate leaned over Twig, asleep in her crib, a tumble of golden curls against her cheek. Then walked to the drawing board where I had an unfinished painting. "Can you really have a husband, a baby and a career?" she asked. "My mother says the two won't mix."

"Well," I said, "I work at home. I think that makes all the difference. When you are a writer you compose in your head a great deal. While I walk with Twig or shop or wash clothes, I'm writing. When she sleeps I type and paint. I admit that you get pulled in all directions. But this is not to say it can't be done."

"Thanks, that's just what I needed to hear. I've been accepted at Yale for graduate school . . . and I'm engaged to be married."

The sixty-three days passed and one morning Gunner turned around on our walk and trotted home with Twig and me at her heels. She curled up on her rug and immediately had a contraction. I called John, and by the time he got home two of five puppies had arrived; both pug-nosed and lion yellow.

"That Lucky's got strong and dominant genes," John said.

The faculty dogs were a motley lot; there was not one purebred canine among them. We decided that the next time Gunner came into heat, we would lock her in the college barn.

February brought sleet, snow and winds that whistled through the many windows of our sunporch living room. And still Twig cried at night. John was losing weight, I was tired and irritable. I wondered if our lives would ever be normal again. One icy morning after I had finished nursing Twig, I made an appointment with the pediatrician.

"I think I'm starving her to death," I said. He patted her plump little buttocks, weighed her, and assured me she was fine. But he had a suggestion.

"Warm some milk, put it in a cup and let her drink it. No use fooling with bottles at this point. Also pull her up to the table and feed her from your plate—meat, vegetables, potatoes, ice cream, anything she'll eat."

Peace descended upon us. We slept from ten to six. I stopped resenting John for escaping to the lab all day. I found time to be mother, wife, artist, hostess, listener and typist for John's lectures, and loved every minute of it.

On sunny days I opened the window and let Bubo fly to the spruce tree where he faced the sun with his eyes and beak open, absorbing vitamin D through the only bare skin on his body, his eyes and his opened mouth.

One night as I crossed the living room in the moonlight for a look at Twig, a billowy shadow hopped across the floor, sending up swirls of warm air. I flicked on the nightlight. Bubo was playing with a dust ball, hovering over it as if it were an owlet.

"Dear fellow," I said, picking him up and hugging him. "I'll get you a night friend." I smelled his sweet feathers and felt him gently tucking his talons under, as owls do when they step into a nest so as not to harm their young. Then he snapped his beak affectionately, and I took out my watercolors and paper, and for an hour or so I made sketches of him.

A few nights later a student called, in hysterics, to say that a bat had fallen down the chimney of her dormitory and was creeping around the room. "Its mouth is open and it has all these *teeth* and it keeps making eerie, horrible screeches."

John went to the dorm and came back with the bat. It was still cold from hibernation, its movements slow and laborious. We put it on a piece of bark in a bell jar, which we kept in the refrigerator until spring. Every time I opened the refrigerator and saw the soft night creature, I would wonder why it chose to sleep upside down. How many millions of years had it taken for the bloodstream to adjust to that?

On a warm April day, when the heat was off in the apartment, I took out the bell jar and placed it on the table. Holding Twig in my lap, I sat watching the winged mammal come awake. Recalling that hibernation desiccates an animal and that the first thing it wants is water, I poured half a cupful into the bottom of the jar.

Around noon, with his blood circulating nicely, his eyes alert and his wondrously webbed feet stretched out into Draculaesque wings, Chiropter (a Latin name again) filled the bell jar with piercing sounds. At this time it was not known that bats navigated by sonar, and so it appeared to be magic that brought the bat down to the water to drink.

Then he was off and around the room, diving through doorways, swinging around lamps, avoiding the clothesline in the bathroom, finally locating the curtain, the only rough texture near the ceiling, where he hung himself up for the day.

Bubo's head screwed all the way around as he followed the bat. Any minute I thought his head would come off and fall to the floor. For the next few nights his life was enlivened by the company of the swooping, darting bat; then one day I opened the vent in the bathroom and from far across the living room Chiropter headed for the empty hole and flew directly out. Like the nineteenth-century scientist I had read, I presumed he had a sixth sense, a mysterious divining rod for openings in walls.

When warm weather came to the Vassar campus I returned to the lawns and gardens with Twig still in the hip sling, my hands free to use binoculars or take notes. John had a basement laboratory under Avery Hall, an old horse barn that had been converted into a theater. It was called the Dungeon and it had become a gathering place for students. I liked to go there myself to talk with them or simply listen. My primary object, however, was to help John finish his thesis. No progress had been made on it all winter and I was becoming frantic. We desperately needed a promotion; John's present salary was hardly enough to live on and promotions at Vassar did not come without a doctorate.

And so I did what I didn't want to do. I pushed him each day to dictate something while I typed it out. I felt aggressive and unfeminine, but I heard my brothers telling me at the time I met John, "You'll have to push him. He's a talented guy and smart, but he needs to be pushed or he blocks."

The typewriter rattled; there would be progress until a student or a faculty member dropped in to chat. At those times I would sit on the floor with Twig, showing her pictures of octopi in the zoology books and seashells from the college collection, and I would try to understand what the trouble was, and wonder all over again whether a woman could really serve her family and her own need to be a person too.

One afternoon while I was typing in John's study, off the main basement lab, I heard female footsteps coming down the steps. They had a flat sound, not the lightness of the usual student.

When they reached the door of the study, I spun around to see a woman with frizzy brown hair and a triangular figure. She had a forced smile and stooped slightly as if to hide her lovely full breasts.

"I'm Dr. Gertrude Banks." Women professors at Vassar didn't ordinarily use the doctoral title, and I must have looked startled as she went on to ask, "Is John George in?"

I said, "He's out in the field with some of the students, checking on a chickadee nest." Something in her face told me I had said too much.

"Oh. Isn't it nearly time for his conservation class?"

"I don't know," I said lamely.

52

"I'm an assistant professor in the Botany Department," Dr. Banks went on. "A bacteriologist. The Third Kingdom." Her smile came and went as she said, "And I'm very much interested in John's conservation course."

Nonsense, I thought, this woman is up to no good. Could it be that she was spying on the young male in the department who was a threat to women's jobs?

"I'll find him and tell him you're here," I said, hoping I could warn him of my uneasiness.

"Never mind. He'll be here for class, won't he?"

John's laugh sounded outside the entrance. Thankfully, I picked up Twig and ran up the steps to meet him.

"Hi," he said. "We've been hunting for a chickadee's nest all morning. The male sings the sotto voce song that means he's about ten feet from the nest; but I'll be damned if we can find it."

"A Dr. Gertrude Banks has come calling," I told him quickly. "And she has not come for nice reasons. She plans to sit in on your lecture . . . like a spy."

"Gertrude Banks?" John saw no woman as a threat. "She's nice; she's all right." He laughed at me, and as he headed down the stairs I followed.

"Be careful," I said. Then I recalled how my mother handled enemies. Whenever a woman flirted with Dad, she befriended her and the flirtation stopped dead.

"By the way, Dr. Banks," I said, coming toward her, "John and I are having a small dinner party Saturday night. We would love to have you if you aren't busy."

She looked startled, and for a moment it was as though she had not heard me. Then she said, "Yes, yes, I can come." Her eyes narrowed, and she walked over to John.

"I wonder if I could sit in on your class, Mr. George."

I flashed a glance at him and mouthed "No."

But he said confidently, "Sure, make yourself comfortable."

I pressed Twig to my hip, tied her on and went out to the Shakespeare garden. I sat down before the great bard of soliloquies and began one of my own.

I cannot do anything more for John, I thought. He must do it for himself. In the end no one can help anyone else. It's time I started writing in my own name and in my own way and let John be what he is without me.

I closed my eyes, feeling the guilt mount. John was enjoying the public lectures and the awards and honors we shared. An amusing and authoritative speaker, he often told audiences how we had written the animal biographies. I had been glad for him. I loved seeing my handsome husband take the leading part in the show we had produced together. But now I had to ask myself whether he knew it was only a part. It seemed to me that he was beginning to believe *he* wrote those books. I shook my head, ashamed of having such thoughts. What difference did it make? We were man and wife, companions and lovers.

Twig had fallen asleep. Her transparent skin, with the tint of her tiny veins shining through, was pink with health. I kissed her and smelled her hair. I loved that smell; as I breathed it, my now empty breasts tingled, although the milk no longer flowed.

I knew now what I was going to write on my own. I lifted my head and looked at the bust of Shakespeare. I'd known it since I was a child on the Potomac River, hunting sagittaria roots with Dad and John and Frank, building bough beds and cooking in leaf pots.

I was going to write the story of a boy who lives off the land for a year—a story of survival, resourcefulness and ingenuity.

But how was I going to get the boy out into the wilderness in the twentieth century without everyone looking for him?

Walking home, I began composing in my head, the book that would be called *My Side of the Mountain*. But it would take a personal revolution for me to get it down on paper.

6

The Evolution of Love

Women who harass male bird-watchers are not all bad. At our Saturday night party, Gertrude peered over her silver-rimmed eyeglasses and told me about her study of bacteria, the living floor upon which the world of organic life rests. Bacteria, I learned, adapted themselves to adverse conditions with awesome ingenuity; some by sleeping for hundreds of years in the frigid soils of the high deserts, until geological change produced the right conditions for growth, others by surviving in the boiling pots of Yellowstone, or living without oxygen. There were bacteria that killed and bacteria that cured human beings. Most reproduced by splitting into two or more individuals. A few reproduced sexually, meeting, touching and exchanging microscopic bits of nucleic acid.

Gertrude's description of a bacterial love affair set me imagining tiny trysts and minuscule meeting places. Evelyn Kivy and her fiancé, Saul Rosenberg, were there that evening. Saul, a composer, pressed for further details of the nucleic acid kiss. Louise veered off. Glancing at a platter of appetizers, she mentioned that she had worked for the Massachusetts Health Department, closing down kitchens and restaurants in which she found coccus or bacillus or spirillum, the three typical forms of bacteria.

I glanced at the platter in my turn. How many billions of death-dealing bacteria were lying amidst the hors d'oeuvres, I asked myself, with Bubo among the company? I now glanced at Gertrude and wondered what she would do if and when she realized he was there hunched stone-still in his dark corner, eyes closed and hardly noticeable. Should I warn Gertrude, or simply keep quiet in the hope that the great bird would not awaken? Sitting still for hours is a survival technique the owls have perfected. I recalled that he had not yet cast up a pellet of bones and fur, the remains of the mice he had swallowed whole at his latest meal. Until he did so, he would not stir to eat. So I took a chance, and I said nothing.

I could not have been more wrong. Hardly were we seated at the table than Bubo's three-foot wingspread unfolded over the bookcase. One flap brought him onto the table beside the basket of rolls where he swung his head around and forward to look at me. He blinked, his hunger signal. Saul burst into hearty laughter, while John, grinning, offered Bubo his fist.

"Gertrude, meet Bubo," I said primly. "Bubo, meet Gertrude." My voice trailed off. While Gertrude stiffly acknowledged the introduction Bubo, following his own protocol, flew to the top of the kitchen door. Paper napkins whirled in the wind of his flight. I excused myself, opened the refrigerator and took out a frozen lab mouse. Bubo dropped to the floor and followed me, hopping like a toad into the bedroom, where I spread newspapers for his feast. I closed the door behind me and returned to the table. After a long silence, I gathered my courage to face Gertrude with a question. "Do owls have bacteria?"

She passed the rolls without taking one. "I've never taken a culture of an owl's foot," she answered and put down her fork and knife.

"Owl's feet and bacteria," roared Saul. "I've never met an owl before, much less dined with one. It is turning into a Lewis Carroll scene. Where's the rabbit with the pocket watch?" Gertrude left early, thanking me for a "very nice time."

"I'm sorry about the owl," I said as I saw her to the door.

"Private homes are clean," she told me. "The only bacteria you have to worry about is *Clostridium botulinum*. It occurs in canned goods and it stinks. Sniff all cans."

As I walked back to the living room, Evelyn and John were discussing a zoology student and Saul was in the bedroom doorway watching

Bubo gulp his now thawed mouse—head first, the tail hanging out of his beak while he adjusted the lower portion inside. Then he closed his eyes and swallowed the tail.

"Barnum and Bailey was never like this," Saul declared, dropping onto all fours to see what would happen next.

As the sun circled toward summer, Gertrude attended John's class less often and I relaxed. But her plans, like her bacteria, could sleep long years without visible sustenance—as I was later to learn.

When fledgling birds could be seen begging on the campus lawns, the Vassar faculty began the annual housing game. John and I applied for a larger apartment, and after much anxious waiting were able to move up the street to a two-bedroom Victorian Gothic house occupying the entire first floor.

In our married life we had already moved six times. Now, at the sight of boxed books, pots and lamps, I became angry. Being a mother brought on all manner of feelings I had not experienced previously, the loathing of moving being one of them. When Evelyn came by the new apartment to tell me she was leaving for Woods Hole Oceanographic Institution where she held a research chair each summer, I found myself complaining aloud.

"Only the caribou moves more than John and I do. Most creatures establish a territory and stay there."

"Many *young* creatures," Evelyn said, "move from place to place before settling down. Even the sessile barnacle does that. It swims frantically in the ocean until it is mature enough to establish itself permanently."

One day in June, just before graduation, I was walking around Vassar Lake when Kate caught up with me. A member of the Daisy Chain, she had been picking daisies and was carrying an armload for the sophomores who would be honored this year.

"I never thought I'd join the Daisy Chain," she said. "I'd made up my mind that if asked, I'd refuse to join."

"Well, it *is* an honor," I said. "Brains, leadership and beauty."

"But I wanted to be different. My *mother* was a member. I was going to change the pattern."

"But you *are* changing the pattern," I reminded her. "You're going to graduate school."

"I was. But now I'm going home to be married. Warren wants me to help him through law school." While Twig pulled the head off a daisy, Kate went on ruefully, "I'm going to be exactly like my mother. I wanted Warren and me to be like you and Mr. George—working together on books, moving and camping around the country, learning together, instead of the nine-to-five routine." She dipped a bare foot into the water. "You're the ideal couple around here, you know."

Ideal couple, I thought, and closed my eyes. The admiring words cut deep.

Not long afterward a letter arrived from my sister-in-law Esther, asking us to come west and camp in the sagebrush beside the log cabin she and Frank had built in the Grand Tetons. When I phoned John and read him the letter, he said without hesitation, "Let's go." I had wanted to mention two important things in our lives. The first was Twig and how a cross-country journey would affect her. The second was the unfinished thesis. I opened my mouth and then closed it without saying anything. One more male decision had been made. I thought of old Charlie, the winter bird, occupying a snowy territory because his timing had been wrong.

That night we began packing the trailer, organizing it in such a way that we could get out stove, pots, pans, sleeping bags and tents to camp each night in a vacant schoolyard or public park. Motels and restaurants were not even thinkable on a lecturer's salary.

The next day I got up early and made a canvas back-tote for carrying Twig up and down the mountains. John and Frank were working on a guide to Rocky Mountain wild flowers for the Peterson Field Guide Series, and the alpine meadows would be their haunt. This summer I would be climbing to those meadows along with them. When I had completed the back-tote, I put Twig into it for a test jaunt around Sunset Lake. She was silent at first, then halfway around the lake, I heard soft gurgles and warm little hands encircled my neck.

"We'll make it," I told her. "We'll be a nomadic family. You, your dad and I will be our own walls and fireplaces."

At dawn a week later, we set off for the West. Twig was lying on her belly in her crib, which had been set up in the back seat. Head up like a turtle, she was peering perkily out the side window. Bubo, tethered to his perch so he could look out of the back window, was sober and quiet. Gunner lay at my feet, whimpering. She was just coming out of estrous; nine dogs had been courting her and were still milling around the house and yard. Now, with Gunner inside, they were milling around the car. As we rolled down College Avenue they broke into a chorus of howling. A light went on in a faculty house, and a professor peered out; a policeman on his rounds turned to stare. We lost three dogs at the first light and three more at the firehouse. The last one gave up at the top of the hill that descends to the Hudson River. We were on our way.

"I hope Gunner is through with this by the time we pick up Laura," I said. Laura was John's sister, whom we had asked to join us on our trip across country—a selfless and generous person who, although she had said she was going west to relax, I knew was really going so as to help me with the chores and the baby. Eleven years older than John, she had gone to work after high school. The Great Depression had just set in, and all the men of the family were out of jobs. Together with her twin sister, Lauretta, she had supported the family for many years, and had never gone to college as she had longed to do.

John, Twig and I settled into her little room at the back of the single-story house in Milwaukee where she, Ma and Pa George, Lauretta, her husband and two children, all lived out of financial necessity. Having grown up with a room of my own, I felt ill at ease with the crowding, but admired the family's forbearance. Only Lauretta exploded on occasion. Ma and Pa were gentle and quiet, Laura giving and joyous, the children noisy but well-mannered. A good Catholic family, they relied on the priest to absolve them of their mistakes and transgressions. Although they were so different from my own family, I was not unhappy among them and eventually made a friend of Pa, an uneducated but entertaining man.

"Know who you are married to?" he asked me one morning. "John, the son of John, the son of John, the son of John, the son of John. To give the name John to a son is to pass on the family blessing. But that's a nice little girl."

Nearly every morning, while I rocked Twig on the front porch, he would tell me stories of building Milwaukee with his huge, gnarled hands. He had been a bricklayer until the Depression ended his career. When prosperity returned he was too old and the industry too modern and complicated and so he had been passed by.

In better times Pa had bought a summer cottage on a Wisconsin lake and taken his family there on weekends and summer vacations. He had held onto it through the hardest years. John learned to love nature at the lake, fishing the waters, following the birds. One winter his interest had taken him to the Milwaukee Museum, where the director spotted him and saw in him the makings of an ornithologist. So John had been encouraged to pursue an academic career, and had become the first in the family to go to college after high school, with Laura pitching in to help.

Visiting John's home always struck some note in me, and I loved him more passionately there than anywhere else.

"Why is it," I started to say to him one night when his lips touched my neck, "that I feel such an overwhelming passion for you when I'm here?" But what came out was: "Does a male's territory make a female more receptive? Is it an aphrodisiac?"

I rolled over and buried my face in the pillow. Why did I resort to such language when I spoke to John about my love for him? What was wrong? Who was I when I was with him?

Several days later we left Milwaukee with Laura patiently jammed into the car along with John, me, Twig, Gunner and Bubo. As we drove down the street my inside voice came on. I see John in knee pants. He is wearing his bittersweet smile and I love him the same way I loved the miller's son. My heart beats wildly as I see him walk through the door of the high school on his way to the track meet where he lost.

The car rolled out of the city of John's childhood. Laura adjusted her cramped legs, and Bubo snapped his beak at Gunner. As the steeples of Milwaukee were left behind, my heart stopped racing and my passion dissolved.

"It's gone," I said to John.

"What's gone?"

"I don't know." But my inside voice said, "a needful child," and I wondered what I meant by that.

By four o'clock I was looking out for likely camping spots. Setting up camp would take about an hour, and I did not want to be late with Twig's supper. It was not until about five-thirty, however, that we agreed on a campsite—a black oak forest owned by the State of Minnesota. Knotty leaves cast shadows on dark tree trunks as we drove down a dirt road into a clearing and got out.

"How's this for the Plaza Hotel?" John said as I anxiously selected a spot under a tree and began setting up Twig's collapsible crib.

Next I unfolded my drawing table, set dishes on it, lit the gasoline stove and heated Twig's dinner. John took out three cans of cold beer and opened the collapsible canvas stools. After Twig had been fed, I began to relax, no longer racing the shadows that were engulfing the crib, or annoyed by John's having passed by so many good campsites. I listened with pleasure to the "kee-yer" of the yellow-shafted flicker and sighed at the sight of tent, sleeping bags and outdoor cooking arrangements. Scenes like this would be our home for many nights to come.

At sundown a many-tongued wind bobbed the heads of the enchanter's nightshade in the clearing. A red fox laughed and Laura pulled her sweater more closely around her. As my fears were relieved, hers increased.

"Hey!" John called from the icebox. "Where's Bubo's food?"

"Oh, *no!*" I struck my forehead with the pad of my hand. "I left it on Ma's kitchen sinkboard."

"This is the second night he's had no food," he said. "What are we having for supper?"

"Spaghetti."

"Forget it." He stroked Bubo, who closed his eyes and hissed his hunger song. John glanced at his watch.

"I can get back to that last town in fifteen or twenty minutes."

I looked at Laura, who was standing beside the open fire staring up into the shadows of the oaks.

"Please stay," I said.

As I stirred water and flour into the sourdough starter for the next morning's pancakes, I dared to glance at Bubo. He was eyeing everything that moved—from a leaf at his feet to the winged seed floating on an updraft.

"Tomorrow, for sure," I told the hungry bird.

When the stars came out I pulled Twig's crib closer to my sleeping bag, and closed the screen top over her. For many minutes she lay on her back looking up into the dark forest canopy. Then she lifted her feet, studied them thoughtfully and rolled onto her stomach. She closed her eyes and I breathed with relief.

"All is well," I said to the last calling birds and slipped into my sleeping bag. Laura was already inside her tent, silent, but in the semidarkness I could see that her eyes were wide open. A wind stirred and an owl hooted. John put out the fire and we were swallowed by the night. Mice came out, nighthawks whistled, and the community of the darkness got up and went about their lives. For three hours I alternately dozed and awoke to listen for Twig. Around midnight I saw John press to his elbows.

"What's the matter?" I whispered.

"Bubo," he said. "I just heard his hunger cry . . . his owlet hunger cry. Strange that he should do that." I rolled onto my belly and stared until my eyes adjusted to the dark and I could see his round head and shoulders.

"Poor fellow," I said. "He's so darned hungry he's fluttering his wings, begging us for food."

"Sssh," said John and we both stared into the night, sensing a presence in the crisp pattern of dark leaves. "A wild horned owl. See it?" he whispered.

"Yes, and another on the ground just below Bubo."

"I hope they don't attack. He's an intruder. They'll kill him."

"They'll feed him," I said. "Like Peggy and Able."

"No chance, only human beings are altruistic—one of the major differences between man and beast."

Then the owls were silent. After what seemed many hours, we went back to sleep.

In the rosy light of dawn Bubo sat upon his perch, eyes closed, his crop bulging.

"I'll be damned," said John. "They *did* feed him."

Still later, far down the highway in the midst of the Minnesota tall-grass prairie, Bubo verified John's observation, by casting a pellet of bones and mouse fur.

That evening I wrote in my notebook, "I always thought owls were altruistic. They are."

7

The Wise
and the Unwise

In autumn Vassar College becomes a genteel stampede of dinners, teas and social gatherings. John and I joined in with gusto, and it was not until early winter that reality caught up with me. One night I awoke to see snow spinning across the window, a reminder that time was passing—that John's salary and our royalties weren't enough to live on, and promotions were coming up.

I awakened John.

"The thesis," I said. "You've got to finish it. It's getting in the way of everything."

He opened an eye, looked at me and smiled. He had a lovely boy's smile at times like these, and I couldn't resist it.

"I'll get to it," he said. "I've been so damned busy getting my courses organized and going to meetings."

"Oh, I know," I said helplessly. I felt guilty for waking him, and for pushing him again. What I could do, I thought, was to write a book on my own, for younger children. The advance I would get on that would help buy clothes for John and the baby, and a washing machine for me.

Still I could not sleep. In the morning I began thinking of my brothers' advice—that John had to be pushed into doing things. I set the typewriter on the dining room table and went back to the bedroom.

"Let's get going," I said, mustering all my enthusiasm. "It's a terrific thesis. You dictate; I'll type."

In the chilly light of that winter dawn, to the hammering of a downy woodpecker in the backyard, John broke through the block that had stymied his work and our relationship for almost a year. The pattern of that day became our model for the following months. I felt exhilarated: we were a team again. John squeezed in work on the thesis at lunchtime and between classes. Together, we ended the day when the bell in the tower of the Episcopal Church two blocks away bonged 1:00 A.M.

Though I hated myself for driving him, I was ambitious for him, for all of us. We would never make a fortune teaching at a private college, but I could live happily with a man who had contributed a fine piece of research to the world.

Nevertheless, as I typed and proofread his thesis, thoughts of myself crept in. "I don't know what John's potential is," I would say to myself, "but I do know what mine is." When he was diverted by a student or faculty member—he did love to talk—I would think once again that I ought to be concentrating on *me*. I knew what I could do.

One night in January, a sticky snow put down two feet of the best snowman-stuff since our arrival at Vassar. That morning I pushed away the typewriter and bundled up Twig and we went out into the whiteness. I had untethered Bubo, and as I opened the door he flew out to alight on the apple tree. There he watched while we rolled snowballs and placed one on top of the other. I held Twig while she stuck buttons into the head for eyes and a carrot for the nose. As a last inspired gesture she took off her hat and put it on the snowman's head. We stood back to admire our work. It was splendid.

Now Bubo, swooping down from the tree, came, his huge wings billowing, and dropped lightly onto the snowman's head.

"Come down," shouted Twig. The owl blinked. She stamped her foot. "Bubo, do you hear me? Come down this minute!"

I glanced from bird to daughter. "Hey," I said, "it's bad enough to have an owl that thinks it's a person, but to have a little girl who thinks the owl is a person, too, is not good at all. It's time for a new baby in this house."

I took Twig's hand. We started back to the door with Bubo riding on my shoulder. I shut my eyes tightly, and said to myself, "Please let it be a boy, to make John happy."

I was facing again the sad truth that I had been managing to ignore ever since Twig arrived: John really did believe that boys were superior to girls. He wanted immortality—John the son of John, the son of John. One could hardly blame him. I need only to look at my father and brothers, who had achieved so much in their chosen fields, to know that this was a man's world. I had been brought up in that world, and I loved them and those achievements.

Now I picked up Twig and hugged her until the snow on our clothes melted and dripped to the floor.

Less than a week later, I happened to find in the library an article in a medical journal concerning sex determination and fraternal twins. I already knew that fraternal twins are conceived when both ovaries are fertilized at the same time, and identical twins when one fertilized egg splits in two. A study of about fifty pairs of fraternal twins indicated that two boys were the result if fertilization took place early in the ovulation period, a boy and a girl if it occured in the middle, and if it occurred at the end of the period, almost invariably two girls. The author went on to say that a woman desiring a child of a certain sex should take her temperature and when it rises—as it does, of course, during ovulation—she should have intercourse accordingly: early in the cycle for a boy, late for a girl. Since the time the article appeared, all of this has been reargued, proved again and then disproved. Never mind—I was off to bed with a lace nightie and perfume, carrying on an intriguing experiment.

One morning in late February I rolled out of bed before seven and throwing back the curtains to let in a dreary morning sun I turned to John.

"It's going to be a boy."

"Now what are you talking about?"

"The new baby. I'm pregnant."

"I suppose it happened last night?"

"Yes."

"And it's going to be a boy, you say?"

"If your fellow scientists know what they're talking about."

John rubbed his eyes and shook his head.

And so I expanded and blossomed like a tulip. After typing for several hours each morning I would walk with Twig down the path around Vassar Lake. I showed her the spring beauties hiding under the brown leaves. We found birds' nests, frogs' eggs and a hole in a tree where she put her collection of beechnuts and pretty stones.

Late that spring the thesis was completely written, typed, proofed and bound. John went to Ann Arbor to defend it before his aging advisory committee. The night he called to say he had passed, I simply slumped down in the chair with an ungainly thump, sighing my relief, and feeling physically enervated.

"Congratulations, Dr. George," I said when he came home. "Twig is coming down with the chickenpox, the phone bill is not paid and I got a parking ticket this morning outside the doctor's office."

"But my promotion came through," he said. "I'm now an assistant professor."

This *was* cause for celebration. So I brought out the champagne I had bought three years ago to celebrate the doctoral degree. After we toasted John's future and my freedom to raise babies and write, he told me, "I'm not quite done. I have to publish the thesis now. It'll need heavy revisions. Do you think you can help?"

I stared at the bubbles in my glass for what felt like a long time before I said, "Sure."

In May, President Sarah Blanding launched a plan to break up the matriarchal society at Vassar. Married couples would replace the single women who had traditionally been house mothers in the dorms. No one was surprised when Dean Tate called John into her office and asked if he and I would like to be "house fellows." "You are the ideal couple for the job," she said.

"No," I said when he told me this. "I need my privacy."

"We'll get room and board free. We can save some money for a house."

I hesitated, then thought further. "I'm not sure it will be good for Twig. If she thinks a normal family includes an owl, what will she think when she has a hundred sisters?"

John paced the floor. "I don't see what harm it can do her. Besides, it's an honor to be asked."

"Honor? Checking in all those girls at night?"

"No, we don't do that. They are their own disciplinarians. We are just folks for them to talk things over with."

"Talk," I said. "Well, I would like that, I think."

The following morning I went on my annual trip to the liquor store for packing boxes.

"When we buy a home of our own," I said to John as I took books off the bookshelves and packed once again, "I'm going to be like the first land-loving Craighead. I'm never going to move again. For two hundred years his heirs stayed where they were born. I seem to have inherited that gene for place."

Within the week we were visited by two interior decorators who wanted to look at our furniture and work out a decor and color scheme for our apartment in Lathrop House. "Your furniture is interesting," said the woman decorator after she had inspected the chests from the Strang farm and the table from an Ypsilanti dump.

"Are there any special needs you have?" asked the tall young man who was her assistant. "Needs that we could satisfy with a niche or personal corner, perhaps?"

"We have an owl," I said. "It would be nice to have a large sand box with a beautiful twisted stump in it for Bubo to sit on."

They did not seem to hear me.

The young man took out swatches of cloth from which I was to choose drapes and upholstery. After he had strongly suggested that we use this one and not that one, that this rug and that end table would be best, I began to realize that the apartment had all been planned, the materials already bought, down to blue demitasse cups stored somewhere in a Vassar warehouse.

"I still like the idea of the sandbox and the stump," I said. "I'm not trying to be difficult."

When we moved into Lathrop House in August, Twig and I carried her stuffed animals into her new room and put them on the sand-colored shelves, where they slumped and stared. After we had placed her books by her bed, we inspected the big bathroom with its huge tub, ran the water, and then bounced up and down on John's and my bed. Finally we went to the living room. Hand-blocked gold and gray-blue drapes hung at the windows. Pale blue modern chairs graced the long narrow room.

The rug was sand, the couch wheat and gray-blue. It was a handsome apartment.

"Where Bubo sit?" Twig asked after a quick run from one end of the room to the other. We searched the hall and study for a box with a stump; needless to say, there was none.

"Our needs are pretty exotic," I said to John that night at dinner, and we laughed, enjoying the elegance after so many years in a tent. I was not sure, however, how I was going to fit into this job.

Bubo was given a perch under the rhododendron bush outside the door of our apartment, and that day Twig and I picnicked with him to help him adjust to his new environment.

Several days later when Twig and I were breakfasting with Bubo, an elderly woman in a dark suit, white shirt and platter hat stopped by. I recognized her as a professor emeritus of political science, who passed our door on her way to the library every morning.

"That's a very wise owl you have," she said as she bent low to peer under the leaves at Bubo. "I come by here every day, and ask his advice on politics."

"What does he say?" I asked.

"He says nothing," she answered, "and that is why he is very wise."

"I'll remember that when the students ask for advice," I said.

The day before the freshmen arrived for orientation week, I heard the sounds of furniture being arranged in the student room next to our apartment, then of a violin playing, and laughter. Presently there was a rap on our inner door and I opened it upon a tall, statuesque young woman with curly blond hair, freckles and small gray eyes. When she smiled I could count all the white teeth in her mouth.

"I'm Sue," she said. "I'm your neighbor. I lived in your apartment last year." I invited her in to see the changes. Having satisfied her curiosity, she joined me in the kitchen where I was making coffee. After a glance at the shelves of Vassar china and glasses, she walked to the window and peered out.

"My God," she gasped, turning ashen. Her pupils contracted, her mouth hung agape.

"What's wrong?"

"I just saw a huge bird."

"Oh, that's just Bubo, our pet owl. A great horned owl."

The perspiration began to bead on her forehead. She was trembling.

"I have a bird phobia," she finally said. "I'm terrified of birds. I get ill."

"You're not the student . . . ?"

"Yes. My psychiatrist says it has to do with my martinet of a father. He's an Episcopal minister."

"You can't scream and yell at God, so it comes out this way?"

"Yes," she said. "But I'll work it out. I'm getting better." She sat down on the gray-blue-and-wheat couch.

"This is terrible," I said. "We'll have to get rid of Bubo."

"That would help. I'd appreciate that."

A second rap sounded on the inner door. A good-looking redhead with neatly plucked eyebrows, a clear skin and sharply penetrating eyes stepped in.

"I'm Lynne. I live across from Sue." She walked into the living room, nodded to Sue, then looked around.

"You're doing this of your own free will?" She laughed. "God, they'd have to tar and feather me to get me to move in with a pack of Vassar women."

"I must admit my first encounter has been nerve-racking," I said.

Lynne quizzically glanced from me to Sue. "What's wrong?"

"They've got a pet owl," Sue said. She was still shaking.

"Oh, my gosh," exclaimed Lynne. "I can't believe it. An owl next door to Sue."

Sue wiped her face and smiled. "You think you've got troubles with me," she said, laughing now. "Wait until you get to know Lynne."

I glanced at the young woman and wondered what could be wrong with her. She looked to me so all-American and wholesome—but then, so had Sue.

"She had no childhood," Sue offered. "So she jokes all the time. Her mother made her practice the violin every day after school. She's never had any fun. But she's brilliant, a wit and a genius on the violin. She's headed for Carnegie Hall next year."

I poured Lynne a cup of coffee and sat down.

"Does this mean you have a phobia too?" I asked. Lynne's eyes twinkled as she lifted her cup and glanced at me over the rim.

"Yes," she said. "Kids." For a long moment I stared at her. Then I burst into laughter. The sawdust that had been draining out of me ever since we took this job stopped flowing. This was going to be a terrific position after all.

That night John and I discussed what to do about Bubo.

"We'll have to turn him loose," he said.

"But he'll come back." I paced the floor. "When we were kids and let old Windy the barn owl go free, he came back to the sleeping porch every night and used our beds to eat mice on. That would send Sue to the madhouse."

"But it's the best we can do. Besides, it would be nice to have an owl in the campus trees."

"I feel dreadful about letting him go." Again I paced the floor. "I've learned so much from him. I know the dark. I can hear mice running on leaves, moths flying to meet other moths. I know where the crickets hide and how the winds come up in the dark. I never knew the night before we raised Bubo."

The following morning, when Sue was out of the dorm, John and I went down the steps to the rhododendron bush. Twig squatted on the steps, watching us suspiciously but trusting us to take care of her owl. Bubo stepped up onto John's fist. Taking his soft body in both hands, I tipped him up so that his feet stuck out. John unstrapped the leash and undid the falconer's knot on his jesses.

To the northeast, three hundred yards away, was a wooded graveyard where generations of Vassar women had learned to drink, smoke and love. The grasses and bushes there supported a large population of mice and sparrows. Here an owl could make a good living. On to the east some ten miles, moreover, the Nature Conservancy had bought a mountainside that was to be kept forever in the condition of a wilderness. An owl could make a still better living there. Although I realized Bubo would fare best on the mountain, I hoped he would pick the graveyard.

News of events traveled swiftly on the Vassar campus. Hardly had John walked into the center of the quad with the owl than the young women began to gather.

"Do you think Sue will be all right if he's free?" someone asked.

Twig pulled my skirt. "What's Daddy doing to Bubo?"

"He's going to set him free," I said. "He'll be happier."

"No," she protested. "No, he won't be happy."

"He'll stay around," I said reassuringly. "He'll probably come home and sit right on his old stump under the bushes and eat lunch with us. He'll be free to come and go."

"No." Twig ran toward the apartment as John held the bird high. The soft wings spread; John yanked his arm downward in a movement so swift I did not see it, and Bubo was launched. He hung momentarily above John's hand; then he glanced around and focused on the trees. With deep strokes he flew, his eyes pinned on some distant spot to the north. He flew on and on, and I knew by the deliberateness of his flight that we would never see him again.

It was autumn. Some force, perhaps magnetic, perhaps something in the rays of the sun was pulling Bubo straight to a distant rendezvous with the owls. A sob stuck in my throat and I turned to hug Twig. She was gone.

After I searched the quad and sidewalks, I started off at a trot for the apartment. Just then the main door of the dormitory opened and Twig walked out, holding the hand of a graceful young woman with brown hair and remarkable black eyes. She was Nina, a child-study major who often played her guitar in the lobby after dinner, entertaining us while we sipped a demitasse, Vassar-style.

As they came close I could see two handsome china dogs clutched in Twig's hand. One wore a blue ribbon, one a red.

"I gave them to her," Nina said, seeing my concern. "She was crying so hard because her owl was gone. Now she has two new pets."

"Oh, Twig!" I was devastated at not having prepared her for this moment. I could have given her a toy owl, or better still a kitten. I reached out but she turned and began talking to her dogs. I deserved that hurtful back. John and I had been so concerned about Sue that we had forgotten the most important person in the world.

"Maybe your mother would like to play with a dog, too," Nina said, sitting down with Twig.

She shook her head, a firm no.

"She's lonely for the owl, too."

A quick glance at me out of the corner of her eyes verified what Nina said. Quickly Twig picked up one little dog and held it up to me. Now I knew that life in the dorm was going to be not only an experience but an education.

And so we took up the life of house fellows in which our interests and own time were taken up not with each other, as they once had been, but with the group around us. Entertaining students, hiking and climbing mountains with them, listening to their troubles, we lived the role of the ideal couple with the bright, lively little girl. We were productive and outgoing and concerned. My mother had been right. If you really wanted something to work, it would.

And then this is what happened. One morning, big and tight with my second child, I was sitting awkwardly on the steps of our apartment with Twig when Perrin Lowry, a handsome and talented young writer, who taught in the English Department, saw us. He walked up the steps and sat down beside me. I remember envying him his flat belly. Perrin had eyes the color of new turquoise that forced you to look straight into them. That was what I did and it was as though he looked right into my inner mind.

As he took my hand and squeezed it, the blood went racing and galloping through me.

"The *angst*," he said. "I see it there in your eyes. I know how painful it is to be a writer and *not* be a writer. We've both got to raise kids, take care of our spouses, earn cash for food. I haven't written a thing in six months." The feeling in the smile he gave me was unmistakable—frightening.

I stiffened, looking down at his sunburned knuckles. What was I doing? Was I sending out signals of some kind, silent signals that I did not even know I was sending? Were those signals being answered? Last week Len, another member of the faculty, had slipped his arm around me.

Could this be? No, it could not be.

I loved John. I did not mean to send out signals. Terrified of the inner self that was somehow being heard, I got to my feet, excused myself, and pulled an iron barrier about the part of me that Perrin had somehow touched. That could not be.

8

Great Experiments by Everyone

"November first is a good day to be born," said Dr. Paul Lass. "Get yourself down to the hospital at six A.M. tomorrow, before this small elephant gets any larger. I'm going to have to induce the birth."

The dawn was streaked with pale red clouds, calling to mind those mornings at the tent with hawkweeds blowing in the meadow. Orange leaves pranced up from the gutters as John sped the car through the streets of Poughkeepsie. I was both happy and furious: happy to realize that I would see my baby today; furious that it was going to be wrenched from me by chemicals.

But when I left the hospital with our handsome son and carried him up the steps of Lathrop House, I was full of advice from the Child Study Department as to how to handle Twig and this new rival for our attention. I put Craig into his newly painted crib and turned to her with my arms open. She pulled back and ran to her grandmother. I took down from the closet a present I had bought for the occasion. I sat down in the rocking chair and leaned over to hand it to Twig. She opened the box and threw the teddy bear it contained under the couch.

"I can't understand all this making a fuss over Twig, just because she has a baby brother," said Mother. "We didn't know jealousy in my day. I don't have time for all this nonsense."

"But you told me you don't remember your early childhood," I said. "Maybe you were jealous and forgot it."

"There has never been any jealousy in our family. We all loved and shared, and so did you and your brothers."

"Except they beat me up and made me eat that stinging elephant-ear plant," I chuckled. "It's all right to be jealous."

"I think this is nonsense."

Twig made her way from the floor to her grandmother's lap. Her blue eyes pierced me with a look of full-blown resentment. Then she took her grandmother's hand and looked up into her face.

"Kill the baby," she said in a loud clear voice.

"Did you hear that?" Even Mother could not help but laugh.

"At least," I said, "someone in this family knows how she feels." But it would be a long time before Twig and I worked this one out.

The day before Mother left for Florida, where she and Dad were now spending their winters, I suggested to Twig that she help us wash the baby. Mother filled the tub and put towels on the table. I put a stool nearby for Twig to stand on and undressed Craig.

"What is that?" Twig said, pointing.

"That's a penis. You and I have vaginas. Craig and your Daddy have penises. Both are equally important."

"Well," said Mother. "This is too much. I just don't think this is at all necessary."

Twig's hands slid off the table, her curly head disappeared toward the floor, and when I looked she was struggling with her diapers. Assuming she needed to go to the toilet, I unpinned her while Mother sponged Craig. But Twig did not go to the toilet. She fled to her room, and when I went to look for her she was seated on the floor, pulling on her flowered pink panties.

And that was the last time she ever wore diapers. If that baby boy needed them, she certainly didn't. And so at the age of two, the wrath of the woman was born in my daughter Twig. Already she knew she was in second place and she was angry. How had she learned it? From John and from me, of course, and from my mother and her mother and *her* mother. The difference between Twig and her predecessors was that she knew she was furious. We had simply accepted the putdown and gone on living with our feelings of insecurity.

The weeks rolled by. Busy all day with two children, with John and the students, I would awaken at night, confronted by a new and devastating conclusion: that I was not doing a good job of raising my children. Once a month John and I met with the other house fellows to evaluate and discuss student problems. The consensus was that all their troubles emanated from the home, and from the mother in particular. One had leaped off the top of the chest of drawers because her mother had not given her enough attention. Another was doing poorly in school, although she had a high I.Q., because her mother had been overindulgent. The student who had brought a young man to her room after hours was the victim of a mother who did nothing but go to the country club and shop for clothes.

I listened in pain, for Twig was now aggressively clobbering her brother and obviously I was the one at fault. One day when Evelyn Kivy, who was now married to Saul Rosenberg, stopped by the apartment, I asked her, as an authority on genetics, which was the greatest influence, heredity or environment.

"They are both important," she said. "Probably equally. Plus one other thing." She paused, then spoke with emphasis. "The spark. The individual who is doing the reacting."

Fortunately, I realized, the little spark that was Twig had already solved her problem. By toilet-training herself she had opened up new horizons. She could now spend the night with her friends, take trips to the city with Nina, go off and leave her brother behind.

She was accepted at the Vassar Nursery School, where being toilet trained, though not a prerequisite, had its advantages. She could be taken on a trip to Pete Seeger's house, where she listened to him playing his steel drums. She could pour the milk at lunchtime, while other children were having their diapers changed.

A year passed and the sibling rivalry intensified. When I discovered that Twig was lying, I hustled across the campus to talk to Bea Stone of the Child Study Department.

She smiled gently. "Of course she lies. You did too. You've just buried all memory of what you thought was a terrible thing. It's perfectly natural. She needs attention in the face of such esteem for a rival. Ignore it."

The guilt was now a leaden coat. It was already too late to ignore it. I had yelled at Twig, sending her deeper into herself, and she had promptly begun to lose boots, coats and sweaters, and to scream like a steam whistle when I corrected her for anything. Several times I started to speak to John about all this. But getting into any discussion of sexual experience was not one of our talents and so I went on living with my sorrow in the dark, reading books in psychology and sitting in on child study lectures.

That spring, Jenny came into my troubled woman's world to give me back a sense of proportion.

Jenny was the mate of Old Blue, the dominant black-capped chickadee of Sunset Lake and the Shakespeare garden. During the winter Blue led the local troop of chickadees, nuthatches and downy woodpeckers through the forest in search of food and shelter. In the breeding season he drove every other male chickadee beyond the edges of his considerable territory over which he reigned with terrible bursts of song. John's students had mapped that territory and posted it in the conservation lab.

"He's the most aggressive male chickadee I've ever seen," John said, and so one morning I went out to watch him.

"He's heavy and he's old," John said as he pointed him out to me. "That's the formula for dominance in the bird world."

While I watched, I was surprised to see a male wearing a yellow band challenge Blue practically on his own borders. "Watch this," said John to Mary, a sophomore, as Blue darted across the lawn, over the laurel and into Yellow's territory. "Old Blue is dominant, but he's going to lose this battle. The bird landowner *always* wins a fight on his own territory, no matter how powerful the foe. That is because the urge to fight wanes as the distance from the home territory increases."

In the conflict that ensued, wings fluttered, bill was aimed at bill, breaths came sharp and fast. Suddenly Old Blue retreated, and Yellow sang victoriously from his own border.

Later in the nesting season, I went out to help find where Old Blue and Jenny had their nest. Chickadees' nests are not hard to find if you sit still long enough, since the birds carry nesting material and/or food right to the site. But that spring nobody could find the nest although John and the ornithology class had spent hours searching for it. There had to be a

76

nest, John knew, since Old Blue would be heard singing the quick song of the male chickadee when he was about ten feet from the nest. The song awakens the female from the stupor of incubation, and he feeds her.

The day was sunny, and the pink and yellow-green of May's buds tinged the trees.

Old Blue, returning from another of his periodic battles with Yellow, flew into a juniper tree that grew along a wooded path between Avery Hall and the power plant.

"I think the nest's in that tree," said Mary, who was a premed student and had taken ornithology because it was the only course that did not conflict with her required classes. The fact that she knew very little about birds was going to be an asset in the finding of this nest.

"Let's search the juniper," I said.

"It's not there," said John. "I've searched it." Hardly had he finished speaking than Jenny appeared on a dogwood limb near the juniper. She was a vivacious bird, her black cap and bib more lustrous than in most of her kind—a reflection of the high quality of the food resources on her partner's land. Old Blue flitted to a limb just below her and scolded.

"She keeps going to that blob of needles in the juniper," Mary insisted.

"That blob is a robin's nest," John replied. "Chickadees nest in hollows that they dig out with their beaks, usually in a rotted stump or a limb."

Mary said, "There she goes into the needles again."

John dropped to his knees to watch Jenny fly through the tree.

"Lost her," he said.

From the dogwood branch Old Blue sang a pensive, almost inaudible melody.

"The sotto voce again." John focused his binoculars. "The nest has got to be ten feet from that bird."

"Let's look again," said Janet, who had been a member of the Audubon Society before coming to college. She marked off a twenty-foot area around Old Blue and we all searched. We looked under limbs for holes, we ran our hands over every trunk and stump, but we found no chickadee nest. After an hour we gave up and sat down on the hillside again. Old Blue returned with food for Jenny, he sang his sotto voce song once more, and Jenny appeared at his side.

"Damn," said John. "She should simply thrust her head out of her hollow. What's wrong with her?"

Eventually because she was not in a hollow, Old Blue once more swallowed his offering, sang half a song and nervously flew off.

"Maybe she's rebelling," said Mary. "If you had had two broods of five kids every year for five years, you'd figure some way to get out of raising another one."

"Maybe she's taking an evolutionary step," Janet said. "If the female phalarope can get away with having her mate do all the incubating and chick-raising, why can't Jenny?"

John lowered his field glasses to glance at Mary, then quickly lifted them. Jenny had winged up from a bush into the juniper, and this time Mary was right behind her.

"Here she is," Mary called. "Sitting on big blue eggs."

John looked at her as if she had said apples always fall up. He did not stir while Jenny flew out of the juniper and Mary peered into the robin's nest again. She now reported, "There are two different sizes of eggs in here."

John leaped to his feet. "I'll be damned!" he exclaimed. "This *is* the nest. There are robin *and* chickadee eggs in here. Unbelievable. Jenny's laid her eggs in a robin's nest." He shook his head.

"She's starting a new trend in chickadee housekeeping," Mary said.

Janet wondered whether this might be how the cowbird got started laying eggs in another bird's nest.

"Too bad Jenny didn't have a better eye for size and pick a wren's nest," she said. "One of her little eggs is smashed under the big robin egg. I think this experiment is doomed to failure."

The female robin hopped over the lawn with her mate, feeding on insects. Old Blue was singing a lusty "Hi, sweetie" song and Jenny was nervously clicking at us, upset that we were so near her nest. We backed off. She flew to the robin's nest, spread her tiny breast feathers and sat down on the vast pile of eggs. She barely covered one-third of the nest.

Old Blue returned, sang his sotto voce song and once again swallowed his offering. Presently the female robin returned, chased Jenny off the nest and, rousing her feathers, sat gently down on the bizarre clutch.

John grinned and shook his head.

"I love nature," I suddenly blurted. "Jenny is my kind of gal. We mess things up with style."

Later in the afternoon I wheeled my two babies out to the hill and, sitting near Jenny, watched her try to cope with her error.

"You've blown your top, sweet thing," I said. "And boy, do I understand you."

The story of Jenny reached President Sarah Blanding's ear by way of her sister Ellen, who had met Mary near the lake that afternoon. After the faculty meeting Sarah asked John about Jenny. Sarah Blanding is descended from a famous naturalist, William Blanding, who had a turtle named after him. Being a pretty good naturalist herself, she appreciated having John on the campus. After listening to Jenny's amazing story, her face brightened and she promptly asked John to come to dinner that night and to bring me along.

"I am entertaining several trustees," she told him, "who would love to hear this story."

As I stood in the green-gray Tudor living room of the president's house, I was approached by a robust gentleman in a well-tailored suit and two expensively-dressed women. Full of wonder of Jenny, I began talking animatedly.

"Jenny is a sleek and well-groomed chickadee," I told them. A gray-haired man joined the group as I went on. "Jenny and Blue have been hardworking, ideal mates and parents for five years. This year, though, she messed up on everything."

Sarah Blanding came our way, carrying a plate of hors d'oeuvres. She said, "Jean, will you please stop talking? Let John tell this."

The circle opened and John stepped in, cleared his throat, and began to talk.

I stepped back to the fireplace. Sarah Blanding's words had hit me like a thunderbolt. "What am I doing?" I said to myself. "What am I doing to John? Am I too much with him? The thesis is done. I hear

79

Perrin's voice. I must get out of his way and begin my own work. Tomorrow John and I must talk. I need his help.''

The next day came and went, and we did not talk. Instead, I walked the campus trails with Twig and Craig, wondering what my own life was all about, what Sarah Blanding had been trying to tell me.

One Sunday afternoon not long afterward, John and I went to a concert in the outdoor theater above Sunset Lake, taking Twig and leaving Craig with his newfound friend, Joan Gordon of the Sociology Department.

In the midst of the concert the sky darkened, lightning plunged through the clouds, and the trees blazed silver as the wind turned up the undersides of the leaves. Audience and performers picked up their chairs and ran; branches rippled like horsewhips and tree limbs snapped. Just as we rounded the corner of Avery Hall and ducked into the conservation lab, the rain pelted down.

"Poor eggs," I said. "I hope Jenny doesn't have the duty now."

In a yellow light of the storm's aftermath, with trees and leaves dripping, I went with John and Twig down the path to the juniper tree. The robin's nest was upside down on the ground, the precious contents smashed and broken. I picked up a tiny piece of chickadee egg and put it in my pocket.

Three days later Old Blue had a new mate. Jenny, who had tried and failed, had vanished.

Several weeks later John, Twig, Craig and I were eating our last dinner in our apartment in Lathrop House. Craig, the youngest of us, was now three. Although I had enjoyed the years in the dorm, I was more than ready for private life. After we clinked glasses and drank, John unfolded the napkin onto his lap and leaned back in his chair.

"Gertrude has been after me for almost a year to let her borrow my conservation lecture notes," he said.

"So?"

"So I gave them to her."

I stared at him across the table.

"You're crazy. She'll do you in."

"What can she do to me?" There was nothing like John's ego when testosterone flowed. No woman could harm him.

I knew very well what she could do. Gertrude had been criticizing John in public for a long time. Now she had his lecture notes. Anyone who is out to get you can find fault with a piece of work.

"Oh, damn it, John," I said, "you should never have done that." Accustomed to winning women over to his side, he had never met up before with a truly ambitious man-hater.

No promotion came for John that year.

"Let's do another book together," he said after the students had gone and we had moved our own skimpy belongings up to Palmer House to begin a more normal life.

I was ready to write my own book; but now I felt guilty about deserting him. He did like the radio talks and interviews we gave; he did like to have his name on the books. Under my own name I had now written two books for younger children; I had illustrated *The Hole in the Tree* and *Snow Tracks;* and I had believed I was ready for that important one, about the boy who survives in the wilderness. Now I said only, "What should we write about?"

"Very little is known about the water ouzel. It's an incredible bird of the high mountain streams and waterfalls. We can get a study cabin at the Rocky Mountain Research Station at Gothic Colorado and spend the summer studying that bird."

"The water ouzel." Images of clear water and bright wild flowers came to mind as I recalled a day when I had waited with my brothers along Crystal Creek in Wyoming. I had looked down into the water to see a small, wrenlike bird walking on the bottom of the stream gathering aquatic larvae. Then he had popped to the surface like a cork, and flown off toward a waterfall, where he had plunged into the pounding water and disappeared. A wonderful creature, a bird at home among cascades and waterfalls.

All the resolves to write on my own now failed me. John could make up for Gertrude's sabotage by publishing a scientific paper on the water ouzel, *Cinclus mexicanus.* Twig, Craig and I could explore the high country. Marty, one of John's students, would join us to help with the children and the research. I would have a few hours each day to slip off and live with the ouzel in that most delightful of all environments, a waterfall.

We left for Colorado and its roaring mountain cascades while the leaves on the hardwood trees were brilliant with June.

The Dipper of Copper Creek, by John and Jean George, won the Aurianne Award for the best nature writing in 1956. And I happily was pregnant again.

One spring day Perrin and his blue-eyed daughter, Annie, came up to the old farmhouse at the rear of the Vassar property where we had our apartment. The household now included a skunk and a possum, and many of the faculty children made treks with their parents to visit and feed the animals.

"Pregnant again," Perrin said, patting my stomach. "Nice."

"I think it will be."

We sat on the steps while Annie inspected Meph II's handsome tail and stubby nose.

"Think you'll ever try for that Newbery Medal?" he said. "You know you've got to write alone. It's never been given to a team."

"Aw, Perrin, it's not for me. I'm beginning to see my limitations. I'm not good enough. Besides, there's John. I can't leave him and write on my own—except for picture books."

"Theodore Roethke didn't encourage you because of your limitations."

"That was college."

"And Thomas Mann didn't answer your letters because you were just another fan. Nor did Karl von Frisch rise to his feet after his lecture on bees and ask to meet John and Jean George, who had written *Vulpes, the Red Fox* because of *your* limitations."

I listened to Perrin hungrily. I longed for just such a conversation with John, but he and I never got down to the depths of each other's feelings. I knew now that I lived alone even though I lived with him. Perrin and I talked for almost an hour about writing and the problems of breaking free from the necessary routines of life to do it. Then he rose to go. "Jeanie," he said, "I'm having a struggle of my own. You and I should run off together to some wooded hillside and write our own books."

"That would be beautiful," I said, terrified because my heart was beating so hard. "But we never would."

82

"We're as square as two wooden blocks." He poked me ever so lightly under the chin, took Annie's hand and walked down the hill to the campus. My eyes followed him until he was out of sight. Then slowly I went inside and got out the vacuum cleaner.

"I asked for this life," I said as the machine sucked up the dust balls from under the couch.

Ten years later Perrin would die in an automobile accident, and although he had been producing good work in those years I cried for the novels that this tender genius would never write.

Now the telephone rang. Dorothy Levins of the Vassar Nursery School was on the line. "I just wanted to say," she said with a chuckle that tripped over into wholehearted laughter, "that Craig is on his way home from school. He tied some branches on his head, told me he was a moose and climbed over the fence. He's almost to your door. I can see him from here."

I ran to the porch and sucked in a cry of love and delight as I saw Craig coming through the bushes disguised as a moose.

What difference did my writing make? What did it matter whose name was on those books? Who cared that I could not tell John my deepest feelings? He and I had something terrific, right here.

The new baby arrived on October 10. Thomas Luke George, a compact and well-formed little fellow, not only was easy to deliver, but shortly after his arrival, he looked me straight in the eyes before snuggling down quietly in my arms.

My grandmother used to tell us that the child at the breast is the adult of the future. "They are already there—complete personalities even at birth," she had said; and she was right. Twig is still vivacious and intense, Craig sensitive and appealing, and Luke comfortable and well adjusted. He fitted into the family without upsetting much more than Twig's trust in me, since I had told her the baby was going to be a girl. When she heard she had another brother she ran to the backyard and hid in her tent. Many days later she discovered that Luke was wonderful to hold, just the right size to sing to and rock.

Hardly had this newcomer arrived than John came home from the office as pale as the white streak on the skunk's black side.

"My contract is not going to be renewed," he said.

Numb with shock, I said, "Gertrude." Then I began shaking. John had been so certain that this woman could do nothing to him that I had come to think so too. Accepting the idea that he would get no more promotions, I decided Vassar College was a wonderful environment in which to raise children. Now that adjustment had proved disastrously unnecessary.

Every morning for the next week, I got up in the dark and paced the floor until sunrise. Many of our friends had protested the decision, and for a short while there had been a vigorous fight to save John's job; then suddenly everyone stopped protesting. I heard no more defense of him. Had Gertrude been right? Was his course not up to standard? I did not know. But no one, not even I, fought anymore.

What I read from the silence was that John had very little insight into himself or his environment. As the chairman of his department said, "You knew this job was not permanent, so why are you upset?"

One day in late May, while John was in New York being interviewed for another job, I got up at six o'clock with the children. Last night's dinner dishes were still in the sink. Twig was cranky. Craig did not want to go to nursery school. I was tired. Three youngsters were taking more out of me than I imagined possible.

"If I could just run away for a few hours," I said, and I closed my eyes and went back to my childhood. I could see the falcons shooting across the sky like crossbows, could smell the wild garlic in the pot of mussel soup Dad was serving in a turtle shell. I could feel the crisp snap of a sagittaria tuber between my teeth and hear John and Frank call from the river that they had a mess of catfish for dinner.

That's how I get Sam Gribley out into the woods, I thought. He runs away as I am doing now. He even tells his father he is going to go, as I had told my mother when I was a kid and marched off into the night—only to turn around and come back. His father will expect him back . . . but Sam Gribley won't turn around. He'll make it.

I sat down at the typewriter and rolled a sheet of white paper into the machine. A boy? I hesitated, now that I was about to begin this long-pondered book. Yes, a boy. Girls were not free to run away and survive except incognito.

"I am on my mountain in a tree home that people have passed

without ever knowing that I am here,'' I wrote as an opener. ''The house is a hemlock tree six feet in diameter and must be as old as the mountain itself. I came upon it last summer and dug and burned it out until I made a snug cave in the tree that I now call home.

''My bed is on the right as you enter, and is made of ash slats and covered with deerskin. On the left is a small fireplace about knee high. It is of clay and stones. It has a chimney that leads smoke out through a knothole. I chipped out three other knotholes to let fresh air in. The air coming in is bitter cold. It must be below zero outside, and yet I can sit here inside my tree and write with bare hands. The fire is small, too. It doesn't take much fire to warm this tree room.

''It is the fourth of December, I think. It may be the fifth. I am not sure because I have not recently counted the notches in the aspen pole that is my calendar. I have been just too busy gathering nuts and berries, smoking venison, fish and small game, to keep up with the exact date.''

And so I ran away to the forest to survive—right in my own home. I titled the book *My Side of the Mountain,* illustrated it and signed it Jean George. When I finished the writing I began another part of the odyssey that was turning out to be me.

9

The Alarm Cry
of the Crows

The crow stepped across the sill of the open window and cocked his eye at me as I stood at the kitchen sink in our own house on a wooded hillside in Chappaqua, New York. An hour's drive from the city and a ten-minute walk from a hemlock-guarded waterfall, it coincided with a wood thrush's territory.

John was now curator of mammals at the Bronx Zoo and he was in the city long hours learning the new job.

The crow on the windowsill croaked to demand my attention. I looked up.

"Hello," said the bird. He had been named New York—because in a world where it is safer to be camouflaged, he dared to be black, canny and conspicuous as the city itself.

"Hello," I answered with a grin of satisfaction. For years I had wanted to know whether a crow could be taught to speak without first splitting its tongue, as the old wives' tale had it. When New York came into our house I set out to learn the answer. After he had been dumped from his nest in the pine woods by a windstorm, John and Craig found him and carried him home and placed him on the kitchen table. He had greeted me with a bite on the hand. He was a real survivor. When I moved closer he rolled onto his back, spread his wings and fought with beak and

86

claw, to an accompaniment of crow expletives. Having exhausted himself, he paused to examine the ground meat I held out to him. After a quick study he stood up and devoured it. Almost instantly, birdbrain cells sent a message to his nervous system, telling him he had a good thing here. Within an hour we had a pet crow.

New York slept in the apple tree outside the kitchen window, and would rap on the framework to come in when he was so moved. In my effort to teach him to talk, I used the opportunity to say "Hello" each time he paused on the sill. For months he listened but said nothing, although occasionally he did waggle the feathers on his throat, as if placing the sounds that I had made. Then he would fly to the sink for water and a bath, or to the table to be fed. After three months I concluded that crows could not learn to talk without having their tongues split and gave up on the English lessons.

On a summer's day just after sunup, Henry, our good-natured milkman, burst through the kitchen door, stared at me and shook his head in relief.

"I thought you were up in the maple tree," he said. "I could swear you said 'Hello' to me from the branches."

"It's the crow!" I exclaimed, and rushed outside, beckoning Henry to follow.

"Hello," said New York. Looking down at us, he preened a feather, then let out a barrage of "Hellos" that sounded just like me and which echoed out across the neighborhood.

"He speaks," I said, the thrill of discovery running down my spine.

"How can he do that?" asked Henry.

"I don't know, except that crows can mimic like parrots and myna birds. Also, the fact that crows have a language of their own with many sounds may make a difference. Some crow words have double meanings. The only other animal that sophisticated is man."

"You ought to teach him to say 'Stick 'em up.' Then you would have a good watchdog."

"Good idea," I said, holding up food and watching New York float down to my shoulder.

"I'll teach you more words," I said to him, "by standing above you on the back porch roof." Konrad Lorenz, the animal behaviorist, had observed that dark objects looming above the head of a crow or jackdaw were frightening, to their eyes, as the shadow of a predator from overhead. Hearing human words, even long sentences, under such circumstances, often had the effect of imprinting the words on the birds, and when moved to do so they would repeat them verbatim.

I headed for the house, and New York flew from my shoulder to the apple tree. Twig was coming down the steps dressed for school. We entered the kitchen together, and she said, "I'll set a place for New York." I went upstairs to dress Luke for the day. Now one year old, he hugged like no other baby in the world. We were locked joyfully together, arms intertwined, when I came into the kitchen. Craig poked him and slipped into his chair, then listened sleepily to the robins fighting over their property line outside.

A tap sounded on the window. New York hopped aside, for he knew that the window opened outward, and Craig let him in.

"Hello," said the crow.

"Hello," we all answered, as if this were how everyone began the day, and then New York took his place at the table.

"It's about time," scolded Twig. "Your scrambled eggs are getting cold."

"I wouldn't eat eggs if I were a bird," observed Craig.

Twig flashed her brother an appreciative look. She was beginning to like him.

"Well, one thing I know," she said, "is that I'm not going to play with New York anymore. He takes all my toys."

"You can get them back," said Craig. "They're up in the apple tree. And so is one of Mom's silver spoons."

Craig now had his chin in his hands, staring at the crow.

"Why does he have eyes on the side of his head?" he asked.

"So he can see to the side, in front, *and* behind, almost all the way behind," I said. "Three hundred and thirty degrees. He can see enemies coming from all directions as well as food."

Craig turned his head from the far right to the far left.

"I can't see anything but a blur."

"New York's eyes are different from yours. He has two focusing points on his retina instead of one."

88

"He sees two things at one time?"

"Well, not quite, but two spots of focus that serve to magnify images. As a matter of fact each kind of animal sees a different world from all others. Animals, including us, see just what we need to see to survive and no more. A toad sees a blank sheet of paper until a fly moves; then he sees it so sharply he can catch it with his tongue."

New York tilted his head almost upside down to focus the highly acute foveae at the top of his eye on a small bit of food. Craig's head spun around too, since Craig was one who gathered what he knew by doing.

"You don't have the right kind of eyes," I said. "You'll still see the same world even though you're upside down."

"I see up your nose," he said. "And that's different." I laughed out loud unconsciously reinforcing Craig's evolving survival technique—a sense of humor.

The clock hands stood at seven-thirty. I made sure of sweaters, combed hair, took lunch money out of the clay teapot, and hurriedly scooted Twig and Craig out the door to catch the school bus.

"Hello," said New York. I opened the window and with a rustle he flew to the sill. From there he flew to the lilac bush. Then, spreading his wings, he traveled low over our lane, caught up with Twig and Craig, and dropped to the ground beside them. Putting one foot ahead of the other in the manner of all crows, he walked them to Spring Road, the narrow forsythia-lined route leading to the main road by the swamp. The three turned the corner and disappeared downhill, walking to the bus stop together. Presently New York returned to the kitchen window.

"Hello." I knew the bus had picked up the children and that they were safely on their way to school. That was what New York's return to the window said to me. I wondered if he knew it. But no matter. The system we were using was the very same one that crows used to communicate. A signal or a deed performed in a certain context conveyed a message. It might be an alarm call given because the crier was frightened—not intended to warn others but causing others, when they heard it, as a warning to depart.

The house was doing us all good. It was most unfashionable: a brown-stained shingle place, built in the manner of H. H. Richardson but without his genius. The Quaker who built it had incorporated such features as a wide front porch, a high peaked roof and a bay window. Inside, the first-floor rooms were connected by spacious doorways that pulled you toward a sunporch. Here I kept my typewriter and easel, and from that window-encased room I kept an eye on the kids outside. I would also check on them inside, by leaning over the typewriter and peering through the divided doorways. Upstairs four generous rooms off a main hall gave each child a room to decorate and paint as she or he pleased. As school paintings and plaster-of-Paris handprints went up on walls, as railroad trains and caves were built, I could feel the setting of my own barnacle glue.

My Side of the Mountain was at the publishers and I was anxiously awaiting the advance against royalties that would pay for painting the woodwork and sanding the pine floors. Advances for children's books are small compared to those for adult books, but good children's books may sell for years and years. In the long run, they do better than most adult books. The small checks coming in twice a year represented future educations, trips into the wilderness, a special dress for me or Twig, a canoe, a camera for John. Yes, the money would be nice. But more important was the book itself. I had taken a major step forward. I was on my own.

One day I glanced through the glass-paned sunporch door to see Luke playing with New York in the sandbox. The day was fine, the frogs were singing. As I stepped outside, New York suddenly cocked his left eye at young Luke and hopped to his knee. He opened his feathers, sat down and began shuffling his body as if brooding. Luke brushed him off, but New York settled back. After a few more shakes, he lifted all his feathers and went into what I knew must be a trance of incubation—a trance so deep that the bird fell over on his side and lay there staring into space.

The great advantage of raising the wild things I wrote about was that they behaved among us much as they would in the wild, so that by translating I would learn about them as in no other way—not even sitting out in the woods. New York was definitely brooding Luke, although Luke was not of his kind or in anything like the usual setting. Thumbing through my books for an explanation, I discovered that most mammals and birds can instantly recognize the sex and age of an individual of any species, whether man or beast. Luke's childlike movements were a universal language that had triggered the now maturing crow into a state of incubation. Wild things have inner clocks that given just the slightest stimulation start up and go ticking along.

Luke went on playing and New York was still incubating when the phone rang. Sharon Bannigan, the juvenile editor at E.P. Dutton, was calling.

"Elliott Macrae thinks we shouldn't publish a book in which a father encourages a son to run away," she said.

I whistled softly. "But the father thinks Sam will be home that night," I reminded her, my voice trailing off. She sounded final. I hung up the telephone and sat down at the kitchen table with my head in my hands.

Hunger makes a writer write. By now it was clear that John was not well suited for the job at the zoo; he was an academician, not the stage manager required for displaying animals. As this became clear through criticism from his colleagues, and demands from the museum's director, I became frightened. A woman with young children is a fear box. Airplane rides, which I had taken so blithely before I had children, were now terrifying. Where once I ran along cliff edges, I now crept on all fours. And yet as I saw John's job dissolving before my eyes, it did not occur to me to go to work outside the house. My grandmother had stayed home with her young children, my mother had stayed home, and I would stay home, too. But I had to do something. I picked up the telephone and called Eugene Lyons. He had been my editor the first year I moved to New York after marriage and had illustrated for *Pageant* magazine, and he was now a senior editor at the *Reader's Digest,* just five minutes away. I had sent him some of our books over the years and he had seemed to enjoy them.

"Gene," I said, "I would like to try to write for the *Reader's Digest.*"

He responded with enthusiasm. "I'll arrange an editorial luncheon for you and your husband," he told me. "We'll discuss what you might be able to do for the magazine."

He gave me a date, which I put down in red crayon on the calendar, then went to my notebook for ideas.

A few days before the luncheon I glanced out through the door to see Twig and Craig stomping about in disgust. A glance at New York's apple tree told me why. Crow-purloined shovels and toy trucks, lead Indians and cowboys bristled in the crotches of the tree—and now New York was following Craig with a cup in his beak.

"Keep it," Craig said to the bird. "I don't want it anyway." Craig stuck out his tongue and climbed to the top of the slide ladder. A breeze fanned the sheath of blond hair back from his face as he zipped to the bottom. When he returned for another run, New York was already there. He was going to try to slide down the board, too—only he couldn't. His avian feet held him to the incline like a mountaineer's boots.

"Ha," said Craig, and the crow flew to the sandbox, where he picked up the lid of a coffee can. Carrying it to the top of the slide, he stepped into it and zipped to the bottom, where he picked it up again.

I gasped. "What a story you are, New York! You're worth your weight in gold."

Then I paused. "Only who's going to believe it?"

A few days before the editorial luncheon, while I was still jotting down ideas for articles, New York came around the corner of the house flying low above the ground. Behind him raced Butch, the SPCA terrier belonging to our good neighbors, the Melvins, whose house was at the bottom of the hill. New York led Butch around the house. After seven more circlings he flew to the apple tree and Butch flopped to the ground.

"He's getting even." Craig had walked into the backyard on the fourth round. "Butch tries to kill New York when he goes to the Melvins'. Now he's killing Butch."

Butch's tongue lolled from his mouth, his eyes rolled back, and I was indeed afraid his heart would stop.

"Vindictive," I said to Craig, recalling another crow who "got even"—an anthropomorphic expression, but true. I told Craig how, many years ago, the expert on crow control in the Department of Agriculture had been a friend of his grandfather's. He was Dr. E. H. Kalmbach, and he lived across the river from Washington, D.C., in Falls Church, Virginia. Like us, he had raised a crow to learn about those birds at firsthand. One day Dr. Kalmbach's bird flew to the neighbor's garden and tore the outside leaves off several cabbages. Hardly had the crow returned home than the neighbor came stamping over to Dr. Kalmbach, his little dog yapping and barking behind him.

"If that crow gets into my cabbage patch again," he told the ornithologist, "I'll shoot him. I raised those cabbages to show at the state fair."

Four days later, Dr. Kalmbach heard the sound of cabbage leaves being ripped asunder, and of a dog barking and yipping. He rushed outside to see his crow with a piece of meat in his feet, flying just above the nose of the neighbor's dog. He was leading him down one cabbage row and up the next, all the while tearing the cabbages to bits. As the leaves flew into the air the neighbor raised his gun, but he could not fire without the risk of shooting his own dog.

"I call it vindictive," Dr. Kalmbach wrote in a Department of Agriculture *Bulletin* some months later.

Or was it just the nature of crows? I watched Craig lean over Butch and pat his heaving sides, until finally the old terrier wagged his tail and slowly stood up. Then Craig led him by the collar, back down the hill where he found Tom, his friend since they had met at the bus stop on the first day of kindergarten.

The telephone rang. After glancing up to make sure that New York was not following Butch and Craig, I went into the house.

"Jean, this is Sharon Bannigan. I told Elliott that it is better for a son to run to the woods than the city. He agreed. We're going ahead with the publication of *My Side of the Mountain*."

I breathed deeply and patted the walls of the house: it was still mine, I could make the next payment.

From our door, the editorial offices of the *Reader's Digest* were five minutes down the Saw Mill River Parkway, across a red maple swamp that belongs to the marsh hawks, and up a ridge. The Williamsburg-style building on its grassy hill looked to me that day like a haven. John had been fired.

The day was clear and sunny. With a few minutes to kill before the hour of our appointment, he and I stood on the lawn under one of the two mammoth white oak trees that had first lured De Witt Wallace, the publisher and editor, to the property. Just before noon Jim Finan, a tall, redheaded Irishman and one of the editors who were to lunch with us, joined John and me under the tree and introduced himself.

"This tree grew up in a field," observed John of the massive oak.

Jim Finan pounced: "How do you know?"

"The limbs spread out horizontally, not upward as they would do if the tree had grown up in a forest."

"How could that be? The tree's more than two hundred years old. This was all forest then."

"It could not have been, according to the tree. The land here was opened by fire or by Indians."

I listened to John's explanation halfheartedly, for it was in every forestry book. At lunch, however, when Jim Finan suggested to Hobart Lewis and Eugene Lyons that we might try a piece inspired by the tree, calling it a "nature detective" piece, I thought of course. "Nature Detective." I could think of many clues of that kind. Where a linden tree stands you will find the nest of a rose-breasted grosbeak nearby. Where the milkweed grows, there will be monarch butterflies.

Excited by Jim Finan's idea, I went home to my typewriter and worked into the night, with John giving his suggestions. When the article was done we signed it John and Jean George. We were together again.

"Nature Detective" was purchased and published three months later. I studied the changes the editors made, returned for many more luncheons to learn about magazine writing and make suggestions for other articles. I sold two more of them.

Then a personal thunderhead roiled up. John opened a letter from a friend one day, and began to pace the floor. "The scientific community is criticizing me for popular writing," he said.

The battle between the scientist and the popular nature or science writer was long-standing, and we had been through it before. Scientists just do not trust those of their coterie who are popular writers. Science is pure, hard information, and needs no embellishments.

"This is a matter of making a living," I said. Then I slumped into my chair. "But I don't want to hurt your reputation. Maybe I had better write articles alone, too." I paused. "Jim Finan said the *Digest* liked the idea of a man-and-wife team. I suppose it might be more difficult for me alone.''

I was feeling truly exasperated with both myself and John. We were together and apart, apart and together. It was then that I suddenly turned upon him with such a verbal assault that I was shocked at myself. All the pent-up anger came out: anger over the situation he had fallen into at Vassar, anger over his losing the zoo job, and over the mortgage we had undertaken, with three children who needed us. Instead of being able to weather these hardships like other women, I simply exploded like a volcano. I saw at last that though John and I dearly loved nature and had that interest in common, we disagreed on just about everything else: on money, on child-rearing (he still took off his belt and spanked the children), on politics, in our tastes when it came to furnishings and art.

I went on shouting at him until I trembled. Then the door opened and Twig came bursting in with a toad she had found. She stopped, took a quick glance at me and then at John. She was not deceived. We looked like two banshees, and she was terrified by our faces. As I looked at her I made up my mind that this marriage would work if I had to be a Tallulah Bankhead, and work every minute at acting the role of the loving wife. Yes, I would do it.

What I couldn't do was support the family with John not working. I had been raised by a strong father and I needed a man who worked, who dominated and took care of us all. I was just as thoroughly imprinted as Lotor the raccoon had been. It was all there inside me.

A few days later, my cousin Barb Hallowell arrived at the house with a little screech owl. She had found it in her driveway and couldn't take care of it herself. Could we? Twig's hands went up to the baby bird as though in reverence. The smallest of the local owls, *Otus,* he had yellow eyes, a gray face and sticklike ear tufts. We placed him on the kitchen table as he blinked and gave the baby owl's cry for food. When he had been stuffed until his crop stuck out an inch, he surveyed the house, turning his head slowly from side to side.

The wild things we raised indoors have always found corners and niches similar to their outdoor habitats. The fox had denned in the fireplace, the mink in the rootlike springs of the couch. The muskrat had

95

crawled into a lodge among the pots and pans. Otus the owl looked around, and after sizing up the premises, flew to the bookcase, where he stepped into a cozy hollow between *Ancient Greek Literature* and *Stuart Little*, E. B. White's gift to children. There he took up residence.

For a husband to lose his job is often a shock to the wife as insufferable as a bereavement. I ached over it day and night. I thought again of going to work, but could not bring myself to do it. I needed John to be the head of the family; but I also needed *him*. When he was offered a job with the Fish and Wildlife Service in Washington, I wrung my hands.

"I'll commute weekends," he said.

"Dig ditches," I said, "but stay here until we can get ourselves in hand financially for another move. I feel shaky and frightened about our marriage. Please, please stay."

John took the job in Washington and began commuting on weekends.

One day, as I worked at my desk with the door open, the sun on my feet and the wood thrush feeding his fledgling nearby, I looked out to see Tom and Merry Melvin and my children catching the tiny toads that had just metamorphosed and were hopping across the land like animated thimbles. Just one element was missing from the scene.

"Where's the crow?" I called to Craig.

"He's gone to a party," was the answer.

"Oh, no!" Only the day before I had received a call from a neighbor who had not known until too late that we had a pet crow. The bird had dropped from the sky into the midst of her cocktail party and had devoured a piece of cheese and two deviled eggs.

"It was horrible," she said. "Horrible. And then the bird said 'Hello.' My husband's still on the wagon. Can you leash him?"

"No," I answered, "but he's quite harmless and friendly. Just hold up some cheese or hamburger and he'll come talk to you."

She answered, "He's dreadful."

Anticipating trouble, I walked across the lawn to listen for voices that would establish the location of the picnic. I paused under the linden tree. Feathers rustled overhead and I looked up to see New York.

"Hiya, babe," he said, leaning down. I stared at him, then laughed right out loud. The voice he used was deep and masculine.

"That's not a very good thing to be saying these days," I told him.

"Hello," he said.

"Hello, sweet bird."

There would be other pet crows in the years to come, but New York has remained my favorite. In addition to his speaking talents, he had an eerie sense of timing. One afternoon the nature artist Helen Van Tyne, who was a family friend, dropped by to pay a call. After settling into a chair, she looked out and saw New York walking along the railing of the front porch. "How does he keep his feet and legs so shiny?" she asked. "I've never seen such black and glossy feet."

With two jumps the crow hopped into Twig's dollhouse, rummaged inside and picked up a hotel shoeshine rag. Holding it in his beak, he walked along the railing, balancing easily and all the while eying Helen, who clutched the arms of the chair and then arose, visibly upset.

"It's just a coincidence," I told her, but she made a polite excuse and was gone.

At five o'clock one morning I was awakened by the loud assembly call of the crows. Stepping to my window, I saw fifty or sixty of them on the lawn and in the trees. When all were settled, a sentinel bird began a repetitive cry, which I eventually concluded must be directed at New York. I presumed that the sentinel was telling him that he was a crow, not a person. The other crows loudly agreed.

I looked toward the apple tree to learn how New York was taking this news and was shocked to discover that I did not recognize him. How could this be? I knew him so well—his movements, his stride, the cocky toss of his head. But every bird in that yard looked just like him. Obviously I was not as perceptive and sensitive as a crow. New York could pick me out of a crowd at the train station, and would alight on my shoulder, whether I was wearing rain gear or a heavy coat. I was still trying to decide which one was New York when the sun came over the hill, signaling the beginning of the crow's work day. By twos and threes and sevens the birds took off, until only one of them remained in the apple tree.

"Hello," said New York from his favorite four inches of limb.

The arrival of the strange crows made me realize that we were not the only individuals in New York's life. Obviously the crows knew him, and there could be no doubt that he knew them.

When Twig and Craig left for school one morning, Luke and I

walked to Flag Hill, the highest spot in town, where we could get a better view of New York's world. From the rocky heights the railroad track was barely visible, the school and stores were smothered in trees, and the houses were but TV antennae and chimney tops growing up through the autumn foliage. Chappaqua was nothing more than a huge crow habitat.

From the railroad station a group of crows beat their way uphill. One or two alighted in the trees in the graveyard behind the Quaker meeting house, and three others sat down in the white pine trees on our ridge. To anyone standing on the hill, it became obvious that every crow could see every other crow, including our New York. He was no stranger in town.

Luke and I started home, delighted with New York's life outside our family. Three crows floated to a nearby hickory tree. Turning around, they eyed us from the backs of their eyes.

"I have an eerie feeling," I said to Luke, "that those birds know us too. We are crow keepers, the worst of all possible creatures."

The crowd of crows did not return for several days. Then, on a cold morning, they once again descended on our yard, this time mumbling softly. It was late October and the need to migrate was strong in them, though they would not go very far, perhaps no more than fifty miles. They cawed and cahed frantically to New York, as if time were running out.

John was in Washington, the children were asleep, and as I listened to the crows I called silently to New York, "Don't go, don't go." I loved the old bird dearly. He was the most intelligent and amusing of all our pets.

At sunup the crows departed and to my relief New York, lured by the memory of Twig's bacon and eggs, reported to the kitchen window. I threw it open and welcomed him warmly.

The next day the crow crowd returned, as they did every day for weeks thereafter. One morning, when their voices sounded particularly frantic, I ran downstairs and picked up John's shotgun. Crows can't be fooled: they know what hunters are all about. Experimenters at the Department of Agriculture had once disguised themselves in women's skirts to get close enough to corn-eating crows so as to shoot them. As soon as they stepped through the door, the crows had departed. The men then disguised their guns as brooms, and tried again to approach the crows. The birds flew off before the experimenters had taken more than a few steps. However, whenever the experimenters approached the crows without guns, either with or without costumes, with or without brooms, the crows did not fly until they were almost upon them.

As for the conclusion of this research it was simply that the aggressive attitude of a man with a gun was what the crows perceived. When a man holds a gun he stalks. The crows read attitudes, not objects.

I opened the back door and walked into the yard with the shotgun. "Ca! Ca! Ca! Ca! Ca!" The alarm cry of the crows sounded. Moaning "Nevah, nevah," they departed in a long black stream up over the trees.

For the next several mornings I repeated the trip to the yard with the gun—until one morning I noticed the crows were less wary. Some did not move at all.

"They can read a person to the bone," I concluded. "They know I'll never shoot." I put the gun away.

One morning I sat up in bed and listened for almost an hour to the voices of the crows. A note of wistfulness was mixed with the lusty caws—a new sound had crept into their voices.

The telephone rang. "Jean," said my neighbor Art Buckley, "have you noticed the crows around here lately?"

"Yes," I replied guiltily.

"Gee, they wake me up every morning at five-thirty. What are they doing here? I've lived here twenty years and we've never had crows before."

I got up and ran to the window. The crows were restlessly pointing their beaks southwest as they lifted their heads and cawed.

I phoned Art back. "I don't think you'll hear them much longer," I said. "They're about to migrate."

"Oh," he said, "so that's what it's all about?"

I did not answer.

Returning to the window, I heard one crow call a soft "Cah, cah," a melodious and pretty note compared to most crow sounds.

"Cah, cah, hello," came an answer. I clutched the sill. New York was talking double talk, literally—crow and English.

Then all was silent. The sun was above the horizon, a signal that it was well past the time for crows to be departing from my yard. Nevertheless, they sat in the trees and on the lawn, as still as doomsday—until there came a roaring of wings as if a thousand kites were being ripped apart in the wind. It was the crows lifting themselves into the morning mist. They pumped and soared, and by twos and tens and fives they circled the house, the yard, the neighborhood, rising higher and higher, until they were above the town. Then they shot off to the southwest.

And the apple tree was bare. New York was gone.

One late afternoon in January, feeling irritated because I was behind in everything, I answered the ring of the phone with a virtual bark.

"*My Side of the Mountain* is a Newbery runner-up," said Sharon Bannigan. "Second-best children's book of the year. Terrific. It should have been first."

I hung up the phone, hummed to myself and danced through every room of the house. So far so good, I thought. We could pay the mortgage for at least one more year. Although there was no honorarium for the Newbery Medal, or the runner-up, receiving it did mean that sales would go up, since almost every library would buy the book.

Hardly had I settled down to my typewriter than Joan Gordon came by the house. She was on her way from Vassar to New York. In her arms was a delightful kitten, a Manx with a stubby tail and turned-up nose. "Where's Twig?" she asked.

School was over for the day, and upon hearing the word "kitten" Twig was downstairs in a flash.

"Want it?" asked Joanie. "I think every little girl ought to have a cat. It is named Trinket."

"John will have a fit," I said. "He hates cats."

But Twig did not care. She bundled the kitten into her arms and curled up on the couch with Trinket.

"John will just have to go along with it," I said. "There's no taking that kitten from Twig."

"He'll go along," said Joan and he did, though not at all happily.

10

A Crane Dies Hard

An autumn hurricane leveled the trees on the mountainside across the river, in spring the blue jays ate the baby robins under my window. And in my own life I felt changes were coming.

My editor at Dutton departed. At that time there were three outstanding editors of childrens' books: Ursula Nordstrom of Harper & Brothers, Mae Massey of Viking, and Elizabeth Riley of T. Y. Crowell. After studying their books in the local library, I decided that Elizabeth Riley produced extraordinarily artistic science books and with a Newbery Honor Book to give me courage I called her on the phone.

"Meet me at the Stanhope Hotel for lunch," she said. "We'll meet uptown where the publishing business spies can't see us." At that time publishing was a "gentleman's business." A writer did not change publishers, nor did an editor steal another publisher's writer.

"You're not stealing me from Dutton," I said quickly. "I am leaving due to mutual uninspiration. The new editor and I don't do anything for each other."

Nevertheless, I met Elizabeth Riley in the elegant dining room of the Stanhope across from the Metropolitan Museum of Art.

"I love secrets and gossip," she said with a chuckle by way of introducing herself, then added, "My real fame is that I am a member of that subversive group, the Needle and Bobbin Club. We are collectors of quilts and lace.'' I laughed with her and relaxed. Later I learned she really was.

Elizabeth was a slender woman with a handsome crown of graying red hair. She moved with the swiftness of a warbler both mentally and physically and displayed impeccable taste. That day she was dressed in a hand-tailored moss-green suit with a flowered silken blouse. She wore gloves and a hat. With executive decisiveness she swept me to a corner table, ordered cocktails and, as we raised our glasses, spied over the rim at me. I spied back.

"My Side of the Mountain," she began, "is a fine book. You maintained it right to the end. Oh, what you could do with a good editor." I saw the Newbery Medal in her eyes.

"I want to write about a young girl training a falcon—my own experiences at thirteen. I have always written about boys hiding behind their adventures and careers. Now I have a daughter and I am changing."

That book, *The Summer of the Falcon,* did not win anything.

"The family was too unconventional," Elizabeth reported when she came back from the meeting of the American Library Association. Since the judges who chose the winner were librarians, a writer had to pay attention to their comments. Thinking about them, I concluded I would never win the medal.

When you have been raised by the men of the family as I was, to shoot rapids in canoes, and to climb trees, to hold the reflectors while an eagle nest is being photographed, when you have gone on desert trips to observe rattlesnakes, you come to see the men of your family as the image of authority.

When I married John I transferred that image to him. But as a professional writer I had to become my own authority and make my own judgments. What I wrote had to be from my own head, not John's. So I began my own study of ethology, the science of animal behavior. My friend Ray Carpenter at Penn State was one authority in a field that included Karl von Frisch, Konrad Lorenz, Rudolf Schenkel and Niko Tinbergen. What they had done was to observe group organization in animals in their natural environments instead of in zoos, where animal behavior tends to be neurotic. What they were seeing was that animal societies were not unlike human societies, with leaders and followers, sacred borders, territories and an ability to communicate with each other.

I had heard much about the remarkable work of Niko Tinbergen in the Netherlands and at Oxford. Now feeling the need to become my own authority, I sat down with his classic, *The Herring Gull's World*.

"The student of behavior is struck by the deep similarity between man and animals," he wrote. "He recognizes himself too often in an animal." From his own experiments with nesting gulls—such as removing eggs and replacing them with wooden cylinders—Tinbergen concluded: "Why does a gull learn so little about its own eggs? The eyes of a herring gull are excellent, probably even better than ours. Why does it not use its eyes always to the limits of their capacity? Why, for instance does it brood a cylinder? . . . all this type of work forces one to the conclusion that behavior, however variable it may seem to be at first sight, is dependent on mechanisms in the nervous system, mechanisms with strictly limited functions. Here, as in so many cases, nature has only developed what is necessary, and no more. I think the bearing of this conclusion is insufficiently realized particularly in human psychology."

I read that the herring-gull community has a function which is to protect and raise its offspring. To this end the gulls are monogamous, and each parent takes turns incubating and feeding the young.

Each pair has a piece of property about two feet square on which they raise their young. The property is zealously protected from gull intruders, young and old. Herring gulls recognize mates, leaders and neighbors as well as their own offspring.

Every herring-gull community, I read, is like a club; it has its president, and follows gull protocol. Its members strengthen the bonds among themselves by yelling across the dunes at the presidents and members of other clubs. The president is the bird that holds his head higher, and puffs himself up to look bigger and more imposing than all the others, who submissively pull in their necks before him.

Once I had finished the book, I packed a picnic lunch and drove with the children to Sherwood Beach, Connecticut, where they caught clams and crabs while I stared at the gulls wheeling and circling on their tapered wings. Where once I would have seen only beauty and freedom, I now knew there were tense individuals adhering to rules and adjusting to complex pressures as each fulfilled its needs. I looked but I saw no order, only chaos. Expecting to discover presidents and ward bosses, I saw only a wild snowstorm of wings, folding, opening, and drifting over the marsh and beach. I could see no organization, no deference to the leader, no bonding. I returned home discouraged.

John was gone all week, and for the next few nights after the children were in bed I reread Tinbergen, writing down in a small notebook some clues that might be helpful the next time I encountered herring gulls.

Calls: Alarm: "Ha, ha, haha, haha."
Predator near nest: "Keew, keew, keew."
Copulation call of male: "Klee'ew."
Mother to young, young to mother: "Mew."

One morning, before going out for groceries, I went upstairs to get Otus the owl in Craig's room, a precaution that was now called for because he and Trinket had taken to playing their own deadly game of Russian roulette. Otus would perch on the top of the curtain in Luke's room and Trinket would sit in the center of the rug in the hallway, paws curled under, eyes focused on the owl. All of a sudden Otus would glide down from the curtain and swoop over Trinket, who with a cat's lightning swiftness would swing a lethal paw at him. Inches separated the two— maybe only millimeters—before Otus climbed to the top of the curtain in my room, where he would alight, turn around and stare at Trinket. But this morning I found both of them on my bed, Trinket curled up on the folded blanket, Otus sitting on the footboard not three feet from her. I concluded that they had arrived at some peaceable understanding and went off without separating them.

As I returned with the groceries, a radio news broadcast was announcing the crash of Flight 101 out of Logan Airport in Boston, caused by birds that had been ingested by the jet engines during takeoff.

"There were no survivors," the announcer said.

As I listened, Twig's sixth-grade class had been tuned to the prelunchtime news and had heard the same report. A curly-haired friend of Twig's ran screaming to the teacher: "My mommy and daddy are on that plane." The teacher managed to convince her that this was impossible, and Mary Lou went off to lunch with Twig. An hour later she was called to the principal's office and told that both her parents had been killed in that crash.

At three-thirty Twig threw open the door and ran to the sunporch where I was working. Her face was white and her eyes were wide with fear.

"Mary Lou's daddy and mommy are dead," she said. "An airplane crashed."

We clung to each other. I had been traveling by air at least once a month on assignment for the *Reader's Digest* or to give talks to schoolchildren. And John was flying home on weekends from Washington.

"Death is," I began. I tried to offer my grandmother's philosophy, that the acceptance of death was part of life. But I could not say it. I was terrified of death and darkness, of never awakening to the sun again, just as Twig was. The sparrow that had died in her hand, the kittens Trinket ate because they were deformed: all the realities of life and death in our small world of living things was of no help.

"I don't have a daddy most of the time," Twig cried. "But now Mary Lou won't have a daddy or a mother at all. Mother, don't die."

I did not know what to say. It was Twig who found her own answer.

"Mary Lou will need some friends," she said. "I'll call all her friends and we'll go and be with her if she wants us."

After Twig had gone upstairs to use the extension phone I filled the scrub bucket and got down on my hands and knees to wash the kitchen floor.

When I realized what I was doing I rocked back on my heels and stared at my dripping hands. How symbolic—to be scrubbing the floor! But it was no joke. I heard Twig's words again: "I don't have a daddy most of the time." I meant it: I was ready to do anything to make this marriage work.

The tragedy of the airplane crash hung over us for a long time. John and I avoided flying together. We made arrangements for guardians for our children, and we kept a flow of letters to Mary Lou, who had moved to West Virginia to be taken care of by relatives.

Not long after the accident, John was called to Boston with other ornithologists to study the hazard of the birds at Logan Airport, and the possibility of scaring them off the runways with amplified recordings of their alarm cries.

The crash of Flight 101 brought to light many more such crashes and near-misses. Herring gulls were in the limelight. With public attention focused on them, research funds became available. One morning I read in the *New York Times* about a scientific task force from the Massachusetts Audubon Society that was studying herring gulls on Block Island, off Rhode Island.

We had vacationed there once, and had been enchanted by its barren landscape, its sagging Victorian houses and its birds.

In June we packed owl, cat, Luke's painted turtle, and the new dog Tonka, a Newfoundland (who had joined the household after Gunner had to be put away), and set out once more as a family.

As the ferry to Block Island pulled out from New London, I glanced up to see a blizzard of herring gulls above us, floating, drifting, and screaming untranslatable things in gullese, and once again I felt I would never see order in the herring-gull society. I still couldn't tell a male from a female.

That evening, after a picnic supper on the cliff overlooking the ocean, John drove the children and me down the narrow road to the gullery outside an abandoned lighthouse at the north end of the island. We left behind the last tree and rode through acres of bayberry and raspberry bushes, passing an occasional gray-shingled house. When the road ended we parked the car and walked westward over sand dunes and spiky grass. From the top of a dune, the nesting ground of the gulls came into view, with several hundred birds plunging and circling above it like flies around a honey jar. They moved as if on a well-planned highway system, each avoiding the other, each coming and going in its own space.

"The city of the gulls," I said to Twig, who looked up at me with a knowing eye.

"Am I going to have to play with a baby seagull?"

"Wouldn't you like that?"

"Well, yes; but after all, I am nearly twelve."

"And she wants to play with *girls*," said Craig as he picked up a stick and whirled it out toward the sea.

The next day while John took the boys fishing, Twig and I packed a lunch and drove to the beach near the gullery. We sought a knoll behind a twisted bayberry, spread out our blanket, and from a safe distance looked down on the confetti party of seagulls.

"Keew, keew, keew," called a bird above us.

"Twig!" I said excitedly. "He's saying there's a predator near his nest. He's talking about us—you and me." And I wrote in the notebook I was keeping for both an article and a children's book, "I have translated gull talk for the first time and the whole island has more meaning than it did yesterday."

The ocean sparkled against the long spit that disappeared into the sun's glare, the sky was clean and fresh. Once more the primordial need to be out-of-doors was being satisfied as Twig and I sat on the hill. I felt a deep comfort. Twig seemed to feel it too. It could have been those Craighead genes reacting to the sea and the wind, but it was also more. Within each person, I believe, there is an ancient twist of DNA that reacts to the beauty of the land and sky, and brings back with a rush our original love affair with nature.

The warning of predators was the only call I recognized all morning. And by the lunch hour I had still not been able to pick out a single individual.

Twig found a little girl on the beach, and I left the two of them playing on an old wrecked boat while I went back to the gulls. I made a grid on a page of my notebook and tried to map out what I thought were mated pairs on their nesting territories. In the process I noticed a plastic bottle near two seagulls; with that as a landmark to help in pinpointing a pair I focused my binoculars. I went on watching and wondering what they were doing until Twig returned sometime later.

"Twig," I said, "what do you and your girl friends do when you meet a new boy?"

"Giggle."

"Do you ever notice what he is wearing?"

"Sure."

"See that plastic bottle?" I said. "Take the field glasses and look at the two birds in front of it. What are they doing?"

A long pause followed.

"One is walking around the other, looking at her."

"The walker is the her. The one being looked at is him."

"Well, he's sure puffing out his chest," said Twig.

"A herring-gull female picks her mate. She looks him over, sizes him up and then bows her approval. He gives her a stick or a stone for a present and they're mates for life."

"The girls pick the boys?" said Twig. "Hmmm."

When I next settled myself at the gullery I noticed a gull pulling grass. That, I knew from Tinbergen, meant a fight. Again, pulling grass was like a man raising a gun at a possible intruder. I cleared the focus. The bird went on steadily pulling grass. I looked for his opponent, but could not find him until a nearby gull with his neck pulled in ran, then flew away. Another small success.

The next time I went to the gullery I spotted a gull with a band placed on his leg by the Audubon Society. Now I had a known individual. I decided it was a male because he held his neck high and aggressively. He was down near the water and had stopped eating. He turned and walked toward his mate, fluffing the lower ventral feathers as he came. Since both male and female gull tend the young, it was natural for the female, on seeing him approach with his feathers in the broody position, to rise and walk away from the two eggs. He sat down on them and she flew off to the beach to feed. For the next hour I watched and made notes; when I reread them, I knew what I had been seeing. "Nest relief," I said, excited by the coordination of the pair. Up to that moment I had been watching each bird separately. Now I watched them together. Such was the intertwining of their needs that they were like a beautifully choreographed ballet. The male stayed on the nest until his urge to brood was supplanted by the urge to eat. Out on the beach, his mate fed until her hunger drive was satisfied and the brooding urge came on. When it did so, she headed for the nest, lifting her feathers—at sight of which something clicked inside him, and he got up and went off to feed.

As I watched this lovely feathered language I felt a deep sadness and loss. They fulfilled one another, these lowly birds who could not reason, talk or use their intelligence as John and I could. Yet they lived in harmony, and John and I did not. The sea was now far out, a silver thread beyond the spit of sand. Watching the gulls come and go, I wondered whether the supreme gift of reasoning that sets man apart from all other animals was a good gift after all.

At the cottage that night, while John and the boys were fishing and Twig was out with her new friends, I reread a paragraph from the introduction by Konrad Lorenz to *The Herring Gull's World*.

"Much of the beauty and wonder of nature is based on the fact that organic life is directed toward goals, toward survival, reproduction and that attainment of higher perfection. This very directedness of life, impelling evolution from amoeba to ourselves, and, we legitimately hope, to something beyond our present selves, is indeed very wonderful."

I knew that day that John and I had lost our own sense of directedness. And I did not know what to do.

A few days before we left Block Island, we were all walking on the north beach when several of the Audubon Society researchers passed us on their way to the gullery. Curious about their study, we followed them up over the rocks to the edge of gull land. Suddenly one chick became frightened, ran off its own circumscribed territory and across the one occupied by another pair. The protective instinct of a seagull parent causes it to strike a strange chick—and before our eyes an adult gull did just that, while John ran to save him.

"Keew, keew, keew."

"Ha, ha, haha, haha."

As John got back to us, fending off wings and beaks, the air was filled with flying feathers, falling streaks of whitewash, regurgitated food and dive-bombing gulls. The farther from their territory we ran, the less agitation among the birds, until peace returned to the gullery.

And so Larus the seagull joined our family. We put him on the floor of the cottage and gathered around while the half-fledged bird, mottled brown and tan, rocked unsteadily on his jointed legs and flapped his huge webbed feet as he balanced himself. Then he fastened his pupil on my eye and stared contemplatively.

"He's real ugly," said Twig, "but I like him." She patted his head.

Larus wiggled his rear end, lifted his tail and squirted a large watery blob of feces across the floor.

"But I don't think he likes us," added Craig.

As I wiped up after him I recalled another of Tinbergen's observations, about the size of the nest site and the rules about staying on it.

"Larus might stay on a piece of newspaper," I said. "His parents have trained him to remain on a spot about as big as the *New York Times*."

"But he *didn't* learn," said Craig. "That's why we've got him."

The idea did not work perfectly, but Larus did at least stay on the paper long enough for me to cook fish for his dinner and mix it with some canned dog food. Making a small ball of the mix, I held it over his beak. He eyed it but did not open his mouth. After a long effort I decided he wasn't hungry and placed him on his paper in the corner. Later, when I turned off the lights and went with the children to their bedroom, we looked back to discover that the little herring gull was fast asleep.

Luke was out of bed early the next morning to feed the gull. I heard him softly talking to Larus, urging him to eat. Presently he was shaking my shoulder.

"He won't eat," Luke said. "Please let him go."

Dressing hurriedly, I came into the living room. "I'll have to force-feed him," I said to Luke. "I've gotten many a little bird started by forcing it once or twice." Gently prying open the chick's bill, I pushed the food deep into his gullet, a hole so enormous that I seemed to be looking at his entire insides. He closed his beak and swallowed. Hardly was the food down than up it came. I pushed more down and it came up. After a dozen tries I sat back on my heels.

"He's going to die," said Luke. "Take him back home."

By late afternoon when Larus still hadn't been able to keep anything down, I decided that Luke was right: I had better take him back to the gullery.

"Either he or you'll be killed," John reminded me. So I went back to Tinbergen, and noted that the adults could not recognize their own chicks up until they were five days old. During that time they would adopt a stranger; after that, they knew their own chicks and struck at all others. Though I did not know Larus's age presumably it was more than five days. I went on reading and learned that downy chicks step from their eggs, dry off and look up, see the red band on the underside of their parent's bill. In response they jump up and strike these markings setting off a chain of events that sounded more like a Rube Goldberg invention than a living process: after the button has been pushed, the parent chokes up food, puts it on the ground and feeds the chick. Until it has been struck in this way, the parent is unable to feed its offspring.

110

"Maybe this is the trouble," I told Luke. "It seems that Larus has to hit a red button in order to swallow and eat." Taking a lipstick from my purse, I made a red mark on the knuckle of my thumb, took a pinch of fish in my thumb and forefinger, and held it above Larus's head. He looked up, jumped, hit the spot and opened his mouth. I stuffed down the fish, he wobbled, swallowed—and kept down the food.

"That's neat," said Luke. And I agreed.

At home in Chappaqua, Larus jumped for his red spot, ate, grew and ran in and out of the door to the sunporch, where I worked. He was so responsive to the color red that he had soon knocked the red print off the books on the lower shelf, as well as the polish on Twig's toenails whenever she painted them.

He was clearly developing along the aggressive lines of the herring gull, throwing fear into Trinket and Tonka by striking each of them once on the nose with that powerful beak. After that once, they kept their distance. Otus ignored Larus altogether, sleeping by day in the bookcase and flying around the house at night when the gull was asleep.

By the end of July, Larus was flapping a great three-foot spread of wings and playing under the hose with the children. One day when he had been standing beside me as I typed, he flapped so hard that the air currents he set in motion lifted him up and onto my desk. This accomplishment left him as surprised as I, but he recovered more quickly. Glancing around, he seized my coffee cup with a quick stab, leaned over and dropped it with a crash.

"He's never seen a gull do that," I said to Craig. "And yet he is acting just like one when it drops clams on rocks to break them. That's what is known as instinct."

After that nothing was safe. Any hard object triggered the clam-dropping instinct, and it became too intolerable to keep him indoors. So Larus was banished to the lawn.

One day, while he was sharing bits of bread from the picnic we were having outside, I asked the children to write down what they thought of Larus.

"I like him, but he doesn't like me except when I have food for him," wrote perceptive Luke.

"He's funny and amusing," wrote Twig, "but he chases my cat."

111

Twig's friend, David Linquist, wrote, "I think Larus never had to figure out anything. He was just born knowing all he needs to know and he's waiting for us clods to learn too so he can have someone to communicate with."

One overcast afternoon in August, Larus found someone to communicate with, and it was not us clods. While he walked beside me as I weeded the garden, with his neck pulled in out of respect for my size and age, he caught a glimpse of four seagulls passing overhead. They were on their way to the Hudson River from the Valhalla reservoir.

When Larus stretched his neck out and flattened his feathers to his body, I knew that he knew what he was all about. Without even a glance at me he flapped his great wings, which carried him upward to the sunporch roof. There he sat and stared in the direction the seagulls had taken.

Around four o'clock he spread his wings and took off, speeding westward in search of his own kind; and we never saw Larus again.

I was sorry to see him go for I had begun fantasizing that he was holding John and me together. While Larus was around we could at least talk about seagulls. Even though John had a circle of new friends in Washington to talk to, I was trading confidences with a friend in Chappaqua whose marriage was also falling apart.

After Larus departed I would be out of bed at six-thirty, get the kids off to school, then look up at the clock on the kitchen wall and know that when the big hand stood at twelve and the little hand at nine, I would settle into a deep depression. My feet would become leaden and my housework would remain undone. I knew now that I could write for a living. I had to. Yet I still shrank from the thought of being on my own.

One day a friend from Vassar, Leslie Koempel of the Sociology Department, came by and found me pacing the floor. She recommended a psychiatrist in New York who had helped her and other professional women. As I went to the telephone to call Dr. Neubauer, I could hear my family scoffing at the idea that I needed help from a psychiatrist; no one in our family had ever had such problems. I got as far as picking up the telephone, then put it back.

That weekend John saw Twig wearing a pair of earrings Gene Lyons, my *Reader's Digest* editor, had brought me from India, and he slapped her—not me. All the resolution and love went out of me. I turned on him like a tigress.

"Something terrible is wrong," I said, hugging Twig. "Twig and Craig are not doing well in school, although you keep telling them they should all be A students. And you strike them. You believe in spanking and whipping. But now you hit the wrong person. Hit me, not her. Tomorrow I am going to see a psychiatrist."

"He'll just tell you what you want to hear," John roared. "You are the one breaking up this family—not me."

The sense of guilt burned in my guts. He was right. I was spending time on my writing, on the children, on having dinner with another man. I wasn't helping anyone.

With that I struck rock-bottom.

When I walked into Dr. Neubauer's office I could barely see for the mist before my eyes. Gradually it cleared and I noticed paintings of children hanging on his walls—big orange heads on stick bodies, dresses that connected to neckless heads, suns that smiled. I smiled.

When he opened his office door and I gave my name, ready for the scolding I felt sure would come, I glanced back at the paintings. "They're wonderful," I said. "So fresh and original."

"They follow very definite rules," he answered, and I realized for the first time that each drawing was like the development of a child physically. Slowly the hand and eye coordinate as the growing child moves toward adulthood. I felt an understanding with this man: he too was a behaviorist.

"My marriage is in trouble," I began.

He leaned forward and held my eyes with his. "Everything is interpersonal." I knew what that meant. I had raised too many young things not to know that each living thing could get hung up on a parent or a sibling and react to all other people from that emotional level.

"You are confused," he went on. I didn't know what he meant but saw hope for enlightenment. He talked on about the human emotions and psychiatry. As I departed I mentioned the interesting color of his office walls.

"You try to please," he said. "It's all right, if you mean it."

By the next meeting I was truly in misery.

113

"My scalp is creeping," I said. "It feels as if it is being tightened, as if I had my head in a vise."

"That's fear. When did you first notice it?"

"I'm not sure. Maybe when I saw my aunt and uncle and their well-regulated life."

We talked briefly about my fear of John and he shook his head. "Don't be afraid of him." The tightening eased.

"We all fulfill needs in life," he said. I thought of the amoeba, of the gulls at their nest-relief chores, of my wish to have children.

"I'll go backward. I'll do anything to make my marriage work."

"You can't go backward."

I was now talking in short, frightened sentences, in the hopes that he had the insight to read deeper. "My husband works in Washington."

"You don't have a husband. He's gone. Hmmm?" said Dr. Neubauer, while I stared. "He's not around."

"He located a house we could buy, outside Washington."

"Where is your work?"

"Pleasantville and New York City. I write."

"So you can't leave. Your work is here." I breathed more evenly. Here was a man who thought a woman was important, that her work mattered, too.

"You are very naïve," he said, and I glanced up quickly. I had not thought I was naïve. I had been knocked around. I had been pushed into cloak closets by amorous newspapermen, had been ripped off by swindlers, had married, given birth, raised children. What did he mean, that I was naïve?

"You have outgrown your husband."

The session ended. I drove home listening to bells ring in my head, as though the coins that had long been caught into the wrong slots were suddenly finding the right ones and clanging into place.

My whole world was turning around. Everything was not my fault. I was a person after all. I had my own importance. And I was still growing and changing.

At the next talk with Neubauer, I wanted him to know just what an ideal wife I had been. When I told how I had helped John write his Ph.D. thesis, he shook his head vigorously. "You shouldn't have done that.

Wrong role. If you had talked to me before you married this man, I would have told you to put your feet up and sit back."

"I see. I am destroying him. I am not letting him grow. I'm his mother or something."

"Your confusion is like the confusion of art and science, the female and the male perhaps," he said gently. I sat quietly as I became aware of what I was doing—being the man *and* the woman. I was indeed confused.

"Did your father work and your mother stay home?"

"Yes." Now I could see where he was leading me, to a path down which I had been going with every observation of nature, but which I could not see for letting myself get in my own way. I was imprinted on the strong male images of my father and brothers. John was imprinted on strong women, on his mother and sisters, who had made all the decisions and kept the family alive through the Depression. I was taking on a male role which was foreign to my own imprinting. John was all right because a woman was taking care of him; but he would not grow so long as I kept doing things for him. The fighting, the arguments, the unloving situation we had gotten into was not the fault of either one of us, but both.

Dr. Neubauer said, "It's time for you to get a lawyer."

"John won't hear of it."

"He will understand that you mean it if you do not sit down at the table and eat with him. The old thing about breaking bread, hmmm?" This was a fascinating symbol. I sat up straight in the chair, thinking about it and wondering if I could do it.

"We fight all the time now. I'm like a spitting cat."

"What do you fight about?"

"Money."

"That's a symptom of deeper problems."

Survival, I thought.

"What else?"

"Sex." I did not bother to go on with that conversation. I did not want to make love these days, possibly because my mother had told me that you kept a man by making love to him whenever and however. I knew now why we argued about sex. He would leave, I thought.

"He also doesn't believe the children are ours." I whispered this for when John had thrown it at me I had been absolutely demolished.

"Does he have reason for this?"

"I knew when each child was conceived. I guess he thinks that means I was with someone else. I don't know what a man thinks."

"Are you working again?" My back stiffened. How did this man know I had stopped working for two weeks, while my head turned round and I saw the world, not through the guilt of my womanhood but at long last, through my own eyes.

"You had better see a lawyer," he repeated. "Get him some help, too. You may remarry him."

I walked the entire distance across his office in stunned silence, passed through the lobby and paused on the sidewalk outside his door. Trucks rolled up Madison Avenue, the sun shone on the brass sculpture displayed in an art gallery across the street. Then these things were gone. A wave poured over them. It came from my eyes, gushed down my cheeks and splashed onto the sidewalk. I rounded the block, sobbing too hard to begin to know where such sorrow came from. Did it go back to the dawn of monogamy, to the legendary cranes who mated for life? It was something like that, I thought, since it came from so deep within me.

Two hours later I found myself staring in the window of an art gallery at a painting whose soft swollen shapes made me want to hold my children. I found my car and drove home.

Not eating with John did get the message across. He agreed to see a lawyer. When I returned to Neubauer, my head had stopped creeping and my depression was gone.

"You have been deeply hurt," he said. "Away back; nothing to do with John." Now I told him of childhood nightmares of fire, from which I would awaken screaming, and of a recurring dream of choking when I was an infant, and of not being held close, but at arm's length.

"So you have lousy parents." His shrug said, "Don't we all."

Someday my children would discover I was a lousy parent, too, and they would love me anyway, and in so doing they would grow up.

The room suddenly seemed much brighter and clearer.

"My brothers were in New York last week," I said, "and I told them that I could not understand the terrible fear I felt about everything these days, because I never used to be afraid. And they asked me if I remembered when they had locked me in the trunk in the attic. I didn't. I don't remember anything."

Neubauer did not shift a foot or finger. "Did you ask them how long?"

"I couldn't. I was afraid to." Again I smiled, and sibling rivalry seemed to fall into its place. So my brothers were just like all the rest—not invincible heroes, just ordinary Joes, no better or worse than anyone else.

I shifted the subject to raising my children without a father, and the problems I would have to cope with. John was only going to pay $150 a month for their support, I said angrily.

"He's a professional man, he can only earn so much." I saw that this was right, and that I did not want him to be economically crippled on my account. I wanted him to find a new and better life. But still I was mad. They were his children. They needed his love whether it was expressed in money or hugs, neither of which he could give.

"He won't help out on their college."

I don't remember whether Dr. Neubauer said anything about this, for I was already accepting the situation and my mind was running toward how I could do it alone, rather than trying to fight him anymore.

On January 10, eight days before our twentieth wedding anniversary, John and I were divorced. I picked up the papers in a Mexican courthouse and walked out of the dark building into the blinding sun.

"Now what do I do?" I said. I felt a great relief, a burden was off my shoulders, but I was scared. A handsome Mexican stepped up to me.

"Congratulations. You free. Come celebrate with me."

I smiled, and even hesitated a moment, he looked so dashing and smiled with such tantalizing abandon. Then I hailed a cab to the airport. Two days ago Craig had been skiing with the family of John Allen, my *Digest* editor at the time, and had fallen and broken his leg. Twig was at home, frightened and angry, wondering what her friends would think of her, now that her parents were divorced. And Luke? Luke had been very quiet when I hugged him and walked out the door. He was eight years old, and I had left him angry too.

I drove home from Kennedy Airport as fast as I dared. Now I would be both breadwinner and housewife. Alone I could do it; with a man I became resentful when I had to mow the lawn, repair the plumbing, earn the living. My grandmother had once said she did not mind washing the floors, she just did not want anyone to see her doing it. I did not mind doing a man's work when there was no man around to harm.

117

About a week later I went back to see Dr. Neubauer. I stopped still as I walked in his door. He was a short man, not much taller than I, with an imposingly handsome face, high, intelligent forehead and benevolent attitude. He had a nose that did not quite fit his face, and a jowl. I grinned. I was no longer in love with him. The therapy was done. But his eyes were still wonderfully kind.

"Do you have children?" I asked.

"Two," he answered and he slipped into his proper role as a doctor, a married man and a father.

"I have one more question." Vivid flowers had been placed on tables and desks. They were symbolic flowers, I thought—a message that bright things were ahead.

"What do you want to know?"

"Where I have been."

"In a cage of your own making. You've known this marriage was not working for a long time. Hmmm?"

"Yes. But I thought I could make it work if I tried."

"You knew from the very beginning." He rose and we walked toward the door. "You must speak up right away. It hurts everyone less."

I nodded.

"And where will all this end?"

"With a peace of mind." He smiled hopefully.

When I stepped out onto the sidewalk, I could not believe I was on the same street. There were trees and flower boxes, doors with polished brass knockers, intricate grillwork and white marble façades.

It was a beautiful street, except for one thing—some stately image of monogamy of cranes that mated for life, was dead.

11

The Private Lives
of Bears and Toads

There was no use being scared, though at times I had to talk fast to hold down my panic at the thought of buckling down and raising three children by myself. The summer after John and I were divorced, the children and I headed west to see my brothers and their wives and children, hoping we would find a niche in the extended family. I decided, however, not to accept my brothers' invitation to stay with them, but to try it on my own with Twig, Craig and Luke, and so I had rented a cabin at the foot of the Grand Teton Mountains.

The wind coming off Antelope Flats flowed steadily up the mountains, spinning the aspen leaves like gyroscopes as I steered my rented car across a wooden bridge and onto a road of glacial pebbles. The car bumped over ruts for a dusty half-mile, then rolled between two wooden gateposts and among the trees and meadows of X Quarter Circle X ranch.

The children stepped out of the car like cautious fawns and peered up at the Grand Teton looming above us, a stone thunderhead in purple, black and white.

"It *is* big," said Craig, who had only seen the Grand from his uncles' cabins on the other side of the Snake River.

"And mean," said a rusty voice. We turned to see the owner of the X Quarter Circle X, Jimmy Manges, a sinewy man with a large head and bright blue eyes. Across his face the desiccating winds of Wyoming had worn gullies and canyons that deepened when he smiled. Jimmy had homesteaded these 160 acres in 1910, long before there was a national park or a road into Jackson town. He had eked out a living on game and a vegetable garden for two decades; then, as friends and relatives sought him out, he had cut down trees and built one-room cabins for them. After the friends and relatives departed or died, Jimmy rented the cabins each summer to schoolteachers, to families and groups of elderly people for the price of a sack of flour or a slab of bacon. His sister, who was managing the place when I wrote for reservations, charged very little more.

This would be the first real test of living on my own with the kids while managing a speculative assignment for the *Reader's Digest.* I was here this summer to get background on an eventual article on John and Frank's research on *Ursus horribilis,* the grizzly bear, in Yellowstone Park for their study. They were making the first such use of biotelemetry—radio transmitters and receivers for tracking wildlife. I was eager to settle into a work schedule that allowed me to take the children on as many assignments as possible, for my sake as well as theirs. I worked better with my children around me, and since I was writing about nature it seemed possible to have them there.

While Jimmy Manges sized up Twig, Craig and Luke, I sized up the X Quarter Circle X. Ten or twelve hand-built cabins were hidden in the trees around Jimmy's cabin, a garden lay to the rear, and near the barn horses grazed. Jimmy said, arriving at his own conclusions, "Come on in and try to make a livin' off the place." He gestured to the woodpile and a log shed bulging with traps and garden tools. Twig, Luke and Craig did not move. They were staring at Jimmy with mouths agape. His white beard was shaped like a W.

"Caught my beard in the clothes wringer," he said, reading their faces. "Never should have bought the danged electric generator."

Taking Luke's hand, he led us to our cabin. He crossed the porch and pushed back the vines to expose a view of the deep canyons and white peak of the Grand Teton. Then he opened the door.

The smoke-hued room had two brass beds, a cot and a woodstove. Under the window that looked out on the mountain were a handmade table and four chairs.

"Here's yer heat, hot water and cookin' fuel," he said, handing Luke and Craig each an ax. "And yer water." He gave Twig a bucket. "The spring's down the hill by that rock."

"You mean there's no electricity?" asked Twig.

"Not here," he answered. "Too much can go wrong with it. It's best to use muscle."

"But it's cold," said Luke, hugging himself.

Jimmy walked across the room and pointed to the pots and pans on a shelf. "Here're yer utensils." He opened the table drawer. "The cutlery," he said. He leaned closer. "And your mouse." He closed the drawer gently. "Every guest deserves a mouse. His name is Jupiter." He turned to Luke. "He'll take his meals after dark." Luke nodded seriously.

While Jimmy was showing me the all-purpose mugs that would serve as bowl, plate and cup, and the kerosene lamps, the dishpan and the washbasin, Craig and Twig opened the stove door, stuffed kindling and paper into the black box and proceeded to light it. The flame took hold, the wood snapped and popped. A warmth spread through our new home, we felt a lot more secure and relaxed.

"The only news you'll get up here," Jimmy said as he turned to leave, "is from the chickarees, the little red squirrels. They'll tell you all you need to know—that the goshawk is coming, that the packrat is stealing again, and the sun is going down or coming up." He warmed his hands over the stove, then left us to cope with the basic necessities of life: food, shelter, warmth and, for the human animal, the right never to be bored.

Having unpacked, we pulled our chairs around the stove and chattered nervously. It was only 4:00 P.M., yet the Grand Teton cast a blue shadow upon us, darkening the cabin and sobering our mood. We were a fatherless family on its own. We sat quietly listening to the sounds of twilight. Around us was good work to do, work that gave instant and satisfying results, wood to chop, fires to build and keep going, water to be hauled, berries to be picked, fish to be caught, fried and served. As we talked about who would do what chores, a sense of well-being began to flower in each of us.

Craig put another log on the fire.

"When are we going to see the grizzly bears?" he asked.

121

"The day after tomorrow. Tomorrow we hike the Grand to the alpine meadows and waterfalls."

"Yikes," said Twig. "I'm scared. Bears kill you."

"We'll see them from a safe distance," I promised. "Besides, they are more afraid of you than you are of them."

"No, they are *not*," she expostulated. The high pitch of her voice triggered the fear of the bear in her brothers. Craig nervously kicked the fire. Luke slipped onto my lap.

"Bears are wonderful," I said, sounding too obviously upbeat. "They are so strong and brave that they were worshipped by the Indians." Suddenly from the timberland a great gray owl boomed mournfully, and in a burst of some mysterious excitement the chickarees screamed.

Twig screamed too, jumping like a trapped fox. "Bears!"

"It's only the forest saying goodnight," I told her, but by now I was unsure.

A coyote howled with a humanlike haha.

"I miss Daddy," wailed Luke, and wrapped his arms around me.

Looking back eastward in my mind's eye, to the land of psychiatrists and child-development specialists, I cried out, "Now what do I do?"

Talk about it, talk about it, they would have said.

"I'm scared too," I said to Luke. "But it's better this way."

"Without Daddy?" he yelled angrily. "It sure is not."

Luke had spoken his truth. Now he was going to mend.

I lit the kerosene lamp and the low yellow light pushed back the darkness. After we had dined on a pot of canned chicken stew, we crawled into our beds and lay still. The winds yelled from the canyons, the cabin beams snapped and the children's breathing came in tight little sniffs. Suddenly the cutlery rattled. Everyone sat up in bed.

"We forgot to leave supper out for Jupiter," I said.

"No, we didn't," Luke answered from deep within his sleeping bag. "Goodnight, mouse," he said, ignoring me. But his voice was not as angry; the cabin was performing its therapeutic work.

I opened my eyes to the sound of a fire crackling and saw Twig coming through the door with a bucket of water. I watched as she put it on the floor, dipped out a panful and placed it on the hot stove for oatmeal. I sniffed deeply of the sweet yeasty smell of the sourdough starter I had gotten from Es, Frank's wife. It was bubbling the lid off the crock. Hopping out of bed, I went outside to the washbasin on the porch and came wide-awake with a splash of icy spring water on my face. I breathed deeply of the fresh mountain air.

"Craig and Luke went fishing in the creek," said Twig, leaning out through the doorway.

"I hope they catch something," I told her. "I'm starved for fresh fish."

Up the path came Luke holding something in his cupped hands. He climbed the steps and showed me a fat mountain toad, which he carried into the cabin and placed on the floor. The toad hopped to the woodpile, where it squared off its elbows and then, tilting back the massive head with its encompassing grin, sat still.

Luke was stalking horseflies for Toad when Craig called me from among the purple fireweeds. He held high a fish.

"A trout!" I exclaimed. "That's great."

After oatmeal and pancakes, both served in the mugs, Craig made sure the fire was right, rolled the fish in flour and cooked it, his face glowing with satisfaction.

"We can really live here," he said. "We really can." Then the sun rose and the ominous dark mountain lit up, as airy and ephemeral in the dawn as it had been satanic in the shadows of yesterday.

We packed a lunch and drove to Jenny Lake, where we had arranged to meet Margaret, John's wife, for a hike to Lake Solitude. While John and Frank were in Yellowstone working on the bear study, Margaret, Es and their children had remained at their cabins on the second bench of the Snake River. From there they drove up for visits when the study permitted. The radio-tracking of the bears was now five years along. Over a hundred of the grizzled carnivores had been marked with ear tags, and about half that number bore radios in collars that were beeping back messages, unlocking the mysteries of their lives.

With Margaret was her son Derek, and Frank and Es's sons Lance and Charlie. All were in their early teens, full of vigor and imaginative enterprise. They burst out of the car when they saw us, and almost as soon as they had greeted their cousins, they were leading them along a path rimmed with pinedrops and ferns to the edge of Jenny Lake. The morning was as fresh as spring water, the sky an intense brassy blue, as we crossed Jenny Lake in a motor launch, and walked up the trail past Hidden Falls headed for the alpine meadows.

"Teach me the alpine flowers," I said to Margaret as she set the slow but never-stopping pace of the alpine climber. Ahead of us raced the children.

As a summer park ranger's daughter, Margaret had spent every summer in the Tetons while she was growing up. With the famous Jack Durrence and parties, she had climbed all the major peaks of Wyoming by the time she entered college. When she was not in the mountains as a child, she had been following her botanist father, learning the wildflowers. Her artist mother, Clara Smith, had taught her to paint, and while she was living with me in New York she had attended the Art Students' League, where the teachers gathered to learn from her the names of the wild flowers: glacier lily, starflower, dryad and death camas.

We had just reached the last of the tall trees and were pacing up the trail in the dwarfted krummholz when the blue sky became blistered with white cloud puffs. Margaret kept an eye on these innocent shapes as we ate lunch. Then we went on climbing.

When we were about a mile from Lake Solitude, our final destination, the puffs piled up and covered the sun. Within a few minutes they blackened and came sweeping like dark horses down the face of the Grand Teton, snorting and whinnying and thrashing up wild winds. A crack of thunder shook the mountain. Lightning flashed down Cascade Creek Canyon.

"Let's get to the woods," Margaret called.

"Let's get under this ledge," I shouted back. "Lightning likes trees."

"But it loves the undersides of ledges," she answered.

A sizzling shaft of light exploded around us, the hairs all over my body stood up on end and the ledge became a dance floor for the lightning. I grabbed Luke's hand, herded Twig and Craig ahead of me, and followed Margaret over the rocks to the woods. Lance, Derek and Charlie were already in the timber.

As I ducked under the low tree, a bolt of lightning jumped from the pinnacle where we had been to the rock slide, lighting Luke up like a pumpkin head. Thunder exploded and hail hit the meadow, bouncing two feet into the air.

"Aunt Jean, come here, we're here," called Lance. Creeping along in the blackness, I finally located him under an umbrellalike Douglas fir. His face was knitted with concern. Luke and I huddled beside him and Twig and Craig dropped to their knees under another tree beside Derek, Charlie and Margaret, while the clouds dumped a Niagara of rain.

"It's dry here," I cried out to Lance. "The dusty needles look as if the rain never reaches them."

"I hope so," he said, and I leaned back against the bole of the tree to make myself as comfortable as possible, with Luke pushed up close.

The crackles of lightning gave way to explosions of thunder, the thunder rumbled over the rocks, and although I was nervous, I did not feel that we were in danger.

When I heard a trickle, a spurt and then a gush above my head, I looked up to see water snaking its way down the trunk of the tree. Like a river, it sheathed the trunk, struck my shoulder, cascaded into my lap and spilled over my knees and feet. In moments I was a waterfall.

"This tree is a lightning rod," I shouted over the roar of the storm. "It's a perfect conductor of electricity. Let's get out of here." I looked around for a place to go. There was none. The floor of the forest was a waterfall and every tree was an electric cascade. The lightning careened overhead, illuminating each needle and arcing from cloud to earth like a live wire. Once more I was feeling absolutely paralyzed by fear; but this time I could do nothing but wait. I wanted to hug Luke but thought better of it. Together we would both fry; if we sat apart, he might survive. Holding my knees I watched in dread until suddenly the rain stopped, the lightning leaped to another slope and the sun came out.

"Wow," said Lance, "that was close." He got up, pinched himself and ran out into the meadow. Luke followed, waving his hands. Like birds' fears, the children's were short-lived. They ran in the meadow, wringing out their clothes, whipping them overhead and leaping like goats in the sunlight. Margaret walked slowly over to me. She knew how close to death we had been.

"Bad," she said. "But the mountain is an old friend." She smiled. "Let's go."

As we headed down the mountain, Twig dropped in behind me. I saw Charlie putting his two feet together as he came down the meadow, jumping from rock to rock like a goat.

"Bears are worse," he said as he passed, and Twig screamed satisfactorily.

The next morning we drove out of the X Quarter Circle X ranch while the chickarees were still chattering about the sunrise, and crossed the river to the Craigheads' cabins. Esther had the station wagon packed with food, and her daughter, Jana, and Margaret's daughter Karen were both with her. The two families of children moved easily from one set of parents to the other, eating where they landed, napping where they found a bed, returning to their own families in winter, when John lived in Missoula, Montana, and Frank at Craigheads in Pennsylvania. I thought the children flowed between the parents because John and Frank were identical twins. Although to all six children they were Daddy John and Daddy Frank, as I watched I saw that they shifted parents because of Esther and Margaret. The two women were not competitive about their own children and each genuinely loved the other's. Twig crawled into the car with the girls, I sat beside Es, and we were on our way to the bears.

Esther had grown up in the suburbs of Chicago and had met Frank while she was a sophomore at the University of Michigan. They had been the first of the family to marry. Constantly asked by acquaintances how she told her husband from his brother, Esther simply replied, "I don't bother." Over the years she became the female center of the family. She kept us together with letters, postcards and dollar Christmas presents, gleaned from the backs of old stores, flea markets, charity sales and attics. Her genius was in finding the appropriate thing. To this day, on the window of my front door waggles a small green hand on a spring and suction cup, which Esther sent during the years when my house was a Grand Central Station for kids, relatives and business associates. "Bye, bye," the green hand reads.

At Yellowstone we found John and Frank in their Canyon Village lab, an abandoned CCC mess hall. Outside it bristled with antennae. Inside it was noisy with the young biologists, engineers and electronic experts who made up the Craighead research team. John swept up Twig and set her on his shoulders. Frank took Craig and Luke each under an arm and swung them around. The surrogate fathers were taking over, and I recalled those foster song-sparrow parents back in Michigan.

"Come see the little grizzly bear cub," Frank said to the boys. Putting them down again, he led the way through the lab, past the flicking and beeping radio equipment and out to the back of the building.

"This is Grizzly. He lost his mother," said Lance, escorting me and a nervous Twig to meet the bear cub, who got to his feet and came prowling toward us on his leash. When he opened his pink mouth and thrust up his round ears, I understood why everyone wants to feed bears. They are devilishly cute.

"Will he bite?" asked Twig.

"Yes," said Lance with a grin, and Twig turned and ran behind me. Karen came out through the kitchen door with a baby's bottle of milk. Slowly, all the while talking softly to little Grizzly, she approached him and stuck the bottle in his mouth. Grizzly rocked back on his haunches and guzzled with satisfaction. Twig peered around me.

"Ah," she said, reacting to his infantileness.

"We want to get some weight on him before we let him go," said John. "Then we'll band and track him. We would like to get some data on the survival of lone cubs. We hope to find how much weight they gain compared to the cubs with mothers. We are also curious as to their status in the bear society. We think they need a mother for status."

John and Frank had launched the grizzly bear study soon after the end of World War II, when they returned from the South Pacific to learn that the great bear was in trouble. Of the tens of thousands of grizzlies that had once roamed the West, perhaps a thousand remained in the United States (excluding Alaska, which was then not a state). After they finished their Ph.D.s, they made up their minds to learn all they could about the life history of this magnificent carnivore, its habitat and social needs, and to save it from extinction.

A bell clanged in the kitchen.

"Soup's on!" shouted Jay Sumner, one of the research assistants from the University of Montana.

"No lunch for any guy until he climbs the ropes," said Frank. He ran around the end of the building, jumped for the hemp rope that hung from the eaves, and climbed to the top and back down again hand over hand.

"We have games to keep everyone who's handling these bears in shape," he explained as one by one the research team went up and down the rope. The young Craighead boys climbed, and then it was Craig's turn. I could read the thoughts of failure on his face as he stood before the rope. Nevertheless, he clutched it and climbed quite a distance before grabbing with his feet. He gained a few more yards and then came down.

"Great," said Frank, clapping him on the back. "Pass the grub to Craig." The pleasure on Craig's face was indescribable.

That night we spread our sleeping bags at one end of the huge lab and watched and listened as the bears awoke and unwittingly sent their signals through the forest. Each beep as it came in was recorded on the huge maps on the wall. The marks increased; the maps came alive. Bears were walking into Hayden Valley, some sending their signals from as far as twelve miles away. Others were meeting in the dark. A muffled signal meant that the bear was digging, a steady one indicated that he was resting. There in the lab the wilderness became a theater of the bears.

Early the next evening we drove to Hayden Valley, where the grizzlies had been congregating in summer for a hundred years, feeding at the park dump on the garbage from the hotels and campgrounds.

As we came over a rise we saw a cylindrical trap made of a steel culvert with a drop-door. The trap had been sprung. A bear growled inside. He had come for the bait, stepped on the treadle and released the door.

The cars came to a halt about twenty-five feet from the bear trap. Gingerly, Twig and I got out of the radio-equipped van and watched as John put an immobilizing drug dart in a gun and shot it into the bear. Almost instantly he fell, unable to move. The anesthetic put him into a deep sleep. Frank opened the trap door; there, without bars to protect us, lay a wild grizzly bear. The assistants heaved him out of the trap into a cargo net and cranked him up to be weighed. I felt safe enough to slide down from the car roof, to which Twig and I had retreated, and walk closer to the stunning black animal.

"Just a little one," Frank said. "Five hundred pounds."

"What's a big one?" He looked enormous to me.

"Old Bruno. He runs better than a thousand pounds."

The bear was given a number and a colored ear tag. After a blood sample had been taken for a physiological study, Jay Sumner and Frank took dental impressions of his teeth and paws, from which other scientists would be able to tell his age.

The bear moaned. "The anesthesia might wear off quickly—or it might not," said Frank. He glanced at the bear and then at Craig.

"Want your picture taken with a grizzly?" he asked. Craig hesitated; then he looked up at his uncle with faith and came forward. Frank put Craig's hands under the bear's head and neck.

"Heave," he called and snapped a picture that not only became a family treasure but did more for Craig's status among his peers than if he had won an Olympic contest. A kid who has lifted a wild grizzly bear has cleared the way for himself.

Tales of bears awakening and charging were part of the conversation at the lab, and so I was relieved when the last picture was taken.

The bear blinked. "Get to the cars," ordered Frank, and we obeyed like robots.

Hardly had I scrambled to my place and turned around than the bear was on its feet. Frank and Jay were no more than a few yards from him and I was terrified for them. A man within the "flight-fight" perimeter of a grizzly bear will be attacked. For *horribilis* the zone extends about fifty feet from the bear. But the bear was still groggy. He shook, blinked and, seeing the distant forest, turned and loped toward it. I blew a long breath and looked around for Twig. She was down on the floor of the car.

On the way back to the lab I asked Frank what had been learned from radio-tracking thus far.

"For the first time we know definitely that bears dig their own dens each year, and that they dig them on the north slopes of canyons," he said. "On the northern slopes the snow does not thaw readily on warm winter days. We know that grizzly bears do not use these dens twice, and that pregnant mothers line their dens with soft boughs, whereas barren females and males do not. We know bears can wander twenty miles a night and that, at least in Yellowstone, they all go to bed on the same day. That is the day of the big storm of the season that locks up the area until spring.''

I walked out to Grizzly and squatted before him, studying the piercing brown-gold eyes that were both remote and aware.

"How did it happen," I asked him, "that you look the way you do, and I the way I do? How did the meadows and forests and oceans evolve each of us? And why?''

For an instant I knew. I was one with the bear. Somewhere in the ocean of time we were one and the same. Then I lost the understanding.

That night, while we slept, the society of the grizzly bear enforced its own mysterious laws. A male (identified by his paw prints) killed little Grizzly in the darkness, as male grizzlies are programmed to do by their instincts.

"We must look at it this way," John said to the horrified children who had gathered at the back door. "We now have firsthand evidence that certain male grizzly bears will kill the cubs of their own species. The story is no longer myth, but science.''

"But I'm still sad," mourned Luke. I took his hand and it was cold.

On the way back to our cabin several days later I asked Twig if she remembered how many bears John and Frank had ear-tagged the first year.

"Lots," she said.

Then Luke leaned over the back seat. "Thirty," he said. "They ear-tagged thirty in 1959 and they knew lots of others by scars on their faces. They knew Pegleg because she had a stiff walk.''

Twig slowly turned her head around and looked at her little brother, who did not stop talking until he had given a long and thorough lecture on grizzly bears.

"Listen to Luke," Twig said. "Listen to our quiet little brother. Mom, he's an encyclopedia." He waited for her to finish, and then went on with a plea for saving the bears. We had another personality in the family. Thomas Luke George was coming into his own.

The summer waned, the birds headed south and the chickarees were defending enormous storehouses of summer gleanings. One day, as they say in Jackson Hole, "There was snow above town." Winter had whitened the top of the Grand Teton. It was the day of our departure—usually a sad day for me, but not this year. I had notes on elk and moose, on goshawks and coyotes. But more important was that the children had gained courage from the mountains and from being part of an extended family.

While I packed, Craig replenished the woodpile for Jimmy, Twig carried the dishpan of hot water to the table and washed up the dishes.

"How come housework is fun in this little cabin?" she asked. "I hate it at home."

"Maybe it's because we can see what we're accomplishing. It's just the right scale."

"Or maybe it's because we have only one mug apiece and it's easy to clean," said Craig.

Twig picked up a shoe and jumped backward, startled.

"Did you see that?"

"What?" I asked.

"Luke's natural vacuum cleaner is working." Four or five small wood crickets were feeding on crumbs underneath the table. When they had cleaned up the crumbs, Toad hopped out from under the woodpile, squared himself, and cleaned up the crickets with lightning stabs of his tongue.

"Wow!" I exclaimed. "Ecology has come out of the ivory tower and proven itself. It's practical. Toad goes home to Chappaqua."

But Luke, who had other priorities, took Toad back to the woods.

12

Castles and
Feet of Clay

On the plane ride home, I looked at the tops of my children's blond heads lined up in the seats in front of me and knew that no matter how much affection my brothers gave us, we were not really part of their family. When the snow fell above town, with the day done and the fires lit, each of the Craighead households would close its circle and we would be left outside. It could not be otherwise.

We were another kind of family, a single-parent family, a lopsided thing requiring a special degree of love and insight, which had to come from ourselves.

The days at the X Quarter Circle X ranch and the chores we did to help each other live in comfort had indeed given strength to our broken circle. The summer had been more than worthwhile, for we had found we were neither Craighead nor George, but a new, colorful group: Twig, Craig, Luke and Jean—the Craighead Georges.

As we sped through the high ice clouds I decided to use the name Jean Craighead George for the children's books I was working on, and to keep the name Jean George for the *Digest* articles. Names are a special problem for a divorced woman who has been using her husband's last name professionally. My friend Beth, who had been divorced, widowed, and then remarried, ended up using the last name of her long vanished ex-husband. At Vassar, the head of the Child Study Department simply added the name of each new husband until she had a name—Mary Fisher Langmuir Essex—that almost encircled her latest book.

I was deep in these thoughts when Craig turned around in his seat to voice a concern that had nagged us all: "I wonder how Otus is?" Had Mike, the owl sitter, been able both to keep Otus in mice and chicken necks and to keep Trinket off his feathery back?

Craig's question was answered when we burst through the front door with our bags, and Otus swooped down the steps from his roost on Luke's bedroom door.

"He's alive!" Craig shouted. A note from Mike, who had gone to work for the day, said all was well and that there was a large supply of mice in the freezer.

Otus hovered over us, then side-stepped and landed on the piano stool. He gave his wivered cry.

"He's glad to see us," exclaimed Twig. We watched as the owl lifted his elfin face, blinked and rotated his head one full circle to the left, then one full circle to the right.

"He's really glad," she added. "That's what that means."

"He's only hungry," I said. "Owls aren't glad."

Twig gathered him up in her hands and tucked him under her chin, her long blond hair falling around him. Otus snapped his beak softly.

"And he remembers how to ask me to scratch his head," she added, sinking her fingers through an inch of feathers to gently touch the old-manlike skull beneath. Otus closed his eyes and went limp—with pleasure, obviously.

"He *is* glad," she repeated, and I had to agree.

Trinket meowed from the dining room. That she had not killed Otus while we were gone was a tribute to Mike. Although she never touched a pet while we were at home, if we left for more than twenty-four hours she systematically wiped out every living creature in the house. Over a single Thanksgiving night she had disposed of three chameleons, five mice, a tank of tropical fish, two hamsters and a garter snake. She was now perched on the rim of the stone pool in the foyer where I kept the indigenous freshwater animals, waiting for the large-mouthed bass to make a miss-swim.

As we sorted packs and the treasures in them—such as bleached antelope bones—Trinket came around the corner of the foyer, striking her paws hard on the floor as though to drum out a message. I well knew the meaning of that signal. Trinket was talking to a new litter of kittens, telling them to follow her. So, five lovely kittens were sitting in the center of the living room rug at Trinket's command.

"Oh, Lordy," I said, putting down Luke's elk horn. "Trinket is going to introduce her kittens to us. Sit down, everyone, we are about to have a cat debut." We all knew what to do, Trinket having given birth to eleven litters to date. Just as a lioness of the African plains makes an occasion of introducing her cubs to the pride, a housecat introduces a new litter of kittens to her pride, which is usually the people she lives with.

Trinket did it by stages. When the kittens were a few weeks old, she would bring them out of Twig's bedroom closet and place them in the center of the hall rug. After a few days she would bring them downstairs to the coat closet, and then out onto the dining-room rug. Finally when the kittens were about two months old, she would lead them to the center of the living room to be introduced. There was no use ignoring the kittens' coming-out party no matter how busy we were, for Trinket would persist in meowing and harassing us until we admired each kit. I sat down on the floor, picked up one stubby-tailed Manx kitten, petted it, admired it, oohed over it, put it down and picked up another. When each of us had approved of Trinket's kittens she led them back to the closet and the ceremony was done.

"Harmony will now descend upon us, the pride," I said, quoting Rudolf Schenkel, the Swiss zoologist who had discovered the coming-out ceremony of the cats on a study of lions in Nairobi Park. He had observed that "after the introduction of the kittens to the pride, all social relations of the adults, who fight and snarl until the debut, seemed to be impregnated with tenderness and fondness and there is practically no room for social conflict and tension."

"Up the cats," I said as we carried our packs upstairs. "Let there be tenderness and fondness from now on."

Over the next month, Otus began to worry me. Though he looked well fed, and his feathers were glossy and rich in color, he nevertheless spent much of his time not in the bookcase but on the windowsill of my sunporch, watching the birds come and go at the feeder. He was going wild, I thought. He was seeing right past us as he reverted to the state of mind of an owl. Always before, Otus had come into the bathroom to join whoever was taking a shower. He had stopped doing this after we returned from the summer. I decided it was time to set him free.

One early winter morning while I was bathing I was surprised to see him on the shower head. Talking softly to me, he flew to the faucet and then to the bottom of the tub, as he once had done regularly. Standing under the shower, scooping with his wings, he splashed water into every feather and vane, drenching himself to the skin. With his bare knees and head exposed between sodden feathers, he snapped his beak, his signal to pick him up. A warm shiver went through me. The owl was still with us. All the same, as I placed the little bird-person on the bathroom rug I had an overwhelming desire to open the window and set him free. He was caged even as I had been, but not by his own doings. Had he not been soaking wet, I would have thrown up the window then and there. He hopped down the hall, found Twig reading on her bed and wivered his attention call. She picked him up, wrapped him in a towel and tucked him by her side. His head was very small when he was wet, and seemed to be all eyes. My urge to let him go faded. The little owl was our connection to a wider world—the forces that made owls owls and people people and to the something beyond our present selves. We needed Otus very much.

Since I was often gone all day and sometimes many days on assignments, as well as into New York City to do research or for dinner and theater dates, I decided to engage one regular babysitter instead of a series of young girls.

It often happens after a divorce that the persons to whom you were closest during that painful process drift away, the problems that brought you together having been solved. My *Digest* editor, John Allen, and I had spent hours talking out what was happening as both our marriages ended. Now that our divorces had come through, the need for each other was ending. I needed a new editor and a fresh start. For a few days though, the babysitter problem delayed my taking any action on the matter. I placed an ad in the paper. A Mrs. Blanche Davidson was the first to apply. She was an older woman, round and motherly, who had raised eleven children of her own. After the birth of her third child, her husband had a stroke and was never able to speak again, much less hold a job.

Blanche Davidson had "sat" the children for about a week before I asked them how they liked her.

"She bakes bread and tells stories," said Twig. "She's neat."

135

"What kind of stories?"

"She grew up on a farm."

"Good, farms make wonderful stories."

"She told us about a dairy maid who gave birth to a baby with a pig's head."

"A what?"

"A baby with a pig's head. She said it was shameful for men to do that." Twig paused, waiting for me to react, I thought. But that was not so; she was thinking.

"What I don't understand is that if the dairy maid had the baby, the father must be a pig, not a man."

"Mrs. Davidson has told you an old farm myth that I thought had died with my great-grandmother. Perhaps the child was deformed and people must blame something; but pigs and people just don't mix. I think we should get another babysitter."

"She sure gets us to brush our teeth," said Luke, coming to her defense.

"How does she manage that? I have to dog and heckle you to get the job done."

"She takes out her false teeth," said Craig taking up the story, "and goes 'clomp, clomp, clomp' with her bare gums. Then she opens her mouth without any teeth in it and says 'You'd better brush your teeth, or you'll look like me.' "

"Boy, you ought to see us beat it upstairs and brush our teeth," said Twig, and all three laughed and shivered at the horror of the toothless mouth.

"I think I'll call Briarcliff College and find a student who would like to earn some extra money."

"But we never watch TV when Mrs. Davidson is here. You ought to like that," said Craig.

"What *do* you do?"

"We watch Mrs. Davidson. She watches wrestling on the TV and she grapples and twists and turns and yells like crazy. She's real funny."

The next week I arranged for Martha, a young woman recommended by one of Twig's teachers, as a sitter. Upon returning from the city I was pleased to find the house in good order and the children asleep. As I drove

Martha home I asked if she would be available for the following Tuesday. She emphatically was not.

"How about Wednesday?"

"No." From the tone of her voice I knew that all had not gone well, and the next morning at the breakfast table I confronted the children.

"How was Martha?"

"She's okay. When is Mrs. Davidson coming back?"

"What happened?"

"We put dog biscuits on our plates and ate them with our mouths," said Twig, her eyes twinkling. "Craig told her that's all you ever feed us and he barked when she spoke to him. She said we were worse than the wild animals in the house."

"She has no sense of humor," said Luke.

"Sense of humor," I said. "I guess not."

And so Mrs. Davidson was hired to come regularly two days a week. Gradually I had to admit her tales were amusing; I even began collecting Mrs. Davidson stories for telling at Chappaqua cocktail parties. But there was more to come, as I discovered one morning when counting out weekly allowances from the teapot where I kept my cash. Twig shook her finger at me and said, "You ought to put that in the bank."

"Why?"

"Mrs. Davidson said so. She said that she used to keep her money in her bureau drawer, and one day while she was out a burglar came in and took it all."

"Where was Mr. Davidson?"

"Well, he can't yell for help or call the cops, so the burglar laughed at him and took all her money. Now she puts it in the bank."

"Good advice," I said, and let it go at that until I was faced with another Davidson adage. The winter froze the duck pond at Quaker and Douglas roads and we all went down to ice skate one Sunday morning. After lacing my skates I stepped on the ice and was about to spin off when Craig pulled me back.

"Never go out on the ice without testing it," he said.

"Aw, come on. I can see how thick it is."

"So could Mr. Davidson," said Twig.

"Okay, what happened?"

"Well, Mr. Davidson does all the shopping because he doesn't need to talk to pick things off the grocery shelves. On the way home one winter day he decided to take a short cut across the frozen pond."

"Yes?" I said.

"Now this is true, because his daughter Linda saw it. Mr. Davidson walked out on the ice and fell through to the bottom, six feet down. In a few seconds he came up through another hole, near land, and walked ashore, still carrying the groceries in his arms. When he got home Mrs. Davidson had to chop the ice off him."

I tested the ice that day and thereafter.

One afternoon John Allen called to say that a flying squirrel article I had worked on for months had not been bought. I was desolate. The semiannual check from my books had been used up in paying bills; now more of them were piling up. Old family training made me compulsive about paying bills on time. When Twig came in from school I was pacing the floor.

"Have you got any more Mrs. Davidson stories?" I asked. "I'm really in the dumps."

Twig put down her books and sat beside me. "Yesterday," she began, "Mr. Davidson forgot to take his digitalis, and he passed out right by the school bus stop where Linda and all her friends were standing. Linda got her mother, and they had to pick him up by the head and the feet and carry him home. Mrs. Davidson was disgusted at him for embarrassing Linda in front of her friends and when he came to she told him so.

"He wrote her a note; he can't speak, you know. He said: 'Anyone who doesn't need digitalis is blessed and ought to be quiet.' Mrs. Davidson said she hugged him and agreed."

"Thanks," I said. "That'll hold me for several days."

The Parkinson's law of divorce is that whoever initiates the proceedings gets the small end of the financial settlement. In our separation agreement John got our stocks, the library, the outdoor equipment, and the royalties from the books I had written using both our names. I don't know why I had agreed to the last, but I had.

For my part I got $150 per month, the house (with the mortgage payments), the car and, after a fight, the royalties from my own books. He wanted those too. "You wrote them under my roof and neglected me as a husband to your own advantage," he said. I guess I'll never forget those words, although by now I've forgiven them.

At times, when the bank account was low, I would be angry with myself for having signed away any of my books. At the time of the agreement I suggested that John might like to use the money to help the children through college. He did not respond, nor did he ever help. Granted, by the time ours were ready for college he had a new wife and two more children to support. But John and I never had agreed on child-rearing.

I give up hard. The day after learning that the flying squirrel article had been rejected, I got up before sunrise and began to rewrite the story once more. On the bookshelf above my typewriter sat the aquarium in which I had two crayfish. They were stalking each other as the light came up; the aquarium was too small for the two.

A college professor had once said that the definition of life was meeting and solving problems—be it an amoeba bumping into the edge of the pond and solving this problem by going another direction, or a human being faced with a low bank balance.

As I leaned forward to watch, one of the crayfish backed off, picked up a small pebble with his claw and placed it between himself and his opponent. He went back for another and another, and before the sun was over the tops of the trees outside the house, he had built a wall so high that one could not see the other. Not being able to see each other meant that they no longer needed to fight. A space had been created.

"There's more than one way to solve a problem," I said, and took a new tack of my own. I drove down to the grocery store and with great embarrassment asked Sam, the owner, if I might have a little more time to pay my bill.

"Pay whenever you can," he said. "I know writers don't get weekly checks." I was touched by his kindness and also by his respect for a writer. Somehow I had taken a hard line on my profession; I had to make good and there were to be no excuses. But I indulged myself in Sam's admiration.

At home I picked up the phone and dialed Hobart Lewis, the editor-in-chief of the *Reader's Digest,* to raise the question I had put off taking up with him. "Hobe," I said, "I seem to be blocked. I'm not producing good stuff for the *Reader's Digest* anymore. I think I can do it. I just think I need a new editor, for a fresh start.''

"I understand," he said. "I'll get back to you in a few days.''

My new editor was Andy Jones, a powerfully built Scotsman with a smile that exposed a yard of beautiful white teeth. A naturalist, hunter and fisherman, he was acquainted with John and Frank, having written while he was in prep school to tell them they were not the only guys with an owl. He had sent them a picture of himself on his bike with his own owl balanced on the handlebars. I well remembered that picture of Andy; his letter had been one of the more memorable of the hundreds of fan letters John and Frank received.

"I want an article on canoeing from you," Andy said as we settled down to a lunch of filet mignon and asparagus in the *Reader's Digest* guest house. This was an old farmhouse on the property, which Wally and Lila Wallace had refurbished with antiques and staffed with chefs for editorial luncheons.

I had just bought a canoe, my pointed gesture to a new life, and had been skimming up rivers with Craig and into marshes for frogs with Luke. Andy discussed how to go about this article. I listened and nodded, excited by the possibility of, as Andy said, "putting myself on eye-level with the wildlife in that canoe.''

"I admire John George," Andy said as we rose to leave. I drew back. John and I had met Andy at one of the *Digest* dinner parties and they had talked at length. This was the first time I had been forced to speak about John since the divorce.

"John's a superb biologist and an excellent teacher," I said. "He's teaching at Penn State now." Once the words came out—not easily, but with sincerity—I was over a huge block. Although that was to be the only discussion we had of the relationship between John and me, I was one further step out of the cage; I had talked about John in a civil way and without anger.

"And the grizzly bears?'' said Andy, getting back to business.

"The answers John and Frank have been asking of the bears are just coming in," I answered. "For one thing, they know what sends the bears off to bed.''

"Get crackin'," he said. "Go see your brothers.''

The canoe piece sold immediately and for a time I stopped adding and subtracting money at night. I paid my grocery bill and left Sam's store with a steak and four fresh artichokes to celebrate with at dinner. Next I drove to the camping equipment store and bought the backpack I'd had my eye on since the summer before. Unlike my old pack, this piece of technology possessed side pockets, space to attach a tent and sleeping bag to, and a large compartment for food, clothes, stove and a pot. It was lightweight, it shed rain, it zipped and fit the back. I propped it against the north wall of my bedroom where I could see it before I closed my eyes at night and when I opened them in the morning. I thought of it as my chrysalis; it would transform me from library research, backyard pets and old notebooks into a new kind of journalist, one of participation. I would explore the environment of the back country on my own. I had camped all my life, but never in solitude. I wasn't sure I could do it without a man, but I would try. And so the backpack was both promising and frightening.

One afternoon I came home to find Twig huddled in the corner of the couch, wringing her hands and close to hysterics.

"My mice," she screamed, grabbing my hand and pulling me upstairs to her room. Covering her eyes, she pointed to the cage in which she had been running an experiment for her science teacher on the population growth of mice. I opened the nest box and looked down at what appeared to be living pink spaghetti, but which was, in truth, a solid mass of mice, fornicating, giving birth, eating their offspring and each other. In place of the orderly spacing of life, birth and death, under crowded conditions they had all been compacted into a biological horror.

We flushed the whole experiment down the toilet and, feeling sick at our stomachs, built a fire downstairs and curled up before it.

"You still think nature's beautiful?" Twig asked when she had quieted down. "It's gross, that's what it is, gross."

"When it gets out of balance it's horrible," I agreed.

"How do you keep it in balance so we won't be eating each other up, some day when there are too many people in the world?"

"No one really knows," I told her. "A balance in nature is so ancient, so rooted in the past and the future, so complicated, that scientists have only begun to understand it. One thing I do know, however, if we had left those mice alone they would have solved their own population problem and come back down to the right number for the size of the cage and the amount of food."

"Ghastly. There's got to be a better way," she said. "And I'm going to look for it and tell everyone."

"That, my sweet Twig, is the best thought of the year."

Friends and animals, and an open house for the children's friends, made my life pleasant and lively. As I became more professional I enjoyed writing more and more. When I sold an article we celebrated; when I did not, we went back to chili con carne and cornmeal mush. The canoe was our recreation—cheap, simple and beautiful. The elusive peace of mind I had sought was descending upon me.

One night Elizabeth Riley ended my career as an illustrator. After dinner she took me on a walk through the darkening streets of Greenwich Village. Lights were coming on in attics and stone buildings; skylights were beginning to glow. She stopped and pointed to a light at the top of an early American townhouse.

"In that room there is Jerry, talent from the Pratt Institute of Art," she said. "Working late into the night for the T. Y. Crowell Company. That pleases me. And down there on Greene Street is an artist from Cooper Union. He is working for us, too, making beautiful children's books." My head was tilted up now, watching the lights come on in small corners of the city. I could visualize artists yawning and beginning their work.

"Jean," Elizabeth said, "your drawings are very nice, but these people are professionals. You need good artists to illustrate your books."

I felt a bit sad, for I loved to illustrate. But she was right; I had a style, but I could not hold a candle to the artists who were illustrating the children's books of the day. I would always love to paint and draw; but, with only a few exceptions, years later, after that night I did not illustrate my own books.

Elizabeth was a genuine taskmaster, a characteristic I have always admired and so I listened to advice. The next time she gave it, I did not take it.

As an author of children's books, I often went with Elizabeth to conventions of librarians when I had a book coming out. On a trip to Detroit, where we were both scheduled to speak to the Michigan Library Association, Elizabeth crossed her ankles and cleared her throat.

"Jean," she said, "you don't write conversation well. I think it's time you shifted to nonfiction for children, such as your *Digest* articles.''

I was taken back. For a long moment I looked out of the window of the plane, thinking about what she had said. Elizabeth was a perfectionist and a successful editor, and so I weighed her words thoughtfully.

"I can learn," I said. "You must teach me to write conversation. I really believe that storytelling is the best way to stimulate children to read and investigate. And I do tell stories."

We said no more about the matter. But not only did she teach me to write conversation, I also wrote thirteen nonfiction books for her; and our relationship continued to be strong and rewarding as long as we worked together.

The finality of our creative years was as stylish as the beginning. One morning Elizabeth called to ask me to meet her at the Stanhope for lunch. As I took my seat at the usual table in the red and gold dining room, she folded her hands in her lap and tilted forward. I waited for some savory piece of gossip concerning the children's book world to fall from her lips.

"Today you are dining with a millionaire," she said, and sat back. "The T. Y. Crowell Company has been sold to Dun and Bradstreet. I owned much of the stock . . . and now I'm retiring."

"A millionaire," I repeated. "Well, you were as canny a businesswoman as you are a great editor. Congratulations."

Before leaving me under the white marquee of the Stanhope, she gestured toward the Metropolitan Museum of Art across the street.

"I'm embarking on a new career," she said. "Curator of quilts and lace at the Met. I am going to forget the whole world of children's books." A few steps down the sidewalk she turned and came back.

"I still think you have another good book in you," she said. "A Newbery." I laughed and shook my head as she walked briskly up Fifth Avenue—a slender, energetic woman who had changed the prevailing standards of children's literature from cute stuff to fine art. I admired her greatly and wondered where I would go now. But that decision was three years in the future.

On a hot afternoon I came home to find Craig in the backyard with his friend Jim Deignam, an older boy who was teaching him chemistry from a college text. They also mixed chemicals. As I opened the door

143

there was the sound of an explosion from the woods. Jim and Craig came running indoors after me, laughing uproariously.

"We know exactly what we're doing," Jim said, seeing my face. "You don't have to worry, Mrs. George."

I took a long look at both of them, wondering where investigative science progress turned into a hazard. "I believe you do know what you're doing," I finally said. "But I don't. Be careful." Just then the telephone rang. The voice at the other end of the wire was saying, "This is Bob Radnitz. How would you like to see *My Side of the Mountain* made into a movie?"

I tried to recognize the voice and pin down who the prankster was.

"Where are you?" I asked finally, beginning to believe this might be a legitimate call.

"Hollywood," he answered, and then asked, "Who is your agent?" When I had given him the name and address, he said, "By the way, your book was brought to my attention not by a Hollywood scout, but a young boy. He said it was the best book he had ever read and that I should make a film of it."

I tried three times before I managed to get the receiver back onto the hook. Then I ran outside, where Jim and Craig had another countdown in progress.

Another chemical explosion rocked the woods, this time with sparklerlike darts flying out from it, as I called out: "A movie. Bob Radnitz Productions and Paramount are going to make a film of *My Side of the Mountain.*"

Twig and I went down to Sam's for lobsters, Chinese peas and a quart of ice cream, and that night we celebrated with as many friends as we could find. It was not until later that I was told what a risky celebration it had been. Options from Hollywood almost never materialized; but Bob Radnitz's did. *My Side of the Mountain,* with Teddy Eccles and Theodore Bikel, opened at the Museum of Modern Art and then moved out across the country. For a month I drove by the local theater each day to stare at the title of my book on the marquee.

It was a few days after Radnitz called that Frank gave me a ring: "If you want to talk about why the bears go to bed," he said, "come on down." I was off to Pennsylvania as soon as school ended for the day.

Esther greeted us in the hallway of the two-hundred-year-old house at Craigheads where Twig had been conceived. Her kids and mine together made so much noise that she opened the front door and let all six of them out into the winter grayness where they ran to the creek to walk logs and climb to Charlie's and Lance's treehouse.

I found Frank in the old kitchen with its walk-in fireplace. He touched off a flame, then settled back onto his heels. I said, "Tell me about the bears."

"On September fifteenth," he began, "I was chopping wood at the Yellowstone lab when I noticed a sudden drop in the temperature. Cold is one of the triggers that send bears off to den. I ran inside and turned on the bear radios. Bob Ruff, one of the assistants, and I waited and listened. You can tell when a bear dens because the beep changes its sound. But the beeps did not change that day or the next or the next, even though the cold spell persisted for eight days. So it wasn't just the cold.

"On October fifteenth the day dawned warm, the birds sang. Then at noon the clouds piled up and we routinely flipped on the radios. A startling thing was taking place for such a warm day." Frank put on a pot of coffee. "Bear Number 202 had left his summer bedding area at Sulphur Mountain and was trotting along Elk Antler Creek. Other bears were on the move: 181 was splashing across the Yellowstone River; 65, a barren female, was running toward a canyonside. We didn't know what to make of it because we didn't know what the bears knew. Then we got the message. At four o'clock in the afternoon a snow fell. We assembled the equipment and prepared to record the denning of the bears.

"But they did not den, they only walked to the denning places. All the beeps came in loud and clear. We sat up all night waiting for those muffled signals that would tell us they were under the roots of the trees. No such signal came. Three days later the sun came out, the snow melted and Bob and I tracked down the bears to find out what had happened. They were all fighting sleep. Heads drooped between their shoulders, they sat on the ground near their dens, moaning as if in agony. They seemed to be waiting for something. What? The cold snap had made them lethargic. Why didn't it send them off to hibernate?

"On November eleventh another storm struck. I flipped on the receiver and heard erratic beeps all over the plateau. One was weak. That meant a bear had denned; at last we were close. Bob tuned in on 202 and his beep said he was heading for his den. We hoisted the receivers on our backs and went out to the canyon where 202 had prepared his den earlier in the season.''

Turning the receivers from right to left, Frank had hiked six miles through the falling snow, hunting for bear 202. The signals indicated that he was nearby, but still Frank could not find him.

"Suddenly," he said, "I saw him trotting between the trees to my left; and I knew what the bears had been waiting for: the storm was blowing and drifting, covering 202's footsteps as he went off to bed.

"In the morning," Frank concluded, "there was not a print left to tell where the bears had gone."

I said, "That's just beautiful."

"It adds up this way," he interpreted. "A cold snap makes the grizzlies we studied lethargic, an early snowfall trots them off to their denning areas, and the arrival of the storm that locks up the plateau until spring is what sends them off to bed."

"How did they know that snow wouldn't melt that time?" I asked.

"That'll remain the secret of the bears for a long time to come."

The article I wrote—"The Day the Bears Went to Bed"—became one of the fifty *Reader's Digest* articles selected for the fiftieth anniversary collection of the magazine. Letters poured in inquiring about my brothers, and the *National Geographic* followed up the *Digest* article with a TV special, one of their first. The morning after it was shown, the knocker clanged, and Margaret Mayburn, a tall, energetic mother of four, walked in and sat down. She had been having trouble with her two older children who had dropped out of high school. The son was smoking pot and her daughter was living with a young musician, an arrangement that was unheard-of at the time. Margaret and her husband, like most of our generation, believed that the secret of a full and successful life was education. They had worked to put themselves through a Midwestern college, and Larry had risen to a highly paid executive position with a large corporation.

"I saw your brothers' TV show last night," she said. "They are perfect—out in nature, teaching their kids. They don't have any problems. They can't have any problems."

"Sure, they do," I said. "People think they live the ideal life, but—" and I recounted one or two difficulties.

"No, they don't have any problems," she insisted. "They live with nature and they're teaching their children to live with nature."

I chuckled to myself. No one ever believed John and Frank lived anything but the ideal life. They were the American dream—man in nature. "You're right," I finally said, giving up. "They don't have any problems."

Sunday morning was bright, and I awoke early and stood at my window. The colors of the trees were just turning; the monarch butterflies were passing on migration, flying due southwest. The knocker banged and a medium-sized man with intense blue eyes and close-clipped hair, wearing a jacket and tie, stood before me.

"I want my daughter Polly," he said. "She ran away from home last night."

"Your daughter? She's not here."

"She crawled in your bathroom window. I know she's here."

"But she's not."

"She's often threatened me with that. You like runaways. You even write books about them."

"I'm sorry. You're mistaken." I started to close the door, then thought better of it and invited my visitor in. "I'll check Twig's room if you insist," I said, and hurried upstairs. Twig was curled on one of her twin beds; the other was smoothly made. I stalked back downstairs.

"She's not here."

"She *is* here." He sat down and folded his arms on his chest. "I won't leave until I get her." I was about to ask him to go when it occurred to me that the pillow on the other bed had been unusually large. I ran back upstairs and uncovered Polly, curled up like a rabbit underneath the bedspread.

"Polly, your father wants you."

"Please." She slid out of the bed and cringed beside a chair. "Don't make me go back with my father." I sat down beside her, wondering what to do, but knowing there was really only one option. I suffered for her, having once had to face my own father after lying to him, and I took Polly's hand and brought her downstairs to her father. As she went out with him, her pretty face swollen with tears, her eyes wide with fright, I heard Twig kick the laundry basket.

"I'll never trust you again," she shouted. "You wrote a story about a boy who runs away from home; and now you send Polly back to her father." She burst into tears.

"That was only a story," I said. Twig stared at me with rage, and I felt a halo falling. I was no longer a being to be worshipped, but just another adult, as full of faults as the next.

That night Otus flew to the windowsill and peered out into the darkness where owls dwell. And once more I was overwhelmed by the feeling that I had to set him free.

"It's time to let Otus go," I said when Twig, Craig and Luke came to my room to say goodnight.

"No," said Twig.

"No!" Luke cried. "He's the same as our brother."

"But wouldn't it be nice if he lived in the trees and came back at nightfall to be fed and play with us?"

"Will he?" asked Luke, who was fond of letting wild things go. Only ten days before, he had opened the back door and set our robin of the season free.

"Sure he will," I said. "When I was a kid at Craigheads we had owls that slept in the woods all day and came back at night to be fed and play on our beds. Windy would run after tennis balls under the covers when we made tents for him."

"No," said Twig.

"He'll come back," I insisted. "And he'll be much happier. What do you think, Craig?"

"Will he really come back?"

"Yes. He doesn't know how to catch his own food, so of course he'll be back."

Craig petted Otus, who was watching the TV screen from the foot of the bed, and smoothed his glistening feathers.

"You're all growing up," I said. "We'll set Otus free; then we'll pack up the car and go to the animals."

"No," said Twig again. "What about Bubo? *He* didn't come back."

Craig and Luke hesitated. Luke thought it might be nice for Otus to meet other owls, and finally Craig agreed: the moment had come. The window opened with a bang that startled the elfin bird. He took off from the foot of the bed, flew around the room, then headed straight through the window. Like a small gray cloud he soared into the darkening day; the owl-person was free.

He never came back; and I have not heard the end of it to this day. Nor have Twig, Craig and Luke ever thought of me as a hotshot since. I must qualify as a centipede where feet of clay are concerned.

13

The Wilderness at Home

The backpack had leaned against the bedroom wall all winter waiting for me. June came and I was out backpacking—alone.

As I rolled up the car windows and locked the doors, I could feel my resolve begin to crumble. Couldn't I do my research for a book about black bears in the Smoky Mountains just as well with a companion as without? A moment ago I had known why I couldn't. Now I did not. Four steps down the trail I turned and looked back at the visitors' tower. Friendly people moved in clusters up the ramp for a look at the view. I stared at them a long while, then slowly turned and began to walk. The kids were growing up; this summer they were off to camp. The time had come to walk alone.

The path from Clingman's Dome westward to Silers Bald is deeply scored by boots. It passes among spruce and fir trees, and through patches of thornless blackberries and large purple-fringed orchis, to a ridge of bald rocks. Then it strikes off for Thunderhead and eventually to Mount Springer in Georgia. That path is the Appalachian Trail, which opened the way for long-distance pleasure hikers in 1922 when volunteers began cutting a path from Maine to Georgia. It would take until 1933 and would finally be 2,023 miles long. The Appalachian Trail can be followed all the way or for a short tramp. I had planned to hike for two days, turn around and come back, in the process of gathering information on the habitat of black bears.

To my right and left the Smoky Mountains rolled out in summits and troughs like the waves of a seascape. More than two hundred different species of trees breathed out a vapor that rose like smoke, and had given the mountains their name. The dripping mixture of greens was so fecund that I could all but feel new creatures coming into being. I stopped now and then to make a note and then walked on. A winter wren sang; gray boulders gleamed in the light; all around me in the mystic vat of the soil, bacteria were at work recycling the debris of the forest to sustain the higher kingdoms of the plants and animals. The miraculous accidents of DNA that brought the human being and the forest into existence seemed almost understandable as I walked the trail. Thoreau was right: in the wilderness one had the ability to make sense of it all . . . almost.

Just when I was grasping how I fitted into the scheme of the planet, a thought came into my head that made me lose track of the whole complex. I had planned to spend the night at the Mount David lean-to about twelve miles ahead. Now what came was the thought of darkness. I stopped once more and looked back. I could not hear a human sound. I was over-whelmed by my need for people, and it took all my determination to stick with my plan and go on toward Silers Bald.

Presently I heard footsteps coming toward me. The leaves bobbed, a jay screamed a warning note—and around the bend came a young man with his hair in a pony tail of the mid-sixties. Sweat made salty rings on his T-shirt, and for an instant I was afraid of him. Then I saw his smile and relaxed.

"Hi." I smiled broadly. He nodded, and I said, "Going to Maine?"

"Nah," he drawled. When he lifted his eyes, I saw that the pupils almost engulfed the irises. In the years to come I would know that those expanded pupils meant drugs. But at the time, a youth on a woodland trail was unimpeachable. I smiled at him and walked on.

Farther down the trail I entered a forest of beech and yellow birch and came upon a path with a sign pointing the way to Double Springs Gap. Following it, I arrived at a cool, fern-encircled spring. A ruffed grouse took off in haste, and a red fox sniffed at me, annoyed, from the other side of the pool. Taking off my pack, I lay down on my belly, drank deeply of the water, and then rolled onto my back to look up through the branches to the sky.

It was there on the mountain that I found the Eden we all yearn for. Birds called, water trickled over rocks, and all suffering fell away from me. But after a while I began to mull over, once again, all the arguments that led to my divorce, the sorrow and the mistakes. I was right back where I had started from, working through the guilts of my married life. I did not believe this could be happening to me, here in the wilderness where I had come for refreshment and peace of mind. The forest was not a healer, but an agitator; it had turned me in upon myself. Slowly I reversed my thinking once more, worked out each problem all over again, and squeezed my way out of the cage. When I got to my feet, finally, I could believe that the divorce was over.

After I walked back to the main trail, I could see two people approaching far down the ridge, their heads bobbing above the low brush. Upon seeing me they quickened their pace.

"There's a huge bear on the trail," the taller of the two women said.

"Good," I answered. "I've come to see bears."

"He's about a quarter of a mile back." She pointed. "And a quarter of a mile big."

In eager anticipation I walked toward the bear. Black bears are not as aggressive as grizzlies, and I planned to stop at a safe distance away and make a sketch. Rounding the next bend, I came upon the bear, swinging down the middle of the trail, head low, black shoulders pumping ominously. I yelled, whistled and shouted to turn him back. But still he came, as though seeing and hearing right through me. When I smelled the greasy odor of his body and heard the dry shuffling of his padded feet, I made a quick decision.

There is today a branch of the Appalachian Trail that originally left the main path about twenty feet in front of the bear. It descends the mountain, then circles back up, about half a mile from where it began. I carved out that trail, at a dead run.

Early in the afternoon a steep, short climb brought me to the top of Silers Bald, where I admired the spectacular view and watched seven turkey vultures winding down on something they had found, until a thunderclap sounded. I turned to see a black storm coming my way, bending and whipping the trees, and decided to make camp early.

I trotted down the bald and pitched my tent in a flat place off the main trail. When the last stake was set, the first raindrops splashed onto the nylon shelter and I crawled inside, delighted to have a cocoon in the storm. I took out my notebook and described the bear. The storm slapped down in gulps and blasts; rain pelted the tent and the wind whistled and stampeded through the trees, to the sound of breaking limbs. The seams of the tent began to leak under the deluge. Puddles formed on the floor. I pushed them out with my hands, finally taking out a shirt and sopping them up.

I ate cheese and bread, and stirred cocoa into a cup of rainwater. Then I curled up in my sleeping bag and listened to the storm. By nightfall it not only had failed to blow out, but had gathered more force; the words "tropical storm" flashed to mind, as I had seen them on the front page of a local paper and then forgotten. I thought of the lights of New York as seen from the air, and recalled the friendly braying of humanity in the city streets. I fell asleep planning tomorrow's journey.

At dawn the clouds were so dense that I could make rents in them with my hands. Water slithered over the forest floor in silver sheets, mumbling and whispering in almost human voices as it went.

That was when I said, "I quit." At least I had learned one thing from my psychiatrist: that it's okay to give up. A few years before, I would have stuck it out. Now it was a relief to pack up and withdraw from commitment to backpack alone.

A few days after my own return home, Twig was back from camp with tales of canoe trips in the rain, and "girls on the pill." I blinked; they sounded awfully young to me. Sex had at least been openly discussed in our family, since Trinket mated and gave birth at least twice a year, and before her Gunner had copulated in the backyard of almost every house we lived in. But we had never gotten down to the feelings of men and women, or to what should and should not be done about them.

I sat at the dining-room table, working on a sketch of the bear. Twig, with her chin in her hands and her elbows on the table, was looking up at me.

"You surely don't want to go on the pill?" I blurted.

"Why not?"

"Well, you're too young. Sexual experiences can be damaging

when you're too young. Emotions have to mature, like your body and mind do, for sex to be gratifying.'' No sooner had I said this than I wondered where it had come from. It was not quite what my mother had said to me, and her mother to her: ''Save your body until you marry. It is a great satisfaction to look down into your baby's eyes and know that you have remained pure.'' But it was close enough, and I promised myself that I would never hang up any child of mine with that kind of guilt. I tried to get out of the morass, and only went in deeper.

''Sex leads to deep emotional involvements, it's a binder for holding the fractious males and females together. It's a bond for monogamous birds, beasts and humans. You don't want to be bonded and anchored emotionally.''

Twig picked up a pencil and began making circles on a scrap of paper.

''I know it. But what about the pill? Will it hurt you? Some women die from it.''

I put down my paintbrush. So that was what she wanted—an evaluation of the effects of the pill. ''I don't know,'' I said. ''It looks pretty good; and it gives the human female dignity, on a par with the bird who does not lay until the nest is built and she is ready.''

Still she was not satisfied. I tried again. ''When you are ready to take this step, go see our doctor. Each woman is different. Maybe another contraceptive would be better. Talk to him and tell him I told you to come.''

''It's just that I don't want *you* to die.'' I sat down with a jolt, reached across the table and took both my daughter's hands. ''I'm sure not going to die, honey, for any reason. But I am also too old for the pill.''

''Too old?'' And we skipped from contraception to menopause.

I feel that I did a poor job discussing sex with my children, especially the boys—not because we didn't talk and pass books around, but because I believe that the best way to educate children on love and sex is through the touches and hugs and kisses, the presence of two loving adults in the house. And that I could not give them.

A letter from the tax receiver a few days later announced a rise in real estate taxes, and as usual where money was concerned, I worried. Our village of resident Quakers and summering New Yorkers was changing into a bedroom community for well-paid executives and their families. I

154

would not be able to support all of us much longer in Chappaqua as a freelance writer. Annoyed but also frightened, I walked to the village and put the house on the market.

As I came up the walk, I stared at the remarkably unfashionable house that was our home, and my feet dragged to a halt. The house had been the one source of consistency in my children's fractured lives. It was their ultimate refuge whenever social life became unbearable. It was a space from which they moved out to explore the world, and to which they retreated when the world confounded them. It was that safety zone which every social animal must have to survive. Baboons have their rocks, beavers their lodges, wallabies their open woodlands. We had our brown-shingled house.

When I walked in the door, Twig was sitting in front of the fire, wearing the huge curlers that straightened out her bountiful, natural curly hair to conform with the fashion. I dropped down on my knees beside her on the sheepskin rug, then flattened out and stared into the fire.

"Things are getting tough," I said. "I'm going to stop freelancing, sell the house and take a job. That way, I'll know just how much money I can spend, and see where I am financially."

"Don't do that," Twig said emphatically. "We are used to feast and famine."

Feast and famine; that's exactly what it was, pulling in the belt one month, and going off to the lakes and rivers the next. Twig always had been a perceptive child; now she had verbalized the ecological niche to which we had become adapted: feast and famine. I surely was not going to take a nine-to-five job with that kind of support. After taking the house off the market I called Elizabeth Riley.

"Can we discuss a new book, about a small ecological niche . . . a stone. Certain plants and animals have adapted precisely to stones. This book would be about a cricket among the ferns and mosses that live on a small planet . . . a stone in the woods."

As I returned the phone to the hook, Twig, who was now unwinding great rolls of hair and grimacing at the pain of it, blinked back a few tears and looked up at me.

"Did Elizabeth Riley like your idea?" I nodded. "Are we going to have roast beef and Yorkshire pudding tonight?"

"We sure are." I picked up the car keys.

"To celebrate the book?"

"To celebrate *you*."

A simple book is difficult. The first draft of the stone book was a two-hundred-and-fifty-page short course in geology and animal adaptations. A year later I had whacked the story down to ten typewritten pages, and was pleased with what I had. Elizabeth suggested that I find my own illustrator—a prerogative she usually reserved for herself—and I searched the library until I found Don Bolognese. (Later we won the World Book Award for the best picture book of 1971.)

The weekend before Craig and Luke's camp ended, I went to visit them. I found Craig enthusiastic about canoe trips and musicals, but underneath, desperately homesick. After he and Luke had shown me what they had been doing in crafts, we sat down and made plans to come home.

"I just can't tell anyone about the divorce," Craig said. "I know I should."

"I have problems, too," I admitted. "It's an awful mouthful to get out."

"That man over there is divorced," Craig went on, pointing to a dark-haired man who sat with his back to us, head down as he talked to his two sons. "His sons can talk about it."

"We'll work on it together. At least we're not the only divorced family in the world."

As I rose to leave, the swarthy man gave his elder son a shoulder squeeze and walked over to me.

"Hi, I'm Bob Krampner. Can I bum a ride to the city?"

"I could go through the tunnel and up the West Side to get to Westchester, I guess."

"You can drop me at the bridge."

When I dropped Bob off at his apartment in Chelsea, he suggested that we have a drink. We sat down in a grim dark bar and looked at each other. I tried to make small talk, but the conversation faltered and died. Finally I got up to go home without further ado. Bob Krampner was somber and unstimulating; and yet he and his sons could apparently talk about divorce. He must have something going.

"I'm in the directory if you want to come to the country sometime," I said.

When Twig began her senior year in high school, she announced that she wanted to decorate the basement and move into it. It had three nice windows that opened onto the terrace and could be made attractive with some color and paint; and it had its own private entrance. I knew perfectly well why she wanted to live in the basement. I added up the pros and cons and came to a decision.

"Good idea," I said. "We'll all help you—me, Craig, Luke and any of your friends. Tell them to come on over."

We were at the dawn of the drug age, and there were no guidelines to carry parents and kids through it. From my own past experience, I recalled that peer pressures had never gotten out of hand when I brought my friends home. If my adolescents were going to experiment with beer, marijuana and eventually the pill, I wanted them at home and safe, free to talk and make judgments.

After school we all painted, hung drapes, whitewashed pipes, walls and furnace. Twig involved everyone, from Luke and his friends to mine. The dreary place brightened and took on a bold and friendly air. Trinket moved her kittens down.

I came to the basement one afternoon to find Twig with a paintbrush, a bucket of flour paste and a basket of colored tissue paper. At one end of the room she was creating a mural that took my breath away. I'd known she had a gift for design, but this showed something more than that. Every parent has a moment of seeing in the child a more miraculous creation than himself—a change of genes, an added plus, an improvement. I held that moment in my mind's eye, for Twig was afraid of success, and I would have to tell her about this some day.

The paste would mildew, the colors would fade; the mural would be torn down and the wall repainted white by Twig herself. From what she had observed so far in her short life, many of the successful women she knew either were divorced or had not married, though marriage was the ultimate desire and refuge for all the daughters of Chappaqua . . . and who was I to tell her otherwise?

When the bed, tables and couches were in place I checked out my accounts and bought a color TV, the first in the neighborhood and, as it turned out, just the right honey pot. Around it swarmed Twig's friends as well as Luke's and Craig's and mine. We were all together again, down in the basement with Twig.

Kids came after school to play guitars, dance, read or simply overflow upstairs. When I stopped writing for the day, I would put a pot of tea or coffee in the middle of the kitchen table. Over the mugs and cups I became educated in the music of Arlo Guthrie, Bob Dylan, the Beatles, and about the terrible ends to which the young men were going to avoid the Vietnam War, from fleeing the country to gorging on aspirin.

Downstairs, the TV became a shock box that delivered trauma in vivid electronic color. We watched the funeral of the assassinated Martin Luther King, and exactly two months later of Bobby Kennedy.

"What's gone wrong?" young Ethel Losing asked me as we stared at coffins for the third time in less than a decade.

"I don't know," I said. "But you don't assassinate leaders without paying a price."

That night I carried the latest volumes of animal behavior to my room and began puzzling over the roles of leaders in animal societies. Fundamentally, I learned, they maintain order and make the decisions. When animal leaders were removed for experimentation, some societies lost land and status; others broke up into fighting factions; still others maimed, killed and even practiced cannibalism. But there were no beasts who shot their leaders.

A few days later Ethel gave me an article by Timothy Leary on the positive effects of LSD. "Maybe this is our answer," she said. With a sinking spirit, I read about the creative idea, sexual experiences and new heights of thinking attained by users of the drug. Noting that Leary was or had been in the same department at Harvard as my old Vassar friend Richard Jung, I put in a call to him.

"Harvard threw him out. He's experimenting with students. Forget him. I'll send you some information about LSD."

I thought I had talked Leary to death around the dining-room table, the kitchen table, in front of the fire and in the basement, when Twig came home one day with Roy, a handsome young man, the son of a talented mother and successful father. As I shook his hand my neck muscles tightened. The pupils of his eyes all but filled the irises.

"Mom, LSD is good," Twig said. "It does make dummies like me into geniuses." I glanced fearfully into her eyes. So far so good.

"You're bright without it," I snapped. "And it doesn't make geniuses, just dropouts." I was getting upset.

"Well, listen to the music Roy writes," she said.

"I'd like to."

Twig edged him to the upright piano in the foyer. Roy sat down, drooped his head and stared for a while at the piano keys. Presently he turned, smiled and began to play and sing. To my horror and grief, I had to admit that he was terrific; and when I glanced across the room at Twig, I could only read "I told you so" in her eyes. The waterfall splashed softly in the pond in the foyer, the fire crackled and I got up to shove a log into place with my foot. For a long time I stared into the fire. After Roy had gone, Twig went to the room off the kitchen to do her laundry and I met her there.

"Tell me something. Did Roy compose before he took LSD?"

"Yeah. Why?"

"Was he better then or worse?" She did not know; she had not heard him before.

I pushed on: "Some studies show that LSD damages the chromosomes; the babies of users are abnormal; and there is some evidence of brain damage."

"Oh, you smoke and drink, and those drugs are worse than all the pot and LSD put together." Twig was getting defensive, but I had to make one more effort.

"Don't try it until all the evidence is in. Please. Okay?"

No answer. But I had said it and it would nag as my mother's advice had nagged and held me in check somewhat.

Slightly more than a week later, as Roy was driving home from a beer and LSD party late at night, he veered off the road. His companion was killed. Although the cellar door continued to open and close, and the kids come and go, most of them came upstairs to talk. Joan Gordon, the sociologist from Vassar, had taken a job with the Commissioner of Addictive Services in New York City, and stopped by often on her way back to Poughkeepsie for a visit.

"Heroin is on its way to suburbia," she said one day. "Where's Twig? Perhaps I should talk to her about it." While I prepared dinner Joan went to the basement and discussed with Twig the symptoms as well as the sequence of drug abuse: pot, heroin, alcohol, brain damage and Jesus freaks.

My friend Barbara, who along with me had been one of the first women hired by the wire services in Washington, seemed to weep from the bottom of her soul as she told me that her talented artist son had just been hospitalized for brain damage. LSD.

I could not believe what was happening. Kids raiding friends' and parents' medicine cabinets to try every drug they could get their hands on, be it digitalis or estrogen. Automobile accidents and deaths were part of our way of life.

One day Bert, a friend's son, walked into my sunporch with Twig and rolled up his sleeve.

"I've got a fifty-dollar-a-day habit." His eyes focused on some far-off world. "But the draft board turned me down."

I thought of Joan Gordon; maybe I could get him to her and a therapist. I got to my feet recalling that there was also a hot line for help.

"Don't, Bert. You'll never get off it."

"I'm strong. I can stop any time." Bert smiled. He did have a nice smile and had been a handsome kid. Now he was pale and puffy. I ached for him and his parents. He took Twig's arm as he walked toward the door. "Help me carry Mom's grandfather clock to my truck. She wants to sell it."

"Sure," Twig answered.

I could not believe it. Didn't Twig understand? I reached out and held her physically.

"Stay here."

That night Bert was arrested for possession of heroin and the attendant equipment. Twig moved back upstairs. My conversations on sex seemed like a game of hopscotch compared to this. Making love was the healthiest thing any kid could do. At night I was no longer counting money. I was counting children.

Just before Twig's graduation she dated Don Carlisle. He was a dapper young man, well dressed, clean-cut and intelligent. I enjoyed talking to him, for he was interested in philosophy and wished to become a college dean or administrator. I welcomed him warmly—only to realize from the comments of other kids who came around that Don was the source of most of the pot and heroin that came into the high school and the community. I was dumbfounded. I had been completely taken in and could understand Twig's own naïveté. I was puzzling over how to get Don out of her life when wild things came to our rescue.

One night Craig and his friend Pete Ehlers came back from Whippoorwill Pond carrying twenty-four bullfrogs in a sack. The science teacher had asked Craig to catch frogs for a class experiment, after which he, the teacher, would return them unharmed to the pond—an offer that made me suspect the experiment was a batch of frogs' legs Provençale. From the sack, a mass of amphibians grinned up at me. I sent Craig to the attic for the large aquarium, into which we dumped all twenty-four frogs, adding enough water to keep them wet, but not enough to drown them. Then we covered the container with cardboard and some heavy pans.

Awakened around three in the morning by the sound of pans clanging and banging, I ran downstairs and switched on the light, to reveal twenty-four bullfrogs hopping around the kitchen, croaking and garumpfing. Grabbing them one after another by their slippery legs, I stuffed them all back into the aquarium, and covered them with a heavy piece of plywood and two cement blocks.

Just before the sun came up I was awakened by the lugubrious song of the bullfrog—a deep and resonant voice that brought back memories of childhood at Craigheads. As I became more fully awake I realized the voice came from the foyer, not the kitchen or my own past. Stealing down the steps, in the dim light I beheld a large green bullfrog sitting on the edge of the stone pond. When he saw me, looming like a predator above him, he jumped into the water and took refuge among the hyacinths.

Then and there I named him: "Twenty-four," I said, "you're a survivor. There'll be no legs Provençale for you."

And so Twenty-four took up residence in the pond, swimming by day, hopping around the house by night to catch the moths that came to the lights. At dawn and dusk, or whenever the light reached a candlepower of three, Twenty-four sang his "jug-o'-rum" song. Occasionally he hopped out of his pond by day and came to sit in my doorway, singing out when I plunked the typewriter. He'd stay until he felt too dry, and then hop back home. After a few days I discovered that when I stopped typing he stopped singing. I ran other experiments, finding that he jug-o'-rummed when I strummed Craig's guitar or when the radio was on. So Twenty-four became a concert performer, and for many evenings we held fascinating musicales in the foyer. He sang even better from a perch among the lily pads.

Don called on Twig one night after I had gone to bed. While she went to the kitchen to make coffee, I put on a robe and started downstairs, intending to confront Don and ask him to stay away from Twig. Before I got there, I heard him get up from the living-room rocker and hurry out. Then I heard him start the car.

"Where's Don?" I asked when Twig came upstairs again.

"I don't know; he ran off." She shrugged her shoulders. "He's nuts," she said, and went to bed.

Don did not come back the next day, or the next month. No one asked where he was. In July Twig made plans to take her freshman year at the Sorbonne in Paris. We shopped, packed and reviewed her French. A few days after her departure, the telephone rang. I recognized Don's voice.

"Mrs. George," he said, clearing his throat, "I have something I must tell you."

"Yes?" My voice was not very friendly.

"This is very awkward."

"Go on."

"The last time I was at your house . . ." He paused; I wondered whether he was going to confess that he had planted heroin in my bookcase and was about to notify the cops. "I was in the living room while Twig was fixing coffee and something terrible happened."

"Really?"

Again he cleared his throat. "This is hard to say. A big green frog hopped across the room right in front of me. A frog, Mrs. George." I did not answer.

"You have frogs in your house."

"So? Were you frightened? I heard you run."

"I was disgusted. Frogs in your *home.*"

"Well, now we're both disgusted with each other."

The phone clicked off. The affair with Twig was over.

Twenty-four, his mission accomplished, hopped through the living room one night, then out through the open sunporch door and leaped off into the darkness. With his internal divining rod he found the neighbor's lily pond. Two nights later I heard him singing from their spring-fed pool. There was a frog who was really a prince.

Wild things also rescued Craig, but in quite another way. During his sophomore year he fell in love with such enthusiasm that, although I had never laid eyes on Marcia Nash, I knew just how she would look. While I was downtown with Craig one day, he slipped behind a telephone pole and pointed to a slender girl with long red-gold hair. She was running across the recreation field to catch a fly ball.

"That's Marcia Nash." His face shone.

"She is beautiful," I said.

"And she likes animals," he added, going on to explain that her father abhorred the entire outdoors, including photographs of animals. "He walked away when Marcia showed him the picture Uncle Frank took of me and the grizzly."

Craig did not need a basement door to go in and out. He was totally open. He simply said "I'll be back" and ran out through the first door he encountered. On a dead run through the house one night, he announced he was going to see Marcia, galloped out the door and was on his way up the ridge to the Nashes' house.

Very soon he was back, chagrined and silent. I had no clue about what was bothering him until he finally asked me how he looked.

"Fine. The knees of your jeans need patching, but so does every kid's in town."

"Mr. Nash won't let me visit Marcia unless I wear a coat and tie."

"Gee, I guess you don't have a suit that fits anymore. Maybe you can get one at the Thrift Shop." I wondered about Mr. Nash's stand. Blue jeans were the uniform of the adolescents, but then a man with three beautiful daughters could demand almost anything. Craig gave me a glance that ended the Thrift Shop suggestion. I heard no more about Marcia until after Christmas, when Craig announced that he was going to see her for a little while, and dashed out in blue jeans and ski parka. I presumed Mr. Nash had relented on the matter of the coat and tie. Not so. Craig had simply earned a special dispensation. After he had been turned down at the front door, Marcia suggested that he climb up the porch and meet her on the roof under her window—an invitation that appealed immensely to a rock-climbing Craig. While they were talking quietly on the roof one evening, Marcia's brother-in-law strolled out onto the porch and into the yard. Craig was sure he would be seen. He rappeled down the post and ran into the woods, where he broke into a lumbering trot.

163

"Bear!" screamed the brother-in-law in a voice of terror. Mr. and Mrs. Nash dashed to the porch and Marcia raced down the steps.

"Where?" she asked, concealing a grin.

Upwoods Craig heard "Bear," turned around and circled back to the front door, where he rang the bell.

"Craig!" Mr. Nash exclaimed as he opened the door. "Come in. Come in. Welcome. There's a bear in the backyard. We need you."

In his patched blue jeans and old shirt Craig ran through the house, onto the porch and straight into the woods. He shouted, pounded trees with sticks and growled. Presently he returned to the frightened family and, brushing off his hands, faced Mr. Nash.

"You'll never see that bear again, sir," he said. "Never."

Fortunately for family history, the ingenious Marcia did not get away. In 1980 Craig's cousin Charlie Craighead married her.

14

Vanishing Images

One night in the spring of 1968 Craig did not come home for dinner. I waited half an hour before serving Luke and his friend Davy Koffend, who spent a great deal of time at our house, going home for security and coming back when he needed to feel independent. As we cleaned up the kitchen, Davy suggested that perhaps Craig was living off the land, an adventure the three of them enjoyed for a weekend every autumn.

"No," said Luke. "Sarah's here." Tonka was now gone, and Sarah was the large black dog who had replaced her. "We take Sarah when we live off the land."

"Yeah," chuckled Davy, "so we can eat her dog food."

"Dog food?" said I.

"It takes too long to cook squirrels so we swap food with Sarah."

I was not surprised at this, for Craig had tasted dog biscuits years ago. I asked, "Where do you go?"

"Up behind Zimmer's on the ridge. There's an overhanging rock and we sleep under it on bough beds. We cook the squirrels and potatoes in a rock over in the ground."

"Potatoes? I thought you only took string, penknives, matches and the air rifle."

"There are potatoes at the bottom of the mountain . . . in a garden. Also apples and carrots."

"You're going to get a load of buckshot some day . . . and deserve it."

"The farmer thinks we're raccoons. We learned to dig and tear the plants just like raccoons do. The farmer sets live traps for us."

The Oliver Twists of the forest were exchanging wise glances when the telephone rang. I snatched it off the hook.

"Hello, Mrs. George?" a young girl's voice said. "Craig told me to call you at seven o'clock and tell you he's on his way to Florida in his car. Tom Ciulla is with him. He'll call." She hung up.

I stood there a long time, feeling the shock. This was out of character for Craig. He was the most open and confiding of the three children, the most sensitive to my feelings. And now this. What did it mean?

Like almost every other young couple there, John and I had moved to Chappaqua because of the exceptional public schools, which were well staffed and isolated in the beautiful countryside, in the belief that children make better students if they are surrounded by natural beauty. But the pastoral look was cosmetic. Every school and house roof bristled with TV aerials, radio receivers, telephone cables. Snapping along these invisible highways into buildings and minds came the whole world—by turns stimulating, violent, intellectual and boring. My children, as one biologist had put it, were walking a multidimensional tightrope, balancing themselves in the midst of a bewildering variety of obstacles. Isolated in that pretty town, many of them were chafing to see a reality other than the cosmetic one of the suburbs. TV, radio and word of mouth beamed out the lure of rendezvous points where kids were clustering like a migration of young Arctic terns. Was that it? Or was the reason simply insecurity?

"Craig," I said, turning to Luke and Davy, "has run away to Florida."

After a long silence Luke's dark blue eyes focused on mine and his angular face relaxed.

"He's a good driver," he said.

I dialed the Ciullas. After an exchange of angry accusations about whose kid had initiated what—an argument born of frustration and concern—I became truly frightened for our sons.

"They can be arrested for driving in Florida," I said. "They're not

166

old enough.'' I had been there the month before, visiting my parents, and I knew that kids under eighteen were being picked up for driving even when they had legitimate out-of-state licenses.

"Can we call the Georgia State Troopers and have them stopped?''

That year was the high watermark in the battle between policemen and adolescents with long hair. I hesitated. Craig had been stopped and his car searched without provocation on the New York Thruway.

"Does Tom smoke pot?'' I asked. Neither one of us knew who did what. Since the kids could be jailed for possession of marijuana at that time, Mrs. Ciulla and I decided we had better wait for the promised phone call.

When Luke was asleep I sat up in bed and looked out the window. The Little Dipper swung slowly around the North Star, marking the progress of the night. The dark hours closed in on me like bats diving and swooping at my thoughts. Where had I missed the signals? I asked myself. Why hadn't I seen this coming? Craig had seemed happy enough in school; he had lots of friends, and was the enthusiastic leader of a group of mountain-climbers and skiers. Furthermore, he was a special person; everyone wanted a little bit of him and he gave not a little but a lot. I was no psychiatrist, but I knew where the trouble was: he did not see enough of his father, and when he did, the meeting was constrained. Men can't hug and cry.

I flopped over onto my back, worried about where he was sleeping this night and wondering where a woman with three children to house and feed, school and guide found a mate. I was either in the woods or at the typewriter, at the kitchen sink or serving and entertaining friends and children. I did daydream sometimes about beautiful clothes and love affairs; but the more immediate concern was always the next deadline, an interview, a wilderness trip to gather information. Moreover, I must say that I liked my way of life. I was not unhappy. My attempts at new relationships had been brief. A divorced doctor wooed and dropped me; a widower from California was too far away.

Just as the sun touched the tips of the trees I heard Luke's latest turtle—a box turtle—heading for the top of the stairs. I started to get out of bed to save him from falling down the steps but then it occurred to me that turtles in the wild were constantly faced with the edges of cliffs and had probably developed some biological radar that warned them to turn back. I had just dropped off to sleep when a crash shook me awake. It was the turtle, clattering down the steps, and onto the landing. By the time I reached him he had righted himself and was walking toward the kitchen.

Of course, I was thinking, turtles were built for falling with the bone carapace on top, and a central hinge on the lower shell that snapped them firmly inside. As I picked up the hardy reptile, my thoughts raced to Craig, with the hope that his own inherited carapace—his agility and quick reactions—would prove as durable.

By 6:00 A.M. there was still no word from him. Meanwhile Luke was up and announcing that the boa constrictor was gone again.

"Look in the laundry basket," I called from the kitchen. I had found the big six-foot snake there twice before.

"He's not in the laundry basket," he said as he came to breakfast. "You didn't hear from Craig?"

"Not yet. But he's lucky; remember the time he won the ski raffle and then found the fifty-dollar bill?"

"But he also broke his leg twice."

"It's a toss-up between his good luck and his bad," I said, and hugged Luke to reassure myself.

By four o'clock that afternoon, I had not heard from Craig, the boa constrictor was still loose and the iguana was not eating. I had written ten pages of manuscript and was tearing them up when the water meter reader knocked at the front door.

"Watch out for the boa constrictor," I said as I let him in. "He's loose in the house."

The man eased toward the cellar door, scanning the floor and walls.

"I've got to quit this job," he said. "It's too nerve-racking. Last week I put out a frying-pan fire for a kid who was about to burn his house down. A month before that a robber crawled through a basement window while I was there, backed into me and scared both of us to death. Now I got to watch out for a snake."

"Never mind," I said. "I see him. He's in the woodpile by the fireplace."

"Gee, that's no help," he said as he fled down into the basement. When he came up he nervously edged past the pond in the hall.

"That fish," he said. "It's a piranha, your son said."

I was about to tell him the fish was our four-year-old largemouth bass and family pet but he was out the door. I had never understood the fear of the piranha until a year before. My cousin Irving's son had had a pet piranha, and had left it alone with what appeared to be sufficient food while he went backpacking for a week. On his return, when he held out food for the fish, it had leaped from the tank and bitten his hand until it bled. Then, falling to the floor, it had grabbed his girl friend's heel.

The phone rang. I wrenched it from the hook.

"Long distance from Miami, Florida. Sergeant Shattuck speaking. Are you Mrs. Jean George?"

I whispered a dry yes.

"We've got your son here in the juvenile prison."

"Oh, thank God. Is he all right?"

" 'Thank God.' You say 'Thank God.' You should beat the tar out of him. He's under arrest."

"Why?"

"Driving under age, trespassing and vagrancy. Found him and his buddy sleeping in their car on the street."

"Should I get a lawyer?"

"Just send us a hundred and twenty-five bucks for a one-way ticket out of here."

"His grandparents are nearby. Can they come and get him?"

"No, lady. We want all these kids out of Florida. We will drive him from here to the airport and wait until that plane takes off with him on it."

"Is it that bad?"

"Send the money." I took down the address. Then I was permitted a brief word with Craig, following which I hung up, slid down the wall and sat with my face buried against my knees, laughing and crying for joy.

I called my mother to explain the situation, and asked if she and Dad would keep Craig's car until sometime in the summer, when he had earned the fare down.

"My grandson in jail!" she exclaimed. "Why, no one in our family has ever been in jail."

"Mom, this is the 1960s. Everyone's kids get arrested today."

"That's a terrible thing for him to do. I'm going to talk to him."

"I'll handle it."

"This never happened in our day. We respected our parents."

"Mother."

"I can talk to him. He likes my lectures. He listens to me."

I met Craig at Kennedy Airport the following day. After a brief greeting he was quiet for the first half of the trip home. When the trees and wooded areas came into view he sat straight in the seat and stared at the forests and lakes, his eyes puffy from lack of sleep, his hair falling into his eyes.

"I'm so lucky," he said. "Two of the boys in the cell with me have been in the juvenile jail for six months. No one came for them. One boy has not seen his mother for three years. He doesn't know who his father is. He steals for a living." I glanced at Craig. He was slumped deep in the seat now.

"We slept on straw mats on the floor. In the morning they made us strip. Then a man hosed us down with Lysol water."

"Hosed you down with Lysol water?"

"To kill the lice. Then they made me scrub the floors and latrines to pay for my food. Then something crazy happened."

I was prepared now for lashings, sodomy, rape; the juvenile jail sounded like a dungeon of the Inquisition.

"What?" I gripped the wheel tightly.

"When the officer called me to the office to get your phone number he pushed me into a chair across from the bulletin board. When I lifted my head after a while, I saw a photograph of Uncle Frank pinned up on the bulletin board . . . the picture from the *National Geographic* where he's rappeling off the face of the Grand Teton. I think they hung it there to show us what good boys do." He gave me a dejected glance. "There was my uncle," he said. "I felt terrible. I had let him down."

"I can't see that you did anything terrible except not tell me what you were up to. Sleeping in a car is hardly a crime. Did you tell the officer who Frank was?"

"No, sir. I sure didn't. They would have locked me up in the kids' nuthouse and you would never have seen me again."

I laughed. "I would have blurted out just who that climber was on the assumption that the officers would have been so impressed they would have opened the doors and set me free," I said. "And I would have been taken to the nuthouse and buried there just as you say."

"That would have been stupid."

"Well, you kids are raising me. This is a whole new world and I'd better learn fast." We rode home in the spirit of lessons to be learned.

The Ciullas punished Tom by refusing to let him see Craig for six months. About a week after Craig's return, while he and I were upstairs in my room and he was telling me his worries as he often had—over being the smallest boy in the class, and now that he was six feet, over having no beard and now he was shaving—he was complaining that school bored him when a head appeared at the window and Tom Ciulla pulled himself up on the sill. He had made a leap from the porch railing. While he hung there precariously, Craig opened the window and Tom jumped lightly to the floor.

"What are you doing here?" I asked sternly. "Your parents don't want you to see Craig."

"My parents can't do anything with me," he said, his brown eyes twinkling, and proceeded to bend over and stand on his hands.

"Let's climb the Grand Teton, this summer," Craig said.

"Yeah." Tom laughed. "That'll make us good boys. This town corrupts. We'll learn more, too."

Craig agreed. "The wild azaleas blooming across the Blue Ridge Mountain were better than school," he said. "Georgia was blazing with magnolias, truck drivers were talking in light signals." Still there had been problems. Craig had dozed off at the wheel once and a truck had nearly run them off the road. The trip was a symptom of deeper problems. Craig needed his father in his life right now. My brothers had helped, but like his father, they were too far away.

Raising children, I kept learning, was not a matter of letting pretty curly tops grow up in the wind and sun, the way my brothers and I had grown up. I called Dr. Neubauer, who recommended having Craig talk to a well-trained therapist in the next town.

By June Craig was concentrating on his schoolwork, had joined the pole-vaulting team and was leading rock-climbing expeditions to a local park in preparation for the Grand Teton. His reading ran to alpine geology and his music ran to Country and Western.

Just as the house had been open to Twig's friends, so it was to Craig's and for the same reason. I wanted my children at home where we could talk at all hours.

Craig took over the attic room. He and Tom Melvin covered all four walls and the ceiling with decorative murals in red, black and gold. They wired the room for sound and as the music flowed Luke and I were lured upstairs to help. I painted luminous spots on the floor and Luke helped to hang the black light. Whereas once the house had rocked from bottom to top, it now rocked from top to bottom. Fortunately I had learned to write in a newspaper office and while kids came and went, I worked between glances up from my typewriter to see who was on his way to the attic now. Some sneaked in, some said "Hi" and some went up and came right back down. In the room a code of behavior was evolving, and those who did not comply quickly left. The personal effort and work that had been expended on the room at the top of the attic stairs had made Craig territorial. He set up rules that were far tougher than any I would have drawn.

One summer day Bob Krampner called to say he had a free weekend, and wondered if he could come to Chappaqua. Craig and Luke were out west, Twig was visiting friends and the free time was precious. I hesitated, then glanced through the window at the flawless blue sky.

"Do you canoe?"

"I'd like to learn."

As Bob stepped off the train in the bright sunshine I saw that his face bore the creases of concern, that his hair was gray and thinning, his girth wide; but he walked upright with his shoulders back and for the first time the worn, adjusted look of middle age had a beauty of its own. I peered at myself in the rear-view mirror. I was there, too, and the marks of survival were not unattractive. I stepped from the car and greeted him.

The canoeing at Sherwood Island, Connecticut, proved to be more wading in the saltmarshes than paddling, for the tide was out; but the gulls were there and the fiddler crabs were performing their one-claw dance of nest defense and the smell of salt air was quieting.

During lunch on the beach I learned that Bob sailed, played chess, was looking for a new job, had a Jewish mother, shopped at Job Lot discount to furnish his apartment and at Sym's discount for clothes. He also collected antiques. In his hip pocket was a book which he read when conversation failed him, which it often did. He talked very little and was dressed in baggy old clothes which declared that he was not a male in courtship feathers. I took the message to mean that he was not interested in anything that went beyond friendship.

Good, I thought.

On the way home I learned that Bob's deepest concern was for his sons. He spoke of his feelings of guilt for not living with them. He saw them often; believing passionately that a father should be a part of every child's life for better or worse, whether divorced or not. He had not left the community they lived in, but stayed nearby seeing them whenever he could or when they wanted and needed him. And so I thought, as I listened, that we would be friends, not lovers. It would be refreshing not to be involved physically.

After dinner, I was closing the kitchen door when Bob pulled me to him gently. He kissed me and that was that. I was involved.

We decided to see each other infrequently, and the next day I took off for a different adventure.

Earlier in the year, a letter had arrived from the president of Penn State University saying that I had been chosen for the Woman of the Year Award, "an honor," he had written, that was given to me "whose personal life and professional achievements and community service exemplify the objectives of the Pennsylvania State University." I was both thrilled and moved by the honor. I, a divorced woman, exemplified the objectives of Penn State? Was one's personal life at last indeed one's own? Even after all these years of being a single parent, I felt very insecure about my status. I could not shake off two centuries of intolerance toward divorce. And yet it had been the right decision. John had a son, a home, a wife who worked in the Home Economics School at the university and did not invade his work world as I had done. John was moving out of his cage even as I was moving out of mine. He was sure and successful with a different kind of wife. I would go to Penn State, meet old friends and accept the honor with pleasure as I stood before a gymnasium packed with alumnae and alumni.

A few weeks beforehand, I had been delighted to receive a phone call from Ray Carpenter, who was still teaching at Penn State but was about to move to the University of Georgia.

He congratulated me and asked if he could meet my plane and take me to dinner. Ray and I had kept in touch through letters after I graduated, occasionally meeting in New York when I had lived there and when he was on his way to Europe. We had not corresponded, however, since I had received word several years ago that his lovely wife Marianna had died of cancer.

As I stepped off the plane in the high mountain airport at State College, I walked slowly across the runway, giving myself time to study this professor and friend who had influenced my thinking and writing. Ray was a large, statuesque man, well over six feet, with a high forehead and warm brown eyes, whose expression as I approached conveyed a mixture of emotions I could not plumb. He greeted me with a friendly hug. His hand was under my elbow as he escorted me to his convertible, talking in his soft Southern accent as though no years had passed. Between the airport and the Nittany Lion Inn we caught up on the intervening years of his research, travel, books and other projects; his sons; on my advance to staff writer for the *Digest,* with a small stipend for security, my own three children.

"But no Newbery," I said. "I will never get it. All the same, it's a goal to keep thinking of."

After dinner we walked across the college golf course hand in hand. Ray had always hoped I would write about the nonhuman primates, and each time we met he would try to entice me with discoveries and information. That evening he told me about a tribe of Japanese macaques that had been studied by the Japanese since 1950. While Ray talked about the alphas, as the leaders of animal societies were called, I realized that I had been puzzling over these authority figures for years. "I can't go to Japan," I said. "So how do I study alphas?"

"The wolves," he answered. "Read Rudolf Schenkel and Raab and Ginsberg of the Brookfield Zoo. The alpha male wolf is the benevolent father, it seems."

A breeze sprang up and summer crickets sang as Ray slipped his arm around me and began to speak of his affection for me first as a student then as a friend. While we walked slowly toward his house, we paused to embrace. We did not make love, but we did plan to see each other frequently. I ran up to my room in the inn with light steps. Here was an alpha—a man of prestige, means and achievement.

I looked at myself in the mirror, noted the drooping lines around the eyes, from age and worry, and they seemed very nice.

Standing at the window, I pushed back the curtains and looked down onto the grounds of the inn. Suddenly, once again I was walking below with my mentor and inspiration, Theodore Roethke, the Pulitzer Prize-winning poet who had taught at Penn State during my four years there.

"It's dark in the woods, Uncle Ted," I was saying as the beloved giant strode beside me.

"Please don't call me Uncle Ted." His voice was pained. "Uncle Ted is so demeaning. I know all the students call me that, but please, not you."

"Okay," I said finally.

"Thank you." He took my hand. "I asked you to walk with me for a reason that's difficult to speak about." His powerful fingers enveloped mine. "I'm sending Maxine to the poetry contest at Cambridge, not you. I am sure you would win with your personality, but her poetry is stronger than yours. You'll win lots of things but she won't. Do you understand?"

I tripped over a stone, slowed down, then speeded up again.

"I understand, Ted," I said—though I really did not.

"You could win."

"I'll win," I said. As he slipped his arm around me in what was meant to be kindness, every muscle in my body tightened. I broke free and ran from him with a hurt goodbye.

Ted and I had also kept in touch after my graduation, exchanging postcards of congratulations, asking questions about publishers. He would call me when he had a poetry reading in my vicinity and I would join him and his admirers at dinner beforehand. Conversation with this witty and caustic man was unforgettable, his performances even more so. At first he would blunder, mumble and all but apologize for living. Moving to the podium he would lower and then lift his eyes and his voice trumpeted a powerful feeling that made us all one with nature.

In 1971 Ted drowned in his swimming pool at Seattle, ending his long feud with words, depression, alcohol and madness. The night I heard the news I walked in my garden for a while. Then I sat down on the granite boulder and I quoted him aloud:

Is my body speaking? I breathe what I am.
The first and last of all things.
Near the graves of the great dead
Even the stones speak.

"Good evening, stones," I said and listened to them speak. If the goal of the Newbery Medal incited me to excellence, so did having known Theodore Roethke.

During the year that followed Ray and I met a few times in New York and once he came to Chappaqua to meet my children.

"You run a big show," he said that evening as we sat down with an after-dinner drink. He turned to lively, lovely Twig, who was, thank heaven, home from the *petites bombes* and anti-Americanism of Paris, and was now packing for Bennington College.

"Twig," he said, "we're beginning a program on Ossabaw Island, Georgia, to help save and study the vanishing loggerhead turtles. It's called the Genesis Program. A group of young people like yourself will live in primitive conditions, raise your own food by tending gardens, and hike the beaches at night to collect turtle eggs. These will be reared in boxes safe from the predators and set free. Would you like to join the group? With your background and intelligence you'd be a great asset."

Twig had not heard such encouraging words from an educator since she left the elementary school at Vassar. Her face beamed. "Next summer?" she asked. "I could come next summer."

"I think we can arrange that."

The program at Ossabaw Island became the turning point in Twig's life. Her career as an environmentalist and educator began there.

The next few years, with Twig at college and Craig and Luke involved in projects at school, and on cliffs and ski slopes, were the most productive since my new life began. Conscious that I had to get three kids through college, I was at the typewriter daily cracking away.

One autumn evening when I was in Washington for a conference, I met Ray, who was attending conferences of his own, for dinner. We walked the mellow residential streets of Georgetown, where the lights were golden in elegant townhouses. As we headed toward the hotel laughing and talking it was as though I had sighted a raft in the ocean. I was safe at last.

Before I left to catch my plane the next morning, Ray tilted my chin upward to look into my face.

"You know what my situation is, don't you, Jean?"

"Your situation?" No, I could not guess.

"I'm married."

I held his hands tightly as the veil of illusion fell away, this time with merciful swiftness. What stood before me now was no longer an authority figure to whom I deferred, but a good friend, an equal. We laughed and kissed warmly.

"I do get the roles of my males all mixed emotionally," I said. "I think I'll go study the alphas."

"Do that." We parted with a hug of friendship, as we would continue to do whenever we met until his untimely death in 1976.

Twig and I cried when we learned of his death. He had opened new worlds, intellectually and emotionally, for both of us.

15

Across the Wide Abyss

My journey to the wolves traversed a third of the globe, through cloud banks under flashes of the sun and stars to the Arctic Circle where my hosts were the scientists of the Naval Arctic Research Laboratory who study the physics, the wildlife and the people at the top of the world. The lab huddles beside the Arctic Ocean, five miles down the beach from Barrow, Alaska, the northernmost town in the United States and the home of somewhere between 1,500 and 2,000 Eskimos known as the Innuits. No roads lead there.

Luke went with me on that journey. He was now thirteen, lean and thoughtful, a walking notebook of information about living things. I had watched his animal interest evolve from earthworms to frogs, fishes, reptiles, birds and now mammals. The boa constrictor and the iguana were gone. Luke's room harbored hamsters and the dog, Sarah, who, he said, was so smart that she had learned to get up on the bed with only one lesson.

Two hours out of Fairbanks, Luke pressed his nose against the window of the plane and stared down at the North Slope, which in 1970 was well known even to an eighth grader for its wells of hot oil and for the controversy over the pipeline that was to be laid across its fragile skin, the tundra.

"The North Slope's white and tan. Ice and grass, I guess," he said, summing it up. A mass of eroded debris from the Brooks Range slants gradually from the mountains to the ocean, it is poorly drained and its soil remains frozen solid except for a while during the summer months, when it thaws to a depth of about eighteen inches, enough to sustain grasses, sedges and a few lowly forbs.

We had been trying to reach Barrow for two days, flying out of Fairbanks only to circle the fog-locked Eskimo town and return to our starting point. On this, our third try, the fog suddenly dissolved and we dropped quickly down the Barrow airport, an opening in the sea of abandoned oil barrels.

We were licked by a damp tongue of icy wind as we left the plane and made our way into the oversized crate that was the Barrow terminal. We saw the town in silhouette against a frosted pile of ice that had been shoved up onto the beach by the ocean. In all other directions lay oil barrels and rippling grass. Not a tree existed under the Arctic sun, not a bush or any living plant taller than the grass and sedge.

Out in that interminably naked landscape, a small Eskimo girl walked toward Point Hope.

"She's awful little to be out there all alone," said Luke as we waited for our baggage. Watching her vanish into the tan and white haze, I identified with that figure who was determinedly going somewhere by herself.

Outside the terminal building a thermometer read 50 degrees Fahrenheit, but Luke and I were shivering with cold. Our winter ski clothes did not fend off the Arctic chill that came from two sources— laterally from the polar icepack and upward from the permanently frozen ground.

Zipping up parkas against the wind, we shouldered our packs and walked past square wooden houses surrounded by broken snowmobiles, boat parts, fenders, airplane tires, gutter jeeps: junk brought to Barrow by the industrial invaders. Our boots clanged on the black stones of the Arctic outwash, as the sound clouds of snow buntings burst up from the grasses and flew away.

Turning left at the store, we arrived at the Top-of-the-World Hotel, a forty-by-eighty-foot box with a peaked roof. The floor boards creaked as we entered a meagerly furnished lobby that faced the midnight sun. A young man from somewhere in the lower forty-eight states looked up as we signed in.

"There are no flush toilets," he said. "Just slop jars." He waited for a reaction from me, got none and tried again. "They're emptied at night . . . carted out and dumped."

Still I did not flinch; having lived in a tent, I knew what had to happen to slop jars. "In a hole in the permafrost, the stuff freezes forever."

Luke said, fascinated, "Freezes forever?"

"Nothing disintegrates up here," the young man said. "Slop, oil barrels, garbage, junk. You throw it in the ocean in summer and it freezes in fall and is shoved right back up in your yard. Can't get rid of anything. Nothing rots except people." Luke turned to look around for verification.

"And if you want a drink," the clerk went on, "it's in the cooler. No running water." He pointed to a watercooler filled with turquoise-colored ice.

"Iceberg," he said. "We get our water by chipping icebergs."

"Isn't it salty?" I asked, thinking of polar ice.

"Icebergs come from glaciers; snow, freshwater," he said, pleased at having finally scored a point.

Now he had an audience. "The glaciers calve in summer. Huge chunks break off and float around the ocean. The winds blow them to shore. The Innuits have been drinking icebergs for over two thousand years. Maybe ten thousand." Luke filled a cup at the cooler. He drank gingerly at first, then gulped with pleasure.

Our room furnishings were skeletal—two cots and one stool—but the sunlight coming through the windows was abundant and pleasant. We unpacked and went to the hotel lobby to observe the sun that whirled around the top of the globe without sinking below the horizon. Although it was noon, the sun stood at about four o'clock, its apogee for a mid-July day. My circadian rhythm was jammed; my midday hunger was gone and I was beginning to slow down for the end of the workday. Nevertheless, we decided to eat, and after Luke had another glass of melted iceberg we joined the hotel clerk on the porch.

"Where are all the Eskimo people?" Luke asked.

"It's noon," he said. "The Eskimos sleep at noon and midnight in the summer. So do the birds and the animals. They go to bed twice a day. I don't know why."

I glanced around for the snow buntings that had flown up from the ground when we came into town. They were nowhere to be seen. The gulls that had circled overhead, screaming and talking, were also gone. The Arctic drummed a strange rhythm.

"There is something otherworldly about this place," I said. Luke nodded as he fell in step beside me and we headed off through town to the restaurant.

In the dark café, Eskimo owners who catered to the schedules of white people were up and about. The proprietor served us reindeer soup on which floated a strong yellow fat. With our bodies still adjusted to the 85-degree temperatures of New York in July, the fat was repugnant. However, after three days of being exposed to the Arctic cold, the yellow globs would taste as sweet as butter and we would gobble them as fuel to keep warm.

From the restaurant we cautiously explored the foot trails between the houses. We came upon two dog teams, hundreds of snowmobiles—most of them wrecked—a department store, a power plant, a hospital, a youth center where the young people gathered to listen to rock-and-roll, a weather station, and the Bureau of Indian Affairs school. Here the Eskimo children learned English and lower U.S. history, and lost touch with their Innuit parents and grandparents. The school was closed for the summer, and with a few exceptions, the American teachers were gone.

Barrow is divided in two parts. One, the south side of town, is a mix of Innuits and whites; the other, Browersville, is inhabited by some five hundred descendants of the New Yorker whaler Charles Brower, who was in charge of the H. Lilbes Whaling and Trading Station in the late 1890s. As we crossed into Brower territory a young boy followed us for a short distance, then ran ahead. He grinned at Luke and beckoned. Apparently a child tourist was not a common sight.

We followed him to the wall of ice on the beach, up ice steps to a floe and looked down on a sealskin boat shaped like a willow leaf. The daylight filtering through it made it glow like a crescent moon.

Beside the boat lay a gargantuan bowhead whale. I gasped to behold this creature of the ocean, which diminished the men to mice. Dressed in white parkas, pants and boots, the whalers were butchering the great mammal. Its spirit seemed to have passed into them, so reverently did they carve.

"My father's," said the boy with enormous pride. Standing on the ice with the whale before me, the dark blue ocean curving toward the top of the earth, I experienced a deep welling-up of emotion that disconcerted me. I dismissed it, not understanding what was happening, and concentrated on the men who were laying open the great whale. Later I would learn that I had been observing a two-thousand-year-old ritual of carving the whale for distribution among the Eskimo people. Until the mid-nineteenth century when white whalers all but wiped it out, the bowhead had constituted not only food but religion, culture and history for the Eskimo. One of the flippers went to the harpooner, the other to the whaling crew, which had already been eaten on the ice according to tradition. The fluke went to the captain of the successful crew, to be kept for the village feasts of Thanksgiving, Christmas and Nalakapaq, which celebrated not only the catch of the whale, but also of walrus, seal, duck and fish. It takes place on the beach amid games such as the famous blanket toss in which a circle of Eskimos hold a skin and flip a person high into the air. The organs of the whale are divided carefully; they are essential because they supply the Eskimos with the vitamins and nutrients otherwise missing from an all-meat diet. Great slabs of meat were carted off by a chain of Eskimos and disappeared somewhere into Barrow. Half the baleen was kept by the captain and half went to the crew. The bones were gleaned by old women in colorful *kuspucks*—Eskimo dresses that fall to their boot tops. Within a few hours the great whale was reduced to a jawbone fifteen feet long and a vertebra the size of a girder. The crew then began to gently rock the great carcass until it moved, then slid it toward the sea. Slowly and gently, they towed it out into deep water. As the great skeleton sank the men bowed their heads and once more I felt an emotion I could not cope with.

"We give the spirit of the whale in those bones back to the sea," the boy said, "so she will give us more. Whales are very rare. For years my father did not see even one whale."

For dinner we ordered whale. It was the tenderest meat I had ever encountered, with an oceany flavor from the krill and plankton on which the bowhead feeds as it migrates northward in June and southward in September-October.

Outside the restaurant a young girl dodged around us and ran up to a tall white man wearing a NARL parka. She held up a ball of grass.

"Five dollars?" she said.

The young man opened the ball and then grinned. "Yes, yes," he said. "Very good, Marty. You've found the first lemming nest of the season." He handed her a five-dollar bill, which she tucked inside the neck of her *kuspuck*. Then she ran off to the youth center.

"Lemmings," I said to Luke. "We *are* far from the lights of New York." I clutched his hand tightly, again wondering why I felt so . . . however it was I felt.

At midnight Luke and I left the hotel and walked toward the beach with a large group of tourists to watch the non-setting of the sun. From the noon position it had now swung to within what looked like inches of the horizon. Clouds stretched before it, drowning it in purples and reds. A dog barked and was answered by another. Then somewhere a wolf howled. I listened; he gave another howl, a low, mournful one that rose higher and higher while my heart beat furiously at the sound.

"Midnight," someone said and cameras clicked. Luke snapped a few shots on our Instamatic camera. I sketched three lines—beach, ocean, ice—and then the sun started up the sky. As the night brightened the sun-guests returned to the hotel, the cold muffling their voices to soft owl sounds. Luke and I followed.

"I can't sleep," Luke called from his cot. "It's too bright."

"Pretend you're taking a nap in the middle of the day."

We closed our eyes, fantasizing, and sleep came quietly. The next thing I heard was the dry, rattling flight song of Lapland longspurs winging past the window. Sleep was over. There was no time; activity had begun again. We were one with the birds, the animals and the Eskimos. Something indeed was happening to me.

Five cold miles down the beach, our jeep taxi bounced through the gates of the Naval Arctic Research Laboratory. Its physical facilities were supported then by the Navy, and its intellectual inquiries were administered by the University of Alaska. The complex consisted of Quonset huts that were both dwelling and workshop, plus airfields and a rectangular building set on pilings to keep it above the snow and ice, which held the offices of the laboratory.

We were met in the lobby by John Schindler, the assistant director in charge of animals. "You're lucky," he said when I told him my mission for the *Digest*. "We have two outstanding wolf men here right now: Dr. G. Edgar Folk of the University of Iowa—he's a physiologist—and Dr. Michael Fox, a psychologist and veterinarian, from Washington University in St. Louis."

Dr. Folk sat on a stool in a large room viewing a closed-circuit TV, his blue eyes intent on the screen.

"I've been up all night," he said, when the introductions had been made. "I'm watching an alpha male wolf interact with an omega, the lowest-ranking wolf. I implanted radios in them both. The radios are reporting their cardiac rates." He pointed to a cardiograph that was printing the track of the wolves' heartbeats.

"The omega's heart raced in the presence of the alpha when I had them alone together in an enclosure," Dr. Folk said. "The alpha's was slow and steady. Now they are back with the pack and the omega has gone slinking off into the crowd. His heart rate has gone down dramatically. The alpha's has shot up as he goes the rounds of his pack, putting this one in place, checking that one."

"We call the fast heartbeat the executive syndrome," said Dr. Folk's wife Mary, who was also an assistant in his work. She smiled. "Ed was asked to be the head of his department last week," she went on. "He turned it down."

"Who needs a high heart rate?" Ed Folk laughed, but quite evidently he meant it.

The Folks took Luke and me to the animal enclosure to meet Michael Fox, a wiry young man with a pointed chin and ears, and eyes lit with humor.

"So you want to know the wolf," he said. "What a beast, *Canis lupus!* He's a social animal who depends on cooperation for breeding, hunting and territorial maintenance for survival."

Mike Fox had raised wolves in his own household, knew their language, and was about to communicate by going into the cage of the big wild alpha. The wolf was steel gray, and like most wild alphas was in excellent health. His ruff and fur glistened. He moved with fluid steps, his eyes and nose in contact with images and scents beyond us, beyond the lab, somewhere out on the tundra. Among us but not of our lien, the wolf weighed about a hundred pounds and stood almost thirty-two inches high at the shoulders. His paws were as big as saucers, and even when he dashed around the cage he moved as quietly as falling snow. He glanced at Luke. The alpha recognized the child in Luke and came toward him unafraid. A man arouses fear in the wolf, since he is traditionally the hunter; a woman is tolerated; but children are enjoyed, especially little girls. The alpha sniffed Luke, trotted off, then turned, pulled back his lips from his teeth and opened his mouth.

"He's smiling," said Mike. "That's a wolf smile. He likes Luke." Waiting for a signal from the wolf, he said, "Wolves truly love each other. They only mate once a year and yet they stay together all year around. It must be love, eh?"

The wild alpha sniffed us and Mike went on with my wolf lessons.

"A wolf says he's the leader of the pack by putting his mouth over the muzzles of the subordinates. They lick and kiss his face to tell him he's wonderful. Subordinates get down on their bellies to him or roll over on their backs in complete submission.

"Wolves also communicate by eye contact. Often it is a warning, a threat. But eye contact also passes messages—to the female, to 'charge' on a hunt, to a pup to stop what he is doing. Wolves look you in the eye. Man is the only other beast that uses eye contact as a language.

"Then, of course, there is vocalization. 'Umph-umph' means that I'm being friendly. An undulating whine is 'Come here.' Puppy growls mean 'I'm afraid.' Growl-barks are a warning: 'Don't come near.'

"Howls have several uses—for location when an individual is separated from the pack, to assemble before the hunt or other wolf events, or for pleasure. Howling is fun. It's accompanied by lots of tail-wagging.

"Scent is also a language of wolves. We don't know much about that talk because our noses are so lousy. We can only get a faint whiff of the ambrosia of wolf scent that tells so much: who the individual is, his status, what he has eaten, probably his age, and certainly his emotions—whether he is angry, fearful or at peace. Territory is marked by urinating, as are other pieces of property—stumps, favorite bones or sticks a wolf plays with. Like dogs, wolves roll in places with foul odors, then come show off to their friends, the way you would wear a new dress.

"Body talk is the third form of communication. Tail high, head held above all the others says the animal is alpha. Tail between the legs, head low means omega, bottom of the pile. Ears back is fear, ears forward is a warning. The flash of the white belly is the white flag of surrender. A wolf on his back has given up. No wolf attacks when he sees the white belly. All aggression stops."

The wild alpha had given Mike a signal, invisible to me, and he opened the door to the cage. Luke clutched the camera so tightly that his knuckles whitened, and I bit my lower lip.

"Umph-umph," Mike whined to the wolf as he confidently stepped into the cage. The wolf lowered his head and listened. Mike approached him, stood above him, then leaned down and put his mouth on the beast's nose.

I held my breath. All this was inconceivable; it wasn't talk, it was suicide. But the wolf heard. He sat down, whimpered "Umph-umph" and licked Mike, permitting him to scratch his ears. The two murmured softly and I knew that somehow, somewhere, I must talk to a wolf in wolf language. That it could be done I did not question. I had called to birds and they had replied. I had brought mice out of their holes by squeaking, and Mary Folk brought little Arctic ground squirrels to her by waggling her finger like a squirrel's tail—a signal which says "all is well, no enemies." But whether a wolf would relate to me I did not know. Wolves are choosy.

Mike was running an experiment on a litter of pups to determine the characteristics of an alpha. We followed him to a cage where a female and four pups were romping. The play spilled over into a fight and the female stiffened. She stood above the scrappers. Pups fight for dominance from three to about eight weeks of age, and the female supervises the conflicts, jumping in to break up a fight that is too rough so as to prevent injury. When the alpha pup emerges from these battles, all fighting ceases. Bites are replaced by snarls, growls and reprimands, signals to stall off battle. The roles assumed during these conflicts are their roles for life unless a pair starts a new pack on new territory. With the arrival of pups the adults automatically become alphas, even as parents are to their children.

Mike placed a tin can, something the wolf pups had never seen before, inside the cage with them, and then withdrew. All four pairs of bright yellow eyes focused upon this new object. Then a dark pup trotted forward and sniffed the can.

"He's the alpha," Mike said. "Alphas are fearless. Note how the others hold back, hesitate, and creep toward the strange object with their bellies close to the ground." Each approached the can according to an emerging scale of status—first the alpha, then the beta and gamma, and finally the cringing omega.

With a burst of energy the brown pup leaped onto his mother's tail. He got a snarl of disapproval. He picked up a bone and ran with it. "Bone ball," said Mike, as the other pups jumped on him. "Wolf pups play games; king of the hill, tag, tug-of-war. The alpha initiates most of the activities. Not only is the alpha fearless, and the initiator, but he sticks to a job longer than anyone else."

"I'll remember that come 1972," I said.

"Don't laugh." He continued. "Leaders of the various social species have a lot in common."

That is what I had come to learn about—alpha-ness, the essence of man and social beast. I was set on finding its evolutionary source, for it had a message for me.

Luke and I now went back to the laboratory to get warm. As we entered the main office another child came in with a ball of grass. John Schindler paid her for it and then turned to me. "We are waiting for the lemmings to boom again. The kids are our scouts. These are the first in many years. Lemming populations usually peak and bust every four years; but it has been five years now and still no buildup to speak of." He sent us to Dr. Steven McLean of the University of Wisconsin for a more extended explanation.

"Last year when the animals should have made a comeback," Steve said, "a series of events checked them. Just as the rodents were beginning to breed—and they have about thirteen to a litter, each of whom have thirteen more in a couple of weeks—ice still covered the grass. So the lemmings starved. Meanwhile the weasels that prey on lemmings were building up their numbers, and they kept down the already decimated prey.

"This was a great disappointment because many studies here depend on the lemming. The snowy owl, for instance. The male swings a lemming before his mate to court her. If she sees lots of lemmings, she mates and lays eggs; if not, she won't lay. The lemmings are birth-control devices for the owls.

"When the lemmings are down, the grass and the caribou are up and the wolves flourish. So you're in luck.''

Before leaving for the night I visited the mother wolf whom I called Silver because of the unusual luster of her pale fur. She was curled loosely in one corner, her eyes on the sleepy pups.

"Umph-umph,'' I whimpered, trying to imitate Mike's efforts. The ears of the female did not even twitch; it was as though my voice were nonexistent.

I tried again. A wolf eyebrow moved. That was all. But it *was* a recognition. Speaking softly, I tried to woo her with singsong, wolflike sounds, but her only reaction was to curl more tightly and bury her nose deeper in her tail.

The following day John Schindler asked Luke if he wanted to play with the wolf pups, and he snatched at the offer.

"There's no record of a healthy wild wolf ever attacking human beings in North America,'' John said as he opened the cage door. "Furthermore, this female is socialized, that is, she has been hand-raised and is accustomed to people. Fear of people is the prime reason for the demise of the wolf in the lower forty-eight. Wolves cannot live near men.'' The count in the lower forty-eight at that time was about five hundred. Since then, with protection from hunters, it has risen to between 1,500 and 2,000.

Schindler entered the cage and stood beside Silver as I came into her domain, on tiptoe, as quietly as if I were stepping inside a private thought. Luke was given a beautiful fat pup to hold. Snuggling it into his arms, he whimpered softly "Umph-umph.'' Luke put his cheek on his head and, holding him tightly, kissed his nose. The puppy licked his face and chin.

"He likes you,'' said John. "You should take him home. You are his alpha. He'd be a devoted pet, a lifelong companion.''

Luke looked at me with hope and expectation, but I shook my head. My friend Bill Woodin of the Arizona-Sonoran Desert Museum had a wolf who had caused problems by bringing him the neighbors' shoes, groceries, schoolbooks, anything left outside. He was taking care of his pack, Bill had said, but it got to be very embarrassing. That was one reason to say no. But Carol Perkins of the Wolf Sanctuary in St. Louis had given me the best reason why one should not raise a wolf.

"Pet wolves are shot," she said. "People just can't handle their fear of wolves."

"Umph-umph," I called to the mother, and this time she deliberately looked away. The hairs tingled along the back of my arms, for by deliberately ignoring me she was saying that I was there and that I mattered.

I talked to Silver several times after that, but got no further with the conversation until one afternoon she lifted her ruff when I whimpered, to say that she had heard. I called again and she rose and came toward me, avoiding my eyes at all cost; for that would have admitted me into her family and she was telling me I was *not* family, not even friend. Lowering her head, she passed me by.

Then, in one unpredictable instant, it happened. Not three feet from me, she turned, pulled her lips back in a smile and lifted her eyes to mine. We each looked deep into the being of the other. Silver wagged her tail. "Umph-umph," she said, and I stepped across an abyss as vast as from here to the moon. I was beyond the language barrier. I had talked to a wolf in her own tongue.

In gestures and movements she talked on; but now I was lost, my short-lived achievement at an end. I could not hear or see what she was so plainly saying, and what I had come to Alaska to discover.

Suddenly, fearlessly, she took the sleeve of my coat, tugged; and then I heard.

"I can't come live with you," I said. The nerves along my spine went off like a sparkler. I was in some other country, in some other era. "I want to live with you; but I can't. I can't. Do you understand?"

She stood still. None of my sounds were reaching her. She heard nothing, but breathed in great drafts from my odor language. Was it the spine tingles she smelled? I did not know, but she turned with a growl-bark and disappeared into her den box. I was back in my personal Dark Ages, but I had tasted the Renaissance, and that would make all the difference.

16

The People of
the Ice and Wind

And someone else at Barrow took up a life within me.

Julia Sebevan tiptoed across the black gravel, toes turned slightly inward, as she came home from work as a nurse's aide at the hospital. Her face was Innuit, round with firm cheeks, her black hair and eyes were the bequest of ancient Siberian ancestors who roamed the polar circle when the Bering Straits were land, and she wore a traditional *kuspuck*. Even at a distance, I felt her strength and warmed to her.

"She will make you a good parka," said her husband, who had been entertaining Luke and me while we waited for her. "She has bird-wing fingers."

Summer sounds in the cold Arctic are soft; bunting whispers, grass blades touching in the wind, ice melting; and so Julia's caribou boots made only a swish as she came on.

"You and my wife must get to know each other," said Mr. Sebevan. "She's a very important person. She is a shaman." He stepped back to greet her, bending just slightly at the knees and waist—movements I might not have seen had I not been observing the deference to leaders in wolves. Julia Sebevan's eyes shone like small half-moons.

"You want a parka?" Her voice, like all the Innuits', was soft and musical. "I knew you would come some day. Come in. I measure you."

Apparently she had been observing Luke and me and had me figured long ago for a parka, although I had been given her name only moments before.

Julia was a short woman but as she spoke she seemed to grow in size, like a bird lifting its feathers.

"You are a shaman, too," Mr. Sebevan said to me as he turned the doorknob on his house door.

"No, no, a writer; a reporter," I corrected.

"But you have been sent here," he said. Apparently the natives of Barrow knew more about Luke and me than I realized. We were, of course, blazingly conspicuous as blue-eyed, blond mother and child, who were staying much longer than the usual tourist.

"Your husband tells me you are a shaman," I said to Julia.

"I saw a ten-legged bear," she explained.

Here my resolve to be scientific tripped me up. "It must have been a mother with cubs standing behind her," I said.

"No, no. One bear, ten legs," she corrected, with a look of disappointment on her face that made me regret having spoken so lightly. I was reaching for words to make amends when Luke stepped closer to her.

"Wow," he said. "Ten legs on one bear; that's terrific."

Julia gave him a warm smile, then looked at me as if to say that any woman who had given birth to such a wise child could not be all wrong.

"I show you," she said, her faith in me renewed. "My son drew a picture of the bear. Come in."

Julia's house was rather small and denlike, just big enough to hold her family and their necessary possessions, and small enough to be heated to a glow by the kitchen stove. The house sat about three hundred yards from the ocean, which now sparkled and lapped on the beach. The tons of shore ice had vanished quickly in the last three days, leaving the Arctic Ocean looking like any other ocean in the world. Through Julia's one window I could see a few townsmen standing by the water. The Northeast Passage was free of ice, and the ship *North Star* would be arriving one of these August days with its cargo of mail-order goods from the Outside.

Julia's kitchen was partitioned off by half a wall of shelves, on which canned goods and supplies were colorful decorations. Two young men in their teens sat at the table, next to a small gas range. They were totally absorbed in the sounds from a transistor radio that was tuned in to some faraway jazz station. They looked up when we entered, and Julia introduced us to her sons. They glanced swiftly from us to their mother to read her disposition and attitude toward us. She lifted her chin and glanced at the far wall where a graceful strip of baleen hung—four feet long, two inches wide, a quarter of an inch thick, and still fringed with long hairs: the sieve of modified teeth from the roof of a whale's mouth. The nearest son rose and took it down, holding it in the light so that I could see the image of a polar bear confidently scratched by a sharp tool through the black surface into the white of the whalebone. Icebergs and hunters floated in the background. The craftsmanship was both strong and inspired.

"The ten-legged bear." I knew what to say this time. "It *does* have ten legs." Julia's smile puckered her cheeks.

"You take it." She pressed it into my hands. "It's an animal spirit." My immediate reaction was to offer to pay for the treasure, but then the air vibrated with signals warning me not to do that. As I glanced from face to face, each pair of eyes met mine straight on. Julia's look held and once more I was hearing another language just as I had from Silver the wolf.

"I am honored," I said, breaking through the deafness imposed by my own culture, as I felt and heard the signals and facial expressions from the Sebevans.

I took the gift of baleen, and although nothing was said, with that act of giving and receiving, Luke and I had been admitted to the Sebevan circle as clearly as the eyes of Silver had welcomed me into her family.

In the living room-bedroom-workroom, Julia measured me for a parka that I could have used on the spot, but which would take several months to complete. Standing with my arms out, turning slowly as Julia swathed me in tapes and paper, I had time to study the room. A double bed along the wall overflowed with the furs of polar bears, seals, caribou and Arctic fox, a palette of life-colors from the North Slope. An old portable Singer sewing machine was on the floor where Julia sat cross-legged to stitch. Around it were scattered scraps of bright velvet, trim, and unfinished parkas and mittens. I admired a black and white checkerboard band of fur that was half sewn to a boot.

"Yes, it's good," she said nodding critically, but well aware of her own skill and worth.

Along the opposite walls two cots, covered with mail-order bedspreads, stood end to end. I presumed that the boys slept on these. Above the cots hung harpoons, paddles, guns, baleen and bright winter parkas. The room was a mix of Eskimo and white cultures, with the warm Innuit culture dominating. The Sebevans were indeed Eskimo.

Julia decided that my parka was to be of red velvet edged with a white wolf ruff and decorated with white and silver kimono trim from Japan. After paying for it and making arrangements to have it mailed, Luke and I stepped outside in the bright evening light. Mr. Sebevan was waiting for us.

"Would you like to see an Eskimo freezer?" he asked Luke, who promptly grinned and stepped to his side. I was uncertain as to what I should do, for his invitation had seemed to exclude me, to say that this was a man's thing.

"Go, too," Julia said, reading my confusion.

On the sunset side of the house Mr. Sebevan lifted a wooden door on the ground to expose a pit, twelve feet deep by ten feet across, chipped and hacked into the permafrost. A ladder led to frozen caribou, half a reindeer, several seals, numerous eider ducks and great slabs of whale meat. At last I knew where the great bowhead had gone.

"You're a hunter," I said, realizing suddenly that this was not an idle man who sat back while his wife sewed and performed religious rituals, but a man who worked long hours on the ice and out on the tundra. Hunting in the Arctic takes not only a knowledge of animal behavior but infinite patience: hours and hours of waiting for a seal to come up to a breathing hole, a whale to blow, an owl to fly close to the ground. The frozen game without their fur and feathers looked almost human, like mummified gods in a tomb.

"It's eighteen degrees down there," Mr. Sebevan said. "All things last forever in the permafrost."

"You use the cold," I said. "It's not an enemy."

"The cold is good, a useful friend." He smiled down at the silent larder, then bowed, paying homage to the spirits of the animals. Luke dropped to his knees.

"What is that?" He pointed to what looked like a surfboard in one corner.

"Whale flipper," Mr. Sebevan answered. Quickly Luke arose and smiled up at the brown, lined face of the hunter. "The harpooner gets the flipper," he said. "Wow, you killed a whale."

Mr. Sebevan's nostrils flared proudly and he nodded, his face serene. Julia was the leader of food preparation, clothing and religion; Mr. Sebevan was the other leader, the provider. Each had a role to play. One could not survive without the other. The harsh Arctic biome had honed not one, but two heads of the household and the male and the female were truly more than the sum of the parts.

We inspected the wooden block where the meat was butchered, looked at bones to be used for carvings by the male Sebevans, said goodnight and turned back toward the hotel.

"These people," I said to Luke, "have to be the most intelligent on earth not only to survive but hew out a culture at seventy below and in darkness." My admiration for their ingenuity mounted as we walked home, in a steady wind that pulled the chill factor down to about ten degrees. Luke was shivering as we climbed the steps.

"Are you Jean George?" asked a lean American woman. "Are you the person that writes the children's books in our library?"

I told her I was, and Ann Patton gave us a warm welcome. Then she glanced at Luke. "You're freezing to death in this wind. Come home and I'll outfit you in our fur-lined winter parkas. It takes years to adjust to this country."

Ann Patton was a schoolteacher who lived with her husband, a NARL pilot, and their two sons, in an apartment provided by the Bureau of Indian Affairs for teachers from the outside. We not only followed her home and accepted her parkas, but stayed on for dinner. Afterward we admired her superb collection of Eskimo sculpture, masks and baleen basketry. Ann was something of a student of the cultural invasions of Barrow from the 1890s down to the present. During those years the Eskimos had suffered three major invasions: the whalers, the military during World War II and the present circumpolar invasion of scientists and educators. Each left his mark and wrought changes; yet most of the natives had remained essentially Eskimo. The cold and the darkness are their creator, and they are what persists. They embraced Christianity, TV dinners, electronic and mechanical gadgets, which they both understand and abuse. But their culture is five million years old, the first and the last of the human hunting societies. And the Arctic still selects them for this role. Physically they are short-limbed like the animals they live with, to cut down the loss of heat. Culturally they will endure until the polar cap melts, and the top of the world turns to the sun or until European and Asian men wipe out the game in one way or another. When that happens, the Eskimo will cease to exist.

The following morning, swathed in our fur-lined parkas, Luke and I went out into the strange sunlight of early morning and trod the tundra, a primeval wilderness of grass, sedge and puddles—a place new and at the same time eternal. And again a strange emotion welled up in me, a feeling I was beginning to understand—almost.

The great North Slope looked exactly the same in every direction, and the sun was always and terrifyingly in the wrong place or moving to a wrong place. After an hour I turned around and we retraced our steps.

After a few yards we plunged knee-deep into a soft whir of wings as the red-backed sandpipers we had aroused flew up, fraying out over the grass to float low against a plum-colored sky, as many as two thousand of them. Heads turned to the right, then to the left, wings tilted and with an upward explosion the birds were on their way.

A tumble of Arctic terns came over and we stopped to stare. To me, before now, these frail sky dancers had been no more than fantasy birds, emerging from the tip of an artist's brush. Yet here they were, plunging into pools to feed on crane flies, one of the few kinds of insects that can survive in the intemperate cold of the Arctic.

"Snowy owls." Luke pointed to two figures on a frost heave. They looked like little Eskimos in white parkas, their yellow eyes shining like snow-glasses. We lifted our binoculars.

"One's got a lemming," Luke exclaimed. He had held one in his hand at the lab; three inches long, it had a short tail, massive head and long face.

"The boom's coming," I said. "The lemmings are on the rise and all the creatures will flourish and reproduce. An abundance of predators will be on the land."

It would have been the male owl, who is somewhat smaller than the female, who held the lemming in his beak. Lifting his feathers to make himself appear large and important, he sidled over to his mate. Drooping his wings, lowering his head, he swung the betrothal offering before her. The female turned her head almost upside down to focus the most precise foveae on it. Then slowly she righted her head, blinked and hopped away. The male swallowed the lemming and all courting ceased.

"Maybe she's telling us something," I said. "Maybe this is not going to be the year of a lemming high after all." I suggested to Luke that we come back to this nest in a few days and check out the birds then. I marked the location by lining up two lakes that had formed where a jeep had broken through the skin of the tundra, and sketching the site in my notebook. Then we started back.

"Mom," said Luke after ten minutes or so, "the poles and towers of Barrow are behind us."

I spun around. "That can't be. Barrow is ahead. The sun." But the sun made no sense at all, nor did the plant shadows or the mosses that grew on the north side of objects in the temperate zone.

With enormous effort I forced myself to turn around and walk the other way—a direction, I was positive, that was 180 degrees wrong.

"It must be a mirage," I finally said to Luke. "Barrow has to be the other way." I turned around, walked a short distance, and then climbed a frost heave for a wider view. Less than a half a mile in the opposite direction the rooftops of Barrow nestled against the ocean. We started off again, keeping an eye on the towers. As I walked I understood the hunter who goes in circles, the scout who smashes his compass because it seems to be broken. I, like them, had gotten lost inside my own head even while my eyes told me where to go.

The junky little town looked beautiful as we came out of the grasses onto the road. Once there, I got back my sense of direction. We were near the hospital and Julia was leaving for the day. Seeing us, she waited.

"Want to see ancient Barrow?" she asked. "Many thousand years old. The town of the Old People, we call it."

Presently we were standing on a grassy plateau behind the berm and the beach, looking at round humps that had once been sod houses, and that had been returned to the earth by time, ice and the growth of plants.

Little holes in the mounds, Julia explained, had been made not by lemmings but by the children of Barrow as they hunted for relics to sell to the tourists.

"Come hunt," she said to Luke, and we dropped down on our knees, pressed our fingers into the rich black peat and dug.

"Luke, you would have been married by now if you lived here," Julia said.

Luke laughed nervously. "How come?"

"Your parents and the parents of some nice little girl would talk together. Then you would go live in an igloo of the girl's family. You would help her men hunt and build boats and make harpoons. If you did not like her after a time you would leave and go to another house, but if you got along after a year or so you would try to run to her bed in the night. Her papa would yell and you would run back and everyone would laugh and have fun playing the game. Then one day you would kill a seal or maybe a caribou. You prove you are a good hunter. That night when you run to the girl's furs the papa does not hear you.

"That's only the beginning of the marriage. A marriage takes many years to complete. You stay with her family and learn, then you and your wife move to your family's house. You hunt and help your family, she makes clothes and food. Finally, when you and your wife work as one and can support each other you make your own igloo and move in. By then you may have children. Like that?"

"I'd rather be a shaman. What do you do as a shaman?"

"Release the souls of the animals to return to the ocean so we can catch them again. I make charms. I dance away pain and evil."

Luke had struck something shiny. Digging more carefully, he held up a slender broken bone with a hole in it.

"Needle," said Julia, clapping her hands and at the same time shaking her head. "How did they sew with *that*?" For a long moment she held the needle in her fingers, and I wondered if she felt about that instrument the way I felt about the single-blade plow that I had found years ago in the barn at Craigheads—a closeness to a more simple life.

"You should put the needle in a museum," I suggested to Julia. "It should not be sold. These relics are your national treasures." She nodded and gave the needle to Luke.

197

Returning from the town of the Old People, we wandered into the youth center for a Coke and sat down with Charlie Edwardson, Jr., the political leader of the Arctic Slope Natives. He had just returned from Washington, D.C., where he had been lobbying to protect the natives on whose land the famous Prudhoe Bay oil had been found. I inquired about his trip, and since he was also involved in the NARL lemming project I told him about the snowy owl with the lemming.

"Do you suppose the lemming boom is beginning?"

"White man is impatient," he said, shrugging as though to say it did not matter. "You can't rush the Arctic. You must be innocent to survive here. And respect the Arctic. The Eskimo is the scientific man of the Arctic."

I laughed, for I was certainly impatient: I wanted desperately to see a lemming high of millions scurrying over the land, to observe their nervousness and restlessness at the sight of each other, to see their numbers build, explode and crash. No one quite knows what causes the buildup, although it is suspected that an antifreeze in their blood, which keeps them alive in the winter, may be released fatally when the lemmings see too many of each other. Others say they simply eat themselves out of house and home.

Charlie was called to the phone, and Luke and I finished our Cokes. A teenage Eskimo youth who worked in the animal pens at the lab came over to us.

"Eskimos are no longer innocent like Charlie says," he said. "Go to Seal Camp if you want to see what's happening to our innocence."

He really did not mean that we should go, only to make a point. But the next day, when Jess Stuart, who worked for the supply concessionaire, asked if we'd like to drive to Seal Camp, I jumped at the offer.

After driving five or ten miles to the north, he slowed down and proceeded with caution. In the gray mist ahead loomed what seemed to be a feudal fortress. As we moved closer, the tops of tents, skin shelters, tarpaper shacks and structures made of oil barrels defined themselves. A wind scooped up the mist to reveal dead seals, eider ducks and fish on the beach, waiting to be carried back to the "freezers."

With a snarling cry and a blur of movement a man leaped in front of the truck, shaking his fist at us. Behind him, screaming and yelling, reeled a woman who was presumably his wife. Behind her came two men with guns. The woman, who was clearly drunk, staggered forward, tripped and fell to the ground. She did not get up. The three men rushed at us, yelling and spitting.

"Rotten people," Jess said. "Let's go. They don't like us to be here."

"I should have known better," I said. "This is the Eskimo hunting ground, the last universal territory. We should not be here."

Jess spun the truck around, with stones firing out from under the tires. I put my arm around Luke in remorse, as the big truck gained speed and rolled down the beach past Barrow to the lab.

When John Schindler let us into the animal compound, Luke wandered over to the big polar bear and I walked to Silver's cage. She was lying with her head on her paws, halfway out of the wooden box den. I whimpered the high-pitched wolf sounds that meant "I want to be your friend." With an exaggerated refusal to take notice, she held her head on her paws, playing "ignore the woman." I barked. Still she did not move. I growled. No response. The brown alpha pup came to see what was up. Lifting the fur on his spine he snarled and curled his lip at me.

"You're growing up," I said at the sight of his lip. Adolescent wolves lift lips, as puppies cannot do.

A wolf howled on the far side of the compound and Silver sat up. The brown pup yipped. Then, one by one, by twos and fours, all the wolves within hearing howled in harmony. They sang of moons and mountains, of ridges to run, of rivers to wade, of pups to romp with, and of who and what they were. They knew what no man knows and they sang of it all.

"Your eyes are watering," Luke said. "Are you cold? I am." He pulled me toward the lab entrance where, just inside the door, Dr. Folk and Dr. Fox were conversing.

"Jean," said Ed Folk, "there's a young man in McKinley National Park who has been studying wild wolves for four or five years. We've just learned he has a wild pack under observation now. Gordon Haber is his name. He's a doctoral candidate, University of British Columbia. You ought to try to get down there."

"A pack of wild wolves?" I said. "I can see wild wolves? I'm going."

A bush pilot who was flying from Barrow to Fairbanks the next day offered to take Luke and me to Fairbanks, where we could catch a train to McKinley National Park.

That afternoon, after we had packed, Luke and I told Julia goodbye. Then we walked to the owls' nest, marking our way with bits of paper so that we would not get lost again. Luke ran up the frost heave.

"No eggs," he called. "White man rush the Arctic." Lifting his arms, he ran toward a flock of gulls that were winging low over the ground. Like snowballs they tumbled away.

At Fairbanks I rented a car, put it aboard the government-run train that links Fairbanks and Anchorage and stops at McKinley National Park, and with a packed lunch I followed Luke up the steps into the coach car.

The train whistle blew, the wheels rolled and we were clicking along the rails into the subarctic, ice-beaten forests of the north that the Russians call the taiga, meaning "little sticks." The sky darkened ominously and the forest closed in. The wild wolves were ahead, and a young man was living out among them. Here was my story for Andy Jones; Barrow had been only the background.

17

The Alpha Male Wolf
and Friends

"The alpha male wolf makes all the decisions," said Gordon Haber. The wind beat down the short curls on his head as he squinted into the sun. Luke and I were standing with him on a slope of dwarf alpine willows looking down and across at the summer den of the wolves of Sanctuary River in McKinley National Park. A rampart of raw mountain rock surrounded the high valley. Gordy was a big man with a firm jaw and gentle eyes. Muscular arms and legs and an alpine sunburn proclaimed the nature of the assignment he had given himself—a study of the wolves of the park that kept him outdoors from April until November, covering five to ten miles a day as he checked on five of the packs of Mount McKinley.

We had found him living in an old ranger patrol cabin in the scrub on the banks of the Sanctuary River, about a quarter of a mile off the one road that penetrates this Serengeti of North America. As he stoked the big wood stove I explained my mission.

"The wolves have had a terrible press," he said. "They don't deserve it. What do you want to know?"

"All about the alpha male wolf, his life and loves and how he orchestrates his pack. That's all."

Luke and I were staying at the park lodge until we could get a camp set up, but that night we barely warmed the beds. We talked to Gordy until sunset, at eleven o'clock, and at sunrise, around 3:00 A.M., we got up to accompany him to his observation site above the den.

The den was the second home of the pups who had been born in May. The first, the whelping or nursery den, was three miles away on a ridge that commanded a view of the Sanctuary River. Gordy did not want us any closer to the wolves than we were now, about three-tenths of a mile—not out of concern for us, but for their sake and for the sake of his study. Wolves move out when people come too close.

After he had taken a spotting scope from his pack and set it up, Gordy scanned the den site for the black wolf.

"The alpha male wolf not only makes all the decisions," he said, "but even decides where the pups will be born." He peered up over the scope to locate the pack leader by eye, scanning the silent tundrascape with a slow rotation of his head.

"Last spring, while I was watching the pack from a plane, I saw the black alpha lead the pack to one of the three whelping dens they'd used over the years. They dove into the tunnels and dens, cleaned them out, then followed him off to sleep on the open ledges and hills as they do in winter. The day before the pups were born, he led the female and pack back to the site.

"Each alpha has his own style; this fellow is an inventor. Listen to this. The female will not let any other members of the pack into the whelping den for two weeks after she gives birth and she won't come out. Food is dropped just inside the entrance. But this old boy dug a hole down to the chamber. I had seen it one summer day and wondered what it was. I found out: it was a sort of telephone. He would stand over it, cock his head and listen. Presently he would wag his tail and the whole pack would wag their tails. I guess he heard good suckling sounds down there and passed the news along."

Gordy watched the huge mountain pass.

"So," I said. "The alpha male wolf makes all the decisions." I felt at once disappointed and comforted—disappointed that one animal dominated the actions of all those spirited individuals, and comforted by the idea that there was after all a "wise and benevolent father" somewhere this side of heaven.

"Look," said Gordy. "The alpha." When I knelt at the scope, my

202

eyes picked out several shapes on the tundra, but not the wolf. His reputation was so great that I expected him to fill the scene.

"He's small," Gordy said, recognizing my problem. "We're far away." I adjusted my mind to something less mountainous, and before me emerged the alpha male wolf of Sanctuary River. He was gazing toward a ravine, his fur twisting in the wind, his head held straight forward as, with all his senses, he guzzled odors, movements, sounds and textures. He stiffened. He had heard something. All wolf eyes turned upon him as each animal waited to be told whether to charge or go back to sleep.

"The alpha male wolf," Gordy went on, "grows bigger than the others for some unknown reason. This fellow is almost a third bigger than the rest. He weighs about a hundred and fifty pounds. The next weighs about ninety or a hundred. Nobody seems to know why they grow bigger. Responsibility? Leadership? Testosterone? What?" He shrugged. "The alpha is bigger, faster, more alert; better in every way. Maybe it's just genetics."

Spontaneously I called the black wolf by the Eskimo name for the wolf—Amaroq. I watched as he rotated his ears forward, once more studying the tundrascape, made a decision and lay down. The wolves relaxed and took up their previous occupations—watching ravines, or pups, chewing at a bur or sedge head caught in the fur.

Behind Amaroq the tundra sloped toward the river where moose and caribou grazed. Surrounding this spacious wild ranch were the mountains; their rocks bent and squeezed up three miles high by ancient compressions deep in the earth. In that revolution they cracked, broke and tumbled, forming the profile of the mighty Alaska Range.

Amaroq and his pack hunted and patrolled more than ten square miles of mountain. Although they worked the land hard, they also ran and cavorted over their domain for the pure joy of it. Borders were marked by urine and no other wolves came onto their land unless invited. Between the property of the wolves of Sanctuary River and that of the wolves of the East Fork lay a broad no-man's-land, a corridor where game was not killed and packs did not trespass. The only wolves to venture into this 2–4 zone would be those waiting to be invited into a pack, or else a pair hiding in the labyrinth, sniffing and testing to find unoccupied land and start a pack of their own. In the unhunted corridor the prey species would recover when their numbers were low.

Gordy briefly watched the ravens that are like flags marking the wolves' whereabouts, as they follow the wolves to the kills.

"The alpha male did not breed this season," he said. "I can't understand it. As a matter of fact he hasn't bred since I've been on this study."

"Who did the alpha female breed with?"

"The beta. The best friend." I thought about that, for most wolf men agreed that the wolves mate for life. Gordy was reflecting too.

"It takes twenty minutes or so to complete copulation," he said. "Maybe that's too long. Maybe he would lose control of the pack in that time. I don't know what's going on." He opened his green Arctic coat.

"Something else incredible," he said. "Last winter this pack lost about nine members. By spring it numbered only four; the alpha male, the beta, the alpha female and a male who is now the babysitter and subdominant to the female, for reasons I don't understand. But what's amazing is that the female gave birth to not four or six puppies, as wolves usually do, but to nine. The pack is now back to normal. Wolves seem to be stable here in the park. In 1942 when Adolph Murie studied this pack there were twelve or thirteen animals. There have been twelve or thirteen all the years I've been here."

"Nine pups," I said. "That's hardly a male decision. Maybe she's the real alpha." It seemed to me that the female determined the genetics of the pack by mating with whom she pleased; corrected the pack's numbers, refereed the battles for the alpha pup; and when prey was low she would not give birth even though she copulated. Those are some decisions! The life and death of it—the future of the wolf.

"We just don't know enough yet," said Gordy, and as he spoke it occurred to me that all the observers of the wolves to date were men. Perhaps I had found what I had come for. Here in this primitive land, unencumbered by layers and layers of complex social adjustments, it could be seen in all its simplicity. The Eskimo and the wolf, both hunters, seemed to have evolved the same social arrangement: the alpha male was the hunting decision-maker, the alpha female the family decision-maker, and their jobs were as one. The Eskimo family and the wolf pack were a single operation.

I was looking back five million years and my own culture seemed at last to have a core.

For the next ten days Luke and I hovered over the spotting scope, discovering the gentility and good humor of the wolves. Around six in the evening, with the sun still casting short shadows, the wolves awakened. One by one they approached Amaroq, rear ends low, reaching up to lick his chin. He mouthed their muzzles. Each tail wagged at its level of status. Milling, touching, talking in body language, they gained confidence until each animal was imbued with the spirit of the leader. Throwing back his head, closing his eyes, Amaroq howled a note so deep and vibrant that the ravens got to their wings. The hunt song began. A bark from the beta soared into a high-pitched howl. The alpha female declared her identity with a yipe followed by triple barks. She moved in closer to the alpha and harmonized with him. The beta took another harmonizing note, the babysitter a fourth. The music soared out over Toklat Mountain, changed key, descended to basso depths and broke into waves of sound like the wind blowing across the lips of a thousand bottles. In all nature there is no sound like the cry of the wolf pack. Even I could feel the force that bound the wolves together before the dangers of the hunt.

The hunt song done, the three adult wolves departed more or less in single file into the valley to seek out the old, the very young, the infested and sick among the grazing animals, the prey of the wolf which sustains the pack and keeps the wild herds fit. Wolves would take healthy animals if they could, but a healthy moose or caribou can outrun a wolf in minutes.

Out in the valley it was Amaroq who called the signals and actually planned the strategy. On one occasion when a moose was feeding behind a small knoll, he gestured to the alpha female to come from the right, the beta from the left, while he slunk to the top. There with darting eye signals he gave the order to charge and the three came down upon the beast. A healthy animal, the moose sprinted easily over the sphagnum bog on the great platter feet that are adapted to such terrain. Wolves miss eighty percent of the time. As Mike Fox said, "You've got to be a super wolf to survive."

Few men have seen wolves kill their prey. But one night Gordy did, and later described what he had witnessed:

"They went for the hamstrings of the moose, then tore into every part of the body. The animal went into shock. I don't think he felt anything."

Once the prey is felled, the wolf will eat anywhere from twenty to thirty pounds of meat at a sitting. The bodies of wolves are adjusted to feast and famine, gorge and starve; they can go for a month without eating.

At the spotting scope, when the hunt song was done, Luke and I watched the wolf hunters disappear, then concentrated on the scene at the den. The vigorous pups played tug-of-war, bone ball and jump-on-the-babysitter, a game which seemed never to end with nine pups on the team.

Every evening the babysitter would try to sneak off with the hunters, only to be turned back by the alpha female, who would lift her head and tail to tell him to stay at the den. He obeyed. Wolf pups are rough and tough and these nine were already old enough to break bones. The babysitter handled them by simply rolling with the punches all night long, lying down, snapping, getting out of the way, moving off. By morning he was worn out. As the pack came home he would drag himself to the top of the rise. Upon seeing them he would wag his tail furiously, then drop to the ground exhausted.

At an indecently early hour one morning, Gordy came to our camp on the banks of the Sanctuary River. Since we had no tent, we had put our sleeping bags under the limbs of a dense and virtually waterproof black spruce and hoped for the best.

"Anybody home?" he called. "I'm going to check out the nursery den. Want to come?"

Luke and I answered with a yes. Then I saw that Gordy was carrying his big Winchester rifle.

"You need a gun?" I pushed up onto my elbows.

"Grizzly bears. There's no place to hide on the tundra and these fellows are unpredictable. But don't worry. I've never had to use it."

That consoled me very little, for several grizzlies had been seen in the area of the spring nursery by one of the rangers. A mother and two cubs had taken over a kill by stretching out and camping on top of it, and although the wolves had fought them off, the bears were still near the den.

Nevertheless we went with Gordy, leaping from one grass tussock to the next, bogging down in the springy sphagnum moss, tripping over glacial rocks. I struggled on into bear and wolf country knowing I could never get away from a charging bear in the deep pits and swales of this ground cover, which the moose and caribou had conquered only after a billion years of shaping hooves that floated on it.

We stirred no bears and it was with relief that I climbed behind Gordy and Luke to the den on the hogback ridge above Sanctuary River. From the den it was possible to see grizzlies in all directions and they us, giving them the opportunity to turn and run before encountering us within their flight-fight zone of about a hundred feet.

The view was stupendous. Rocks and canyons rose above a vast tundra on which a ribbon of trees marked the riverbank. Glaciers and snow fields burned white on the mountain peaks. Clouds floated everywhere. Some snowed; others rained or gusted, misted, thundered, sparkled or flashed. If the alpha male had selected this site he was a poet.

The whelping den, a tunnel with a chamber at the end, had been dug into a white sandy soil that gleamed around the entrance. Wild flowers grew beside it and upon close inspection it seemed as if the wolves had deliberately stepped around them, leaving them fresh and untrampled. On top of the den green grass sprayed upward and above that, a krummholz of wind-twisted and ice-dwarfed spruce trees. Among the trees were the saucerlike sleeping cups of the adult wolves and around them were little holes made by the pups as they developed their digging skills.

"Do wolves have a sense of beauty?" I asked Gordy, and answered the question myself.

We stayed on the knoll only about twenty minutes. Gordy did not want to linger for fear our presence would cause the wolves to abandon this den site. He started off.

"One second," I called. "I want to look out on this valley as if through the eyes of a mother wolf; to see what she sees." As I gazed, a distant wind pulled down an anvil of clouds and revealed beautiful Mount McKinley, an altar of blue-green ice and snow. I stood up.

Then I saw him—a massive grizzly bear, gold-brown with reddish ears and a chest like a mountainside. He was traveling about ten miles an hour, straight toward us.

"Grizzly," I rasped in a frightened voice and planned my retreat into the whelping den. "Come here. Hide." Gordy spun around. Scanning the landscape from east to west, he shouldered his pack.

"We've got to run," he said. "We must get ahead of him. We don't want him ahead of us. He'll turn and come back; and then we've had it."

Luke and Gordy took off like deer before the wolves. I followed; but my feet were not moving, they were embedded in the ground; and yet I passed a jay bird flying on wing and arrived on a hummock almost simultaneously with Gordy and Luke.

"Wow, you sure can run," said Luke.

"Adrenaline," said I. "Good stuff."

Gordy checked out the grizzly. The huge bear was chest deep in willows, headed off in another direction. I sat down and caught my breath, grateful for the terror that had propelled me out of danger.

"This is the spot," Gordy said, "where I learned that, to a wolf, a two-legged upright animal is a man, otherwise it is not. I was down on my hands and knees fixing my movie camera when I heard a soft bark and looked up to see the wolf pack gathered around me. They were obviously curious to find out what this new four-legged creature was. Then I stood up. They saw and took off."

Standing on the ridge where we had been was the alpha female of Sanctuary River and her nine pups. Startled to see us, she barked in alarm and leaped high, turning in midair and then disappearing over the hill with all but three curious pups. They cocked their fuzzy heads from one side to the other as they studied us.

The female reappeared; her ruff went up and she snarled. The pups obeyed, tails between their legs. A moment later one trotted back for a last look, barked and ran away.

"That's got to be the next alpha," I said.

That night Luke and I lay on the banks of the river listening for grizzly bears and making frightened hallos and bellows, until I heard the jays calling softly to each other in the pale semidarkness of the Alaska night.

"Go to sleep," I said. "The jays will scream if a bear comes near."

The river water from the distant glaciers tumbled stones and bubbled out talklike sounds, words I almost thought I could make out if I could only listen hard enough. But I couldn't. Luke fell asleep, the night things moved, the wolves howled. My mind's eye saw the beautiful alpha female wolf of Sanctuary River. She was on the ridge, rearing up, startled, her huge paws poised at her chest, her ears erect as she barked alarm information to her young.

The wolf pack was not the follower of the alpha male wolf; rather, it was one living organism made up of complex parts, all working toward the survival of the whole. There were reproductive parts, planning and thinking parts, parts that supported the planning and thinking. The pack was held together by a tripart language that ran like blood through an organism made up of individuals capable of changing and adapting to the environment; or even of dying out if necessary—all but a male and female—until the environment changed again. A single wolf is not a wolf, just as a totally solitary human being is not truly human.

18

The Amoeba
at the Edge of the Pond

On the long flight home I began composing an article on wolves that would open with a scene Gordy had observed: the black wolf gliding up a glacial moraine, carrying a chunk of meat to his wounded beta to save him from death.

The plane left behind the glaciated anvil clouds above Alaska, the billows over New York City came into view, and the summer of 1970 was over. Twig was at Bennington; Craig and his cousins Charlie and Jana were enrolled in Utah State University at the foot of the Wasatch Mountains.

I unpacked the camp pots and stove and placed them in a kitchen cupboard above the toaster. I wanted them within easy reach, for they represented a new life for me as the children one by one departed. Bob Krampner and I were hiking the Appalachian Trail that passes ten miles to the north of the house. On weekends he would come out from the city where he was now an estate lawyer, and he and I would walk for miles along the trail.

We camped beside white waterfalls, fought our way over ankle-breaking rocks to the tops of mountains and listened at night to foxes and owls. We also saw Off-Broadway shows in New York full of playwrights telling tough messages for tough times. And we built memories, something I had not done with a man for a long time. We also argued. I had learned to speak up and was finding that to disagree did not mean the end of a relationship. Our disagreements seemed to be clashes over roles— over which way the tent should face, how to put the canoe on the roof of the car, which foods were best for camping. We agreed on the important things—what it meant to sit in silence in a four-hundred-year-old white pine forest, and to stay close to one's children.

Since my children did not see their father very often, Bob became the man to whom they reacted for better or worse. His was a difficult role, and one that was not always appreciated even by me; for Bob and I, unlike the Eskimo and wolf pairs, could live without each other. Such were the forces within us and without. As single parents we had grown independently into an extended family of friends, bosses, organizations, routines and habits. Bob had adjusted to his orbit, I to mine. We could not go backward to a simpler life, nor could we howl in unison. We were two alphas looking for a pack. Whenever we talked about marriage, we would once more clash over which way to set up the tent and I would growl in resentment at the passing of my innocence, for I would never again see a man as an infallible figure of authority.

As I put away our Sierra Club cups, stacking one inside the other, already thinking about a climb up Kent Mountain, the telephone rang and Andy welcomed me home.

"Let's talk about wolves," he said. I closed the cupboard on the camping equipment and set out for the office.

As a newspaperwoman I had learned to write while a noisy, moiling parade passed through a city newsroom, and so the hushed and elegant offices of the *Reader's Digest* usually intimidated me. But not on this day; I was noisy inside myself with the doings of wolves. I waved and called hello to editors sitting in silent offices where messages were passed on paper rather than by voice, and knocked on the doorframe of the office where Andy was at his typewriter. He spun around. I said, "Don't get up."

But he did, and we joyfully hugged in greeting. I inquired about his three children, especially Audrey and Seaver, who were my camping friends, and he inquired about mine. Then we sat down.

"Same greeting ceremony," I said. "Except wolves don't hug.

211

Chimpanzees, however, do. They get up on their hind feet when they meet, shake hands and hug—and I always thought Emily Post thought that up!''

"What the devil are you talking about?''

"Ethology, animal behavior, sociobiology and the wolves.''

We had talked for half an hour or so when I said, "Wolves are friendly and loving,'' and Andy said, "Get crackin'. Loving wolves is a story.''

Back home I was diverted from going straight to the typewriter by Luke and his friend Davy Koffend. They were dumping three suckers, seined from the stream at the bottom of the hill, into the pond in the foyer with Bass, our largemouthed pet who now tipped the scale at five pounds. Suckers are bottom-dwellers that live off debris and death. Promptly these fish sank to their own stratum where they roiled up the sediment with their tails, fins and suction-hose mouths. The clear water turned a poisonous yellow-gray.

"They suffocate their food,'' I exclaimed. "They don't wait for death. They initiate it.'' I got down on my knees with Luke and Davy to watch nature's polluters at work.

"Where and how,'' I asked, "did they learn that oxygen and sunlight sustain life?''

"We aren't as smart as you think,'' said Luke. "This guy pollutes for a reason. We just pollute.'' He scooped them up and returned them to the stream.

About a week later Andy called. "Stop working on the wolf piece,'' he said. "While you were away some yo-yo bought an article on the wolves. It's going in the magazine. Yours is out.''

I slid down the wall where the phone hangs and sat with my feet stretched out.

"Who wrote it?''

"L. David Mech.''

"He's the best,'' I heard myself say. "He did the classic study of the wolves of Isle Royale.''

"Nevertheless, mistakes like this shouldn't happen,'' said Andy, breaking into a roar. Andy's temper is marvelous. It clears the air for miles around. I don't know how he felt when he was done, but *I* felt better.

My generosity about the mistake did not last. I was devastated and—as usual after a rejection—overwhelmed with worries. There were college bills to be paid and also therapy for Twig, who was having problems. And there was my obligation to the scientists who had given me so much of their time; had it all been for nothing?

I was the amoeba that had come to an obstacle, and must either change course or die. I picked myself off the floor and called Andy back.

"How about snowy owls instead of wolves?" I said, and rattled off what I knew about the lemmings, the owls and populations. "There should be a lemming high this year in the Arctic, it's long overdue, and when that occurs there's a boom in the owl population and the surplus comes down into the States. There's not enough food for them in the Canadian forests where they winter."

"We'll have snowy owls next fall? Let's go with it."

Late in the afternoon, after organizing my notes, I reached for the phone to call Twig and tell her about the demise of the wolf article.

"I owe so much to the people who helped me," I said.

"Mom," said Twig, "there are still some chipped plates in the lower right-hand corner of the china closet . . . the ones you gave me to smash when I got mad, instead of the good ones. Remember?"

I did and we laughed.

"Well, take them out and smash them all."

"Good idea. But it won't help the wolves or my wolf friends."

"Well, then, write a children's book about wolves."

"Best idea yet. Pat Allen called earlier this week. She once worked with Elizabeth Riley and is now at Harper and Row. She wanted to know if I would write for Ursula Nordstrom now that Elizabeth is retired."

"The Ursula Nordstrom who was E. B. White's editor for *Stuart Little* and *Charlotte's Web*?"

"And for Maurice Sendak, Shel Silverstein, Arnold Lobel, Charlotte Zolotov and on into the night."

"Do it."

The feeling I had thrust down in the Arctic suddenly welled up again, and this time I knew what it was. Inspiration. I loved the Arctic, its people and animals. I did have another good book in me.

The next day I climbed the wooden steps to the Children's Department in the old Harper building on Thirty-third Street and entered a large room partitioned off into offices by glass walls and bookcases. It smelled of paper, rubber cement and printer's ink; its colors were red, yellow and blue against smoky brown. I felt at home.

Pat led me along a winding course to Ursula Nordstrom's office deep inside the busy labyrinth. She was bent over her desk in concentration, her gray hair grooved where her fingers had pressed. Hearing us, she turned around and her penetrating eyes met mine head-on. She nodded to say she knew who I was and why I was there.

"I want to write a book," I said, "about an Eskimo girl who is lost on the Arctic tundra. She survives by communicating with a pack of wolves in their own language."

"Will it be accurate?"

"Yes."

"I'll write up your contract and advance now. Who is your agent?"

Never before had I been offered a contract and advance before a word had been written. But I, like the alpha wolf of Sanctuary River, worked best when kissed under the chin. I went home and began writing *Julie of the Wolves*.

The book was finished in time for the spring thaw and a hike with Bob. It took us from Kent to Falls Village, Connecticut, along a granite ridge above the Housatonic River, down into hemlock ravines and out over farm roads. On the top of Barrack Mountain, above the rolling New England valley, we caught our breath and unpacked the lunch.

"If we do twenty miles every weekend," I said, "maybe we'll get to Bennington before Twig graduates. The Appalachian Trail goes right by her house."

"I'd rather walk from Bear Mountain south," said Bob.

"Well, *I'm* going north." I meant it, Bob meant it, and when the opportunity arose he did indeed walk south, whereas I never got to Bennington because I was writing every weekend. To compensate, fortunately, a dog came into my life. A friend had found her at the SPCA. "She's a terrific medium-sized Airedale with good breeding and lots of personality," my friend had said and opened her car door on Jill.

I brought her home for Luke's approval. When I asked whether he liked her, he said, "Of course. But you wouldn't take her back even if I didn't."

"True. When you bring a dog home, that's it. She was a circus dog, the SPCA said." The dog cocked her head at me. "She also dances."

"Dance," said Luke and held up his hand, whereupon Jill got to her hind feet. Flailing her front paws, she hopped around the room. We broke into laughter and I asked the dog to dance again.

"We can hire her out," said Luke.

For two days Twig and her Bennington friends had been in Washington, D.C., for May Day demonstrations, and I was anxiously listening to stories of arrests all day on the radio. The dancing dog was just what I needed.

"Dance harder," I said, then caught the little dog in my arms. "I do not know which was more difficult, watching children grow up at home or having them away," I said to the Airedale.

That night Twig called. One of her friends had been arrested for throwing a stone. Twig ducked the police and ran straight into a lawyer, a member of the Bennington Board of Trustees, who had taken her home to his wife, housed and fed her and gotten her friend out of jail.

"The world's a mess," she said. "We've shot all our alphas, Jack and Bobby Kennedy, Martin Luther King and the young war protesters. We've failed the Chicago Seven. Greg, John, Denise and I have come home to work on ourselves; that's the only thing we can change."

I did not say how difficult that was.

Jill settled into the household, went on walks with Bob and me and learned to balance in the canoe. One night while I was preparing dinner Luke ran downstairs to the kitchen.

"Jill watches TV. She barks at the animals in 'Wild Kingdom.' "

"Impossible," I said. "I did some research on animal vision . . . even wrote an article about it. Dogs and cats can't see TV images because the muscles that pull their eyes are not synchronized with the movement of the dogs that make up the image on the screen."

"Well, come here." I turned down the heat under the fried chicken and walked upstairs. Jill was indeed sitting in front of the TV, her ears up.

"She hears it," I said, then a flock of ducks arose from a lake and flew through the air. With a leap and a snap of her jaws Jill lunged at the tube. The ducks flew off the screen and she ran behind it to find them.

"You're right. She sees TV. Now what do I do?"

"Write another article," Luke said. "Say she only likes animal shows. Watch what she does when the commercials come on."

I did not have to wait long. Jill lay down and went to sleep.

Some weeks later, Luke reported that he had put his mouth over Jill's muzzle to see if she understood wolf talk.

"What did she do?"

"She sat down."

"I'll be damned."

"And watch this." He dropped on all fours and sniffed Jill's nose in wolf greeting. She grew very excited, wagged her tail furiously and sniffed back. Then she whimpered a high-pitched Silver greeting song. "Umph-umph—"

"The wolf is still in the dog," I said. "That's wonderful. Some people say they are not related. Jill says they are."

"She turns around and around in circles, just the way the wolves do before they lie down."

"And she digs dens," I added. "There are little holes all over the yard."

"I wonder why anyone would want to give her away?" Luke said and hugged her affectionately.

His question was answered the very next morning at breakfast. My hand slipped from Jill's head to her side. Something kicked within her. Quickly I moved my hand to her mammae. They were swollen.

"Luke, I know why Jill was sent to the SPCA." He glanced at me curiously. "She's pregnant. Tossed out into the darkness and snow, never to darken her master's doorstep again."

"Great," exclaimed Luke. "We'll have a pack of our own."

The pups must have been the ugliest ever born to any of the *Canidae*, with molish whiskers, bowed legs and protruding hips. At the sight of them all thoughts of a noble pack died in Luke's heart. I spayed Jill and placed the pups on a farm where they would be useful for fending off intruders.

The publication date of *Julie of the Wolves* had quietly come and gone. Then I had a call from George Woods, the children's book editor of the *New York Times*.

"Don't you think it's a little much to have the heroine get down on all fours? I mean . . . where's your artistry?"

"It's true," I told him. "The scientist at McKinley was approached by wild wolves when he got down on his hands and knees . . ." But my voice trailed off and I said no more. Obviously I had failed to make the wolves convincing. I started another book.

On an unseasonably warm afternoon late in January, Luke came in with a hibernating little brown bat curled softly in his hand.

"I still wonder what forces of darkness got these little mammals off the ground and onto wings," I said as I studied the cold, silken creature in my hand. The bat opened its mouth and emitted a sound beyond the range of my own ears—but not Jill's. She came rushing from the kitchen and danced around my hand, sniffing to catch the scent message from the squealer.

"Your dad and I used to keep the hibernating bats in the refrigerator until spring," I said to Luke. "Then we'd let them go. Want to do that, too?"

Luke refused to lock Sputnik, as he named the female bat, in the refrigerator. Instead we hung her in a fold of the drapes in my room. She opened her mouth to utter a sound out of human range, then turned and hung upside down.

Later in the evening, as I spread a piece of newspaper underneath her, to catch the droppings if she happened to defecate, I noticed an article reporting that in Utah it was a felony to overdraw a bank account. I tore it out and read it to Luke, who was doing his homework downstairs at the dining-room table. This was a habit he had developed when Twig and Craig were at home and the house was buzzing with activity. Not only could he concentrate in the midst of bedlam; in fact, he concentrated better that way.

"Do you think I ought to call Craig and tell him about this? I don't want him in jail. You know how he is with money. He never keeps track of it."

"Is that what a felony means—jail? Yeah, call him."

Just then the telephone rang. "Long distance," I said to Luke, covering the mouthpiece with my hand, and we both envisioned Craig behind bars.

But it was Priscilla Moulton, calling from Washington, D.C., where the American Library Association was holding its winter meeting. "Oh, no," I said, and Luke rose and stared at me in horror. I covered the phone again. "It's all right, Luke. I've won the Newbery Medal for *Julie*."

I recalled that Luke once had a teacher—I believe she was a

217

substitute—who at the end of a long and exasperating day, slumped into her chair and offered the class a piece of advice. "Look, kids," she had said. "If you'll just read all the Newbery Medal books, you'll get a good education." Then she had reeled them off, beginning with the first award in 1922—*The Story of Mankind, The Voyages of Doctor Doolittle, The Dark Frigate, Tales from Silver Lands*—right down to that year, *Up a Road Slowly*. Luke had taken her advice and knew the scope of the honor that had just been conferred upon me. He danced with Jill.

Later that night, when Luke was in bed and I had taken a look at the bat on her drape, I went downstairs to pour myself a celebratory drink of bourbon. I opened the refrigerator for ice. There, on the second shelf, lay the book I had been reading when the phone rang. On the kitchen table sat a plate of what I had thought were cookies when I offered them to a neighbor who had dropped in for coffee. They were dog biscuits. It appeared that I had not taken the news as calmly as I imagined; in fact, I was overwhelmed. To me the Newbery Medal meant more than the Nobel or the Pulitzer Prize because it reached into childhood, into those years where books and characters last a lifetime.

Every night I awaken around 2:00 A.M.—a habit that dates back to the days when the children were young and I would get up to cover and kiss them. The habit persisted when they were in their teens, though during those years I would stand in the doorway to look down on their sleeping forms and thank God that the cars they had ridden in had not gone off the road, that they had not succumbed to the temptation of drugs. I would then walk downstairs and sit alone with my thoughts in the dark house. I still do this. I do not read or write; instead, I look out the windows at the stars or at the moonlight on the lawn, at the rain or the snow, and enjoy the quiet embrace of the unraveled night.

The night of the Newbery Award announcement I awakened on schedule and went downstairs. I lit a fire in the fireplace and, sat down before it hugging my knees, feeling very happy. In the months and years to come, the happiness would take new directions. The wolf would be placed on the list of endangered species in the lower forty-eight states and an awareness of wolves and their habitat would enrich many minds. As for myself, there would be a movie contract, a filmstrip, and the comparable awards in Germany and the Netherlands for the outstanding children's book of the year, the Jungbuch Prize and the Silver Skate. And at long last I would have the peace of mind that comes with financial security—not wealth, but an end to feeling anxious. *Julie* would sell. An unrelated but very important development that year was being made a roving editor for the *Reader's Digest*.

The heat from the fire must have uncurled upward into my room, for suddenly Sputnik was winging around me like the unerring spacecraft she was. She circled my head and then swooped to the living-room curtain, where she alighted and once again produced her inaudible squeak. I went to the refrigerator for the mealworms we kept in a cardboard box for the bass, and tossed one up in the air near the bat. She winged out, caught it in her tail, leaned down (I knew, though I could not see) and took it in her mouth. Returning to the curtain, she finished eating and rubbed her whiskers clean with that wondrous hook on the wrist that bats have evolved to hang by. Again I was provoked by thoughts of how a creature with breasts and fur and the characteristic shyness of mammals had attained two ears that could penetrate the night and wings that could intercept an insect. When I tossed a piece of bark toward her, the bat turned her ears and clung to the curtain; when I threw her a mealworm, she flew out, caught it and returned to the curtain. I was reminded of a night eight years ago, when the phone had rang at almost this very hour.

"Jean," my neighbor Danny had said. "I hate to call you this late, but I'm desperate. How do you get rid of a bat? I can't hit it with anything. Not even a blanket."

I said I'd be right over. Putting on my boots and coat I had run across my yard and woods to find Danny and Amy huddled down in terror in a corner of the living room while a little brown bat circled the room. When it careened in too close, Danny swung at it with a tennis racket, while Amy screamed and I simply thought and wondered. A young Harvard student, Donald R. Griffin, had just startled the scientific world by stating that bats "see in the dark" with their ears—not through some other mysterious and unknown sense as was believed at the time. With the discovery of echolocation, the bats came out of the ignorance and mystery that had surrounded them and took their rightful place as the inventors of sonar. I opened the front door and held it wide. An opening, I surmised, must have a special sound to a bat. Fluttering those webs between feet and finger tips, scooping and pinging sounds off the walls, the bat came from the far side of the living room into the hallway, and darted through the front door into the dark.

"He saw the door," exclaimed Danny.

"He heard the open door," I said, marveling myself.

"Pretty cute," said Danny.

"I still hate them." Amy pulled her dressing gown closer, shivering with relief.

That night in January when I won the Newbery Medal, Sputnik was a lovely diversion. I watched her until dawn.

To be the centerpiece of the Newbery Award dinner was as tremendous an experience as watching a bat find an open door. About three thousand librarians were seated at a sea of tables in the Las Vegas hotel; those at the far end of the room seemed to be awash in a mist. I can still feel my body quake as I walked to the microphone to read the speech I had written, and I can still feel my trembles stop as they did when I looked down from the dais into Twig's bright face. Smiling confidently up at me, she sat with Esther and Margaret and Aunt Dot, my mother's sister. Even though I had been told that I was an old pro and a Newbery Medal would not rattle me, it did and it still does.

Fortunately I could not dwell on it for long at a time. A young man named John Dean was sitting before the television cameras in Washington, D.C., reporting that there was a "cancer" on the Presidency. Between book signing, cocktail and dinner parties, everyone at ALA watched the Senate investigation of the Watergate affair. Richard Milhouse Nixon, the nation's leader—its alpha—was being revealed as his own Brutus. He had struck at the Presidency.

When the ALA meeting was over, Twig, her boyfriend John Housekeeper, Margaret and I left the throngs to hike down into the Grand Canyon's awesome landscape, where silence becomes a presence.

Layer by layer of stone, we walked back three billion years, to a time when there was no life on earth.

19

The Crazy Season

Shifting into gear after the Newbery Medal, like hiking up out of the Grand Canyon, was difficult. Fortunately, in 1974 the editors of the *Digest* germinated a series of ideas that kept me busy, and there were the young people who had fallen in love with our wildlife. The summer after the Newbery, I set off to find two of these young people.

After six hours of putting one boot before the other, of painfully inhaling thin air, of feeling a high as weather-sawed peaks came into view, I reached the turf of Gunsight Pass, in Glacier National Park, Montana. I was there to observe the female-dominated society of the Rocky Mountain goat, *Oreamnos americanus*. I had climbed with Luke, Margaret Craighead and a goat expert, Doug Chadwick. Here above timberline, among purple beardtongue and Indian paintbrush, we would make camp and live with the goats.

As I paused I saw huddled at my feet small alpine plants whose inscrutable intelligence had brewed a red pigment to fend off the blazing light and hold heat. The trees, bowed by submission to the wind and ice, crept on their bellies, sending down roots from flattened limbs in the lee of their body masses. Up the mountain from these survivors there were no more trees, only grass, alpine wild flowers, glaciers, snowfields and rock. Lichens grew on the rock above them, in what was known as the

221

aeolian area. There was constant wind. Although I was standing more than a thousand feet below it, I could hear the fiendish laughter of the winds that were its only inhabitants. I shivered to think that the goat found a home up there.

"Goats!" Doug called. A tall, powerful young man with intense eyes, curly brown hair and a wide smile that revealed fascinatingly irregular teeth, Doug was in his mid-twenties, and he brimmed with energy and ideas. He pointed to the left of the glacier that hugged the pass. The steep wall was veiled in the washout of a cloud that had thundered with electrical discharges while we were climbing from the lake to the pass. Spent now, it was disintegrating into threads, uncovering five nanny goats and five kids, hiding from the rain on five separate ledges.

"See that big kid with the nubbin horns?" Doug said, and then when I nodded, "He's going on two and still with his mother. He should be off with his peers, but in early June his mother lost her kid of this year and he took up with her again. This happens. Apparently it's a good thing. It's a dangerous life up here and the longer a kid stays with his mother, the more skilled and healthier he becomes, for a reason you will see."

"He's got a Roman nose," I said. "Let's call him Romulus. He should be Oedipus, I guess, but that's too humanistic."

The nannies dropped down the wall with kids at their heels, each group keeping a distance between itself and the next as though choreographed by a ballet master. Every animal has its own space requirement. Some, like spiders, are voracious about it and will devour members of their own species that press too closely. Monkeys, on the other hand, can be physically jammed together; they make their space by withdrawing into themselves and staring blankly at their feet, as people do on a subway. The Rocky Mountain goat had worked out a spacing that allowed for leaping down rocks yet keeping in touch with other goats.

As we watched, a kid became separated from his mother. He bleated, ran to a passing female, and smelled that she was the wrong mother. He bleated once more, and from a ledge below the right one answered. Now the long-legged kid jumped into the air, and landed precisely beside her. Luke and I gasped in unison.

"They seem to recognize each other by scent and voice," I said, and Doug nodded.

Luke asked, "How do they stick on these perpendicular walls?"

"Their feet are adapted to sticking. They've got a convex pad like a rubber ball within those two toes which are like pliers. Together the invention holds them to almost anything."

Luke walked slowly out to meet the goats. He was almost six feet tall now, lean and agile. He had graduated from high school in June and had been accepted at Reed College in Oregon. During the summer he had made his way across the country, stopping off here and there to work, climb mountains, fish and run rivers. I had caught up with him at John and Margaret's home in Montana. After persuading Margaret, the mountaineer, to join us, we three had driven north to Glacier Park to find Doug, who was completing a master's thesis on the decline of the Rocky Mountain goat. He and his wife, Beth, were two of those young people of the ecology decade who were living in the wilderness for months and years to study and learn more about the wild animals that live on the ark of this planet with us.

"We must find out who and why we are from these other forms of life," Beth had said, "before they are gone and it's too late to understand ourselves."

As we set up our mountain tents to face west across a steep glacial cirque to the valleys and mountains of Idaho, the goats came down the mountain and grazed peacefully among us. Marveling that they trusted us, I concluded that fear of man must be learned, not inherited. Here, they lived in a national park where animals were not hunted. When camp was made, complete with a kitchen whose tables and chairs were all stones, I took out my notebook and sketched the goats in their social clusters. As I drew, their personalities emerged and I named them Remus, Jason, Orion—names to express the mythological otherworldliness of creatures living high above all others.

I breathed deeply; this was the first expedition I had made into the wilderness to study an animal for a children's book entirely out of my own earnings. When I first talked to Doug on the phone, while I was doing research for an article, he had said, "The goats are declining rapidly.

Unlike deer, who have no natural enemies anymore and who need to be harvested by hunters or they'll ruin habitat for other wildlife, the goats of Montana, Idaho, Utah have built-in population controls—avalanches, falling off cliffs, butting, and a limited supply of food. They should not be hunted. Come out and see for yourself.''

I had been going to take his word for it until he added, ''Goats are a nanny society. The females raise the young and make all the decisions.''

''I'll be out this summer,'' I had told him.

As mountain goats evolved over the eons, they adapted to the terrain above those occupied by the bear, the wolf, the mountain lion and all but the hardiest of human hunters. Not until logging roads admitted four-wheel-drive vehicles to mountaintops could numbers of people reach this white-furred trophy animal with its black spear-shaped horns, jet black hoofs and eyes. It had been a scarce animal even before European man came to North America, dwelling only in the Rocky Mountains from Idaho to Alaska. It was not a true goat, but rather, like the chamois of the Alps and the takin and serow of Asia, a goat antelope.

Up among the rocks and alpine plants, the nanny-dominated society had succeeded for at least 140,000 years (the age of the oldest-known fossil), and I was in Gunsight Pass to learn why.

Luke and Margaret were boiling water for freeze-dried Creole shrimp when Beth came down from a snowfield on Gunsight Mountain. She looked dynamic, weather-burned and very beautiful as with dust on her legs and eyelashes she climbed to our meadow camp carrying a thirty-pound movie camera.

Beth was making a film about the goats that would eventually become a classic, in which she was letting the kids write the script as they war-danced, jumped and butted, nursed, and were kicked to be weaned.

''Doug!'' she called out. ''I just saw the biggest billy of them all. He's absolutely gorgeous; huge shoulders, massive beard, great muscled rump. He must stand as high as your chest.''

''That's Old Gore,'' he said. ''He's the boss of the mountain. Leaves holes in lesser goat-gentlemen.''

The breeding billies of this female society were out on their own, climbing in solitude to rock steeples or to secret gardens on ancient ledges, and sleeping a higher level than the nannies and young. In the fall, they would join their harems to breed and then depart. They might come back to them in summer whenever nannies discovered a supply of salt.

"Old Gore, where are you?" Doug yelled, and a tingle of expectation ran through me. I saw a puff of vapor and there on a nearby pinnacle stood a goat, enshrined in a white halo as the sun backlit his fur.

"Aha, Old Gore!" Doug trumpeted, and I was right back where I had started—admiring the male of a species through the eyes of a male.

Old Gore looked out toward Idaho; then, vigorously, he turned and leaped into space. I watched as he bounced downward, striking rock, slope and monolith in sequence, all the way to the bottom of the cliff, then trotted across the trail and up into our meadow. His horizontal pupils flashed as he sprang to a boulder ten feet away. There he froze, head down, horns aimed.

"I think he's threatening you, Doug," I said. "You're an adult male in the midst of his harem."

"None of that interspecies stuff. He's here for salt."

"Salt?"

"In our pee. If you want to bring these goats to you, all you have to do is urinate."

The winter forage has little or no mineral content, and so in summer the goats' search for salt in rocks and urine becomes urgent. Luke, who had been listening wide-eyed, walked to the spring that bubbled out of the rocks, leaned down and drank deeply.

"Man, am I going to get pictures," he said.

Meanwhile Doug stepped closer to the massive Gore. As he did so, a nanny trotted up to Doug, and Old Gore bucked.

"Ow!" Doug clutched his knee, and a trickle of blood seeped out between his fingers. But he was grinning.

"He does interact," he said incredulously. "I *am* a rival." Doug glanced from his wound to the billy. Once more, the chasm to another world had been bridged, as when Silver spoke to me, and I felt the common denominator of all living things back to the primordial seas.

That night I stuck my head out of my tent to watch the enormous stars and to listen to the winds as they howled upstairs in the peaks. Books are written in the head long before they get to paper, and in that way I produced long paragraphs about a young married couple living with the goats, finding, like the goats, a way of life above the level of the predators.

For the next few days I looked for the leader of the nannies. But no single individual stood out; the group simply flowed with the active one of the moment. If one female initiated a trek to the snowfields, all the rest would follow. Another might walk to the meadows to graze, and her action would motivate first one, then another. When a storm threatened, however, all of them simultaneously sought shelter. Goats can endure snow but not rain, and may die from a drenching.

As the days passed, surrounded by flowers and absorbed in goat-watching, I still had no answers as to why a female society was able to function so well in this hostile world. One midafternoon, a thunder cloud bore suddenly down upon us, driving raindrops into the rocks like nails. I dove for my tent, but then I heard Doug shout, "Follow the goats!" and a minute later I saw him disappear over the brink of a two-hundred-foot rock wall—the rim of the lower glacier cirque—hard on the heels of the nannies and kids. Luke, Margaret and Beth were close behind. I hesitated, feeling safe in my tent, then thought otherwise and ran to the brink. Seeing no one, I called.

"Here!" shouted Luke from a cave. I eased over the ledge, dropped onto a mat of grass and discovered an overhang, where Doug, Margaret, Beth and Luke had taken shelter along with the goats. I moved in beside Luke as the rain shot out over the cliff, soaking the world beyond but leaving us perfectly dry. I realized then that the goats had known much more than that a storm was coming—they had also known from which direction. This shelter would have been no protection against a storm coming in from Idaho.

"A kid without a nanny dies," said Doug, passing me a bag of raisins. "A hunter shot the mother of the only kid born to a herd of thirteen goats that Beth and I were studying in the Swan Mountains. The kid eventually died. Kids need their mothers for at least eleven months. The mothers teach them where the food grows, where the rain shelters are, how to avoid avalanches."

"So nannies are teachers," I said. "That's the female society—education. Up here it takes a long time to get a degree."

"You've got it," said Doug. "This is a teaching society."

The kid I'd named Romulus, who was watching the storm not far from me, proved the point. He was larger and stronger than his peers. Following his mother at this late age meant that he still had access to the best fodder, to the driest caves and to the sources of much-needed minerals and salt. He had an advantage that would give him an edge all his life.

The next day I climbed Gunsight Mountain and found Beth crouched among the rocks, her camera focused on a kid who, having rounded a boulder, stood face to face with a marmot. The reactions of the kid were the universal sequence of surprise, then curiosity, then curiosity satisfied. There, but for hooves and fur, went I.

After she had filmed the encounter, Beth joined me under a rocky ledge, where we looked out on the breathtaking world of the mountain goat: avalanches, cliffs, meadows, lakes and pinnacles.

Reaching into a pocket, she said, "Would you mind reading one of my poems? I'd appreciate your criticism."

Among the rocks and white chickweeds, with the sweat of Beth's anxiety warming the air, I read the poem of a young woman crying from her cage.

"Beth," I said, "this is *very* good. You must go on writing."
She looked away.

That winter, while I was completing *Going to the Sun*, the story of the young married couple and the Rocky Mountain goats, I received a letter from Beth: she and Doug were divorced. Reality had superseded the imagining world of my book; the children had written their own ending. Doug and Beth eventually found new partners and new careers. Beth wrote and codirected a movie, *Heartland*, one of the ten best films of 1981 on the real-life story of a pioneer woman in Montana, and Doug, following his study of goats, became a writer for the *National Geographic*.

When Luke departed for Reed College at the end of that summer in Glacier National Park, my last child was gone. I flew home, picked up Jill at the kennels and walked into the lonely house. Windows rattled in the autumn wind; empty children's shoes haunted the closets. I built a fire and sat down, ready to cry. I've written thirty-five books and over fifty articles, I thought, psyching myself up for a bout of self-pity. But without my kids around, I feel no more motivation. I waited for a reaction. No tears came, only a long, honest sigh.

The telephone rang; Bob, after welcoming me home, suggested that we join a Sierra Club canoe trip into the Okefenokee Swamp.

"That's just what I need," I said. "It's dispersal time for the young and I am more than ready."

At an editorial luncheon with Andy a few days later, I suggested an article on the dispersal of immature birds and beasts in fall.

"The crazy season?" he said. "The time when birds bang into trees and the skunks get into the cellars? Let's go with it."

In the years to come, Andy's phrase "the crazy season" would apply to me and mine as Twig, Craig and Luke went off and came back again, fell off mountains and got broken ankles, fell in love, brought lovers home, fell out of love, worked, loafed and went back on my budget for their "union card"—advanced degrees. The geneticist J.B.S. Haldane once said that if he had been going to breed for any quality in the human being, it would be for a long adolescence, that stage of life when we are most capable of learning. Conscious or unconscious, the Craigheads and Craighead-Georges were breeding older adolescents. My parents had been in their late teens when they were out on their own; I had been past the mid-twenties; my children would be nearly thirty. And theirs—if this keeps up, who knows how old theirs will be before they have flown from the nest?

That autumn, my first as a childless single parent, I renewed old acquaintances—among them Louis Untermeyer, the poet, humorist and anthologist, and his wife, Bryna, a writer of children's books. I had first met Louis through Theodore Roethke while I was in college. Years later, at the end of a letter praising *Julie of the Wolves,* he had invited me to Newtown, Connecticut, to meet his present wife, and his three cats. Now, as I strolled through the garden with Louis and Bryna I admired the pond nestled among reeds; a heron was walking there.

"That," said Louis with a perfectly straight face, "is Lake Inferior, where Bryna and the ducks swim." Then he sat down on a bench and rattled off limericks by his friend Ogden Nash. As I listened to his voice rapping out the punch lines, the rewards of the crazy season seemed sweet indeed. There was much ahead.

Returning home, I stopped by the Chappaqua station to pick up a train schedule and saw on the platform, spread out like something in a poultry store, a naked, pot-bellied house sparrow, species *Passer domesticus*. I truly expected to see him die at my feet. Instead, he chirped. I took him home, stuffed him with canned dog food, and put him in a shoebox with an electric light for a mother. I named him Straggler, since it was September and he was obviously from the last brood of the usual three of four that house sparrows produce per year. By December, however, I had changed his name to Darwin. He had one motivation in life: survival. He grew rapidly, and was ready to nest far ahead of schedule in comparison with the robins and cardinals we had raised. Male house sparrows take part in the home chores, and Darwin accordingly began nest-building as soon as the sun had passed the winter solstice. He gathered paper, paperclips, pop tops, string, socks, stamps and earrings, and out of them fashioned a series of sloppy nests—on the mantel, behind a book (naturally it was *The World of Birds*) in my library, on top of the hanging pot of ferns. The house had never been tidier.

As the nests multiplied, so did Darwin's aggressive behavior. By mid-January he battled anything that even faintly resembled another sparrow—pencils and pens being the most challenging, since they came to a point like a beak. By the end of January I could not sit at a table to write a check without Darwin's arriving to perch on the pen, wildly flapping his wings as he struck the rival dead. With so many pens being regularly wrenched from my hand, I finally shut myself into the bathroom to complete my accounts.

A person's hand moving toward Darwin would also set him off. Apparently the fingers looked to him like five birds coming at him all at once. So I learned not to pick him out of the typing paper box or from behind a book. He also hovered over the knife or fork when I was eating, but since they were not so finely pointed as a pencil or fingers his battles with the cutlery were not so wholehearted.

It was, however, potential nesting sites that set off his most clearly erotic behavior. These were to be found in pockets and lapels; but long hair, which came into the house on the heads of young friends, was most inviting of all. Davy Koffend came by the house one day to inquire about Luke, and Darwin, seeing a gorgeous mass of hair, flew to Davy's shoulder and wooed it with soft, surly peeps. Davy grinned. Seeing that Darwin was about to become a tenant, I grabbed for the bird to get him away.

"No, don't," he said. "He's cute."

"You don't know what you're saying," I sighed, and Darwin took possession.

The arrangement continued satisfactorily until Davy was ready to leave. He reached for the bird with all five fingers and Darwin, like the dervish he was, drew blood from the forefinger before Davy could pull it away. He went back into Davy's hair and chirped softly from deep within it. Davy reached in with the other hand and was again attacked.

"Hey, what do I do?" he said helplessly. I grabbed his hair and lifted it over his head. The nest gone, Darwin flew chirping to the mantel.

One Sunday afternoon when I had been telling the Untermeyers about Darwin, Louis leaned forward in his chair and said, "I must meet him." We made a dinner date for the next weekend.

Louis, a man of impeccable taste, arrived for the evening dressed in a handsome suit with a pale blue shirt, and a beautiful Pucci tie, knotted loosely in the vogue of the day.

I showed Louis the "poetic license" that Craig had made me, complete with a hand-drawn New York State stamp and a list of things I was exempt from—among them bad jokes and bad critics.

"Where's my license?" Louis asked. "I need one more than you."

"You have to apply," I said, and as he took out his pen, Darwin came winging from the sunporch, shot across the dining room, hit the pen and whacked it to the floor. His enemy vanquished, he sat on the arm of the couch and eyed Louis. Louis pleasantly eyed him in turn.

In a moment Darwin had drooped his wings and lifted his feathers in his house-takeover posture. I lunged to grab him. Too late. He was inside the knot of the Pucci tie. Now what, I thought, as Louis leaned back happily to admire the sparrow. At dinner time I suggested removing him. Louis shook his head. Walking carefully so as not to disturb the visitor, he took his seat at the end of the table.

It was around nine, and Bryna was making motions toward departure, when Louis at last reached for Darwin—with all five fingers. The wrath of the sparrow was instantly upon him. Undaunted, he tried again, and once more had to snatch away his hand.

"How do I extricate him?" he asked, with more chuckle than wince.

"I don't know," I replied. "I've never had this problem before. Just long hair. I can't lift your tie over your head."

"I guess there's only one solution," said Louis. Loosening the Pucci tie, he whipped it over his head and handed me both nest and tenant. "That's for the bird," he said. "And I really love him."

As I was crawling into bed that night, my mother called from Florida. She and Dad had moved to a retirement community during the summer and were now settled in a small apartment there.

"Your Dad thinks this place is corrupt," she began. "We are getting none of the services we were promised. There's no infirmary, no nurse, no dining room. Instead, we have a tennis court. And me and dad almost eighty-four and the other people all over seventy."

My father came to the phone. "Something is seriously wrong here," he said. "The manager of the village owns the construction company and the landscaping company. He sells bonds to religious people all over the country and has a mansion of a place in Canada."

Mother got back on the phone. "Your dad is not well."

"I'll be down," I said, and thus I entered the post-crazy season. The children were grown, and my parents' problems were mine for the first time in my life. Before leaving for Florida, I opened the window to release Darwin. Without hesitation, without looking back or even so much as a chirp to acknowledge the momentous flight from his provider, he shot out of the window and hopped upon a female at the bird feeder. Apparently he had been courting her through the window for months. Now he was ready to toss his seed and continue life.

"So the sparrows will inherit the earth—not the meek," I told him.

20

The String Game

Between three trips a year to Florida to help iron out the problems Mother and Dad were facing—the financial collapse of the retirement home because of fraud, the purchase of a new home and Dad's failing health—my front door opened and one by one the children returned.

Twig would eventually get her master's degree from Bank Street and then work with me, learning to make filmstrips. We would incubate and hatch fifty baby quail that ran like miracle toys all over the floor and yard. We would track down salamanders on the forest floor and sea turtles on the beaches of Ossabaw.

Craig came and went, moving in and then out again. Luke foraged quietly on his own.

And Bob? Older and less fractious, we still walked the trails. He was helping his son Jon through journalism school and his son Mike through law school, and seeing his parents out of the world. Mike, at twenty-six, would be named County Judge in Casper, Wyoming, and thus become the youngest judge in the United States, and Jon would become a first-rate journalist—achievements Bob claims as his own claim on immortality.

I was traveling almost every month for the *Digest*, to gather material for a children's book and to speak to children, librarians and university

232

students. Whenever I found myself near one of the national footpaths on such a trip, I would take off a few days and walk. I decided that my feet would attend me to the grave. Both my parents were actively trotting down trails and over sidewalks in their eighties, and I now saw the trails into nature as a way of keeping mentally alert.

The day I flew home, after coming down from the John Muir Trail in Yosemite, I put in a call to Jack Macrae, the handsome nephew of Elliott Macrae, who was now president of E.P. Dutton. Years before, when he was an editor at Harper & Row, Jack and I had plans which never materialized for doing a walk book. When I raised the possibility of a book on our national footpaths, he said, "I like it. Come in. Let's talk."

The *American Walk Book,* as Jack promptly titled it, became the book of this, the post-crazy season. Twig and Craig, who were still trying to find a direction in life, worked on it—hiking, taking notes, making maps and sketches. My father and mother worked on it. I walked with them on the Florida Trail, taking notes as Dad talked about the flora and fauna around us. Bob worked on it. Not only did he walk with me, but he read four thousand pages of observations by hikers on the Appalachian Trail, covering the entire distance from Springer Mountain in Georgia to Mount Katahdin in Maine. He enjoyed every one of them, he said.

Returning from a trek on the Potomac Heritage Trail, I found a letter from Luke, who was majoring in nuclear physics at Reed.

"Dear Mom," he wrote. "I'm changing my major. I can't stay locked up in a lead lab with this destructive force. You brought me up wrong. I want to be out in the hills and mountains. So, guess what? I'm switching to biology."

"Dear Luke," I wrote back. "Welcome home. Get out on the Oregon Trail; note the trees, the birds, the people and the trail's history. John, Frank and I used to joke about inheriting a love-of-nature-gene from twelve generations of Craigheads. It's no joke."

The summer of '75, while I worked at the typewriter in my sun-porch, a young chipmunk thrust his nose out of his mother's den in the rock garden and glanced around. Since he was paler than most chipmunks, I could identify him quite readily and came to know him well.

He was in the midst of his crazy season. Each day he would leave his mother's den, traveling across the yard, with his tail up like a flag, to a den he was digging below the rock pile near the tool house. Most mammals get up and leave home, period; but this fellow came and went, carrying his cheek pouches bulging with the seeds he was carrying from his mother's pantry to his. Compared to the grizzly bear who runs her cubs up a tree and leaves them, or to the fox who turns on her young and drives them off the land, the chipmunk's dispersal was gentle, as befitting an animal that makes provision for the future.

After several mornings when the pale chipmunk did not appear, I walked to the toolshed to see if he had at last made it on his own. As I approached, he volley-balled across the yard and into his natal den. I was wondering if his mother would ever get rid of him when around the corner of the house came Jake Ehlers, Twig's escort to the high school junior prom. I had not seen him in years.

"I'm working my way home to St. Louis from Nantucket," he said. "I learned to shingle houses there." We both glanced at my house, the back bore shingles as black and crisp as burnt potato chips.

"There's a job for you," I said.

Jake took a book on carpentry from his pack and turned to a page of nineteenth-century Gothic houses, whose shingling featured fish scales, circles, triangles and walls-of-Troy designs. "Decorative shingling," he said. "I have always wanted to plan and execute walls like this; but on Nantucket no one will stand still for it."

I studied the book, and that day I drove around town, finding other examples of decorative shingling. I went to the library to read about it. "Next year's the Bicentennial," I told Jake, as we sat down to a meal of roast duck and corn-on-the-cob. "Your book says that decorative shingles are a celebration."

"They were first nailed up to celebrate the end of the corrupt Grant administration."

"So I can celebrate not only the Bicentennial but the end of the corrupt Nixon administration. The designs are symbolic?" Jake nodded.

"How about some purple-mountain majesty, some hip-hip-hooraying—something for the writers and poets; a line from Christina Rossetti, 'Does the hill wind upward all the way? Yes, to the very end.' "

"I can do it." He grinned, already planning. "How about your providing the materials, room and board and a small labor fee?"

We shook hands on it.

Jake moved into the Sioux Indian teepee Twig had lived in one summer on Antelope Flats—the Craigheads West, as the young people called the cabins at the foot of the Tetons. On her return, she and Luke had raised the structure on the side lawn for their guests. Jake now built a stone fireplace in the center, and on the sacred ground opposite the door he laid a shingle cut in the shape of a dancing figure.

The scaffolding went up the next day, and in a few weeks the mountain majesty and amber waves of grain were nailed in place. Jake was cutting Revolutionary cannonballs, one of his innovations, for the east side of the house when Twig got wind of the project and came up from the city to pry off old shingles.

From January to June Jake worked on another shingling job, and it was not until Craig graduated from college and came home that the enterprise went forward again. Between bouts of work on the house Craig drew biotic communities and maps for the *Walk Book*.

Luke, hearing the hammering and sawing over the telephone when I called one day, hitchhiked home from Portland to join in the work on the celebration.

As he came up the road to the house he picked up a baby robin that had fallen from its nest. He named it Rocket. Within two days it had taken the imprint of the shinglers and would sit high on the scaffolding with the industrious crew whom it had adopted as parents. And everyone was back on the payroll.

Craig came home one afternoon with a baby raccoon that had tumbled from a tree den after her mother had been killed by a car. We all fed Hands from a doll's bottle and in a few weeks she too was climbing the scaffolding to sit with the shinglers. The scene of the post-crazy season was complete.

In the midst of all this, a forceful image had taken possession of my mind.

The alpha male wolf of Sanctuary River is running over the tundra. His spindly legs move from the shoulders and hips, swift as a flashing light. The beta male barks to him, agitated. The attitude of the black wolf is strange. He suddenly gets to his feet, glances at the young alpha female, at the three pups and the six other supportive members of his group. Then he turns and runs, not stopping to investigate the urine on the willow at the border of his territory.

The beta barks again.

The black wolf does not bark back.

Over the next year, that image came and went.

On a hot August day, when the hammers were drumming, the jigsaw screaming and the robin chirping, I picked up the telephone and dialed my parents' number. "Once you held the telephone out the window to let me hear the sound of a hundred-mile-an-hour hurricane," I told my father. "Now you are going to hear the sound of the Bicentennial." I thrust the phone out the kitchen window and the cacophony of industry cannonaded all the way to Florida.

"Like it?" I asked.

"Someone's not working," quipped the alpha of the work ethic. "You and me," I said. "Get off the phone."

The shingling was finished the autumn of '76 when Jake nailed up the hip-hip-hooraying design—little men and women with arms and legs outstretched, making Whoopie. He centered them high in the peak at the back of the house. I brought out the wine, the roast beef, the bread, salads, pies and casseroles, and called in neighbors and friends to celebrate with a special toast to the Reverend Alexander Craighead, who had preached revolution for Americans.

The day before Luke returned to college, he and I sat down at the outdoor table with Jill, the Airedale, the raccoon and the robin, to admire the house. The mountains *were* majestic, the celebrants joyous; the hills did go upward all the way.

Rocket took off from the apple tree, aimed for Luke's shoulder swooping low over Jill. She reacted to her breeding, jumped, slammed her teeth shut; and the bird was dead.

"No!" Luke cried out; but it was too late. "So that's how it is," he said. "Alive one moment; then nothing." Slowly he picked up the feathered body and walked toward the garden.

I saw the black wolf splashing along the edge of Sanctuary River; his huge feet left prints in the soft silt. They were the size of a man's palm.

That year, the Governor of Florida and the commissioners of Collier County declared November 16 to be "Frank C. Craighead, Sr. Day," in recognition of Dad's fight to preserve the environment of subtropical Florida. When John, Frank, Es, Margaret and I convened to celebrate our father's lifework, John left a note on Mother's pillow. "You should be celebrated, too. You've been a great mother and wife."

She laughed it off. "I've done nothing," she said. And I knew where three generations of female insecurity had come from.

I saw the black alpha flick his wrists, then swing around to bite a flea that was burrowing into his rump. He smelled the grass and lay down. Again, the image faded.

I moved Mother and Dad to their condominium in Naples when they were both eighty-eight. Dad's health was deteriorating rapidly; but he made it to his new home by the cypress forest. Upon moving in he walked into his sunny bedroom and slept for an entire day. Mother, although alert and in excellent health, was frightened. She was far from the security of their friends at the retirement village. To move at eighty-eight is a traumatic event.

"What am I going to do?" she asked as we unpacked books. "We're all alone here. How will I get to stores and the doctors? I'm not going to be permitted to drive much longer."

"The neighbors will take you."

"What neighbors? The people who own all the other apartments are Northerners. They come south for only a few months each year."

She was voicing my deepest fears. I was alarmed by the empty apartment, the lack of public transportation, Dad's health. I should stay. I should remain with these old parents and help them over that last mile with dignity.

We hung up the landscapes my mother had painted of the Everglade habitats—the alligator holes, sawgrass prairies, hammocks, pine woodlands. Mother had taken up oil painting in her seventies to pass the time while she waited for Dad to hike the back country to take notes and collect plants. She had made many adjustments in their lifetime together, and yet had maintained her own spirit: going to parties alone when he refused to socialize, defying him when he asked her to type and be his secretary.

I saw the black wolf. He was lying on his belly, his yellow eyes watching a ptarmigan as it crossed the newly fallen snow. His head was on his paws and he was no longer attuned to the vast valley where the moose and caribou had been his life. He was a lone wolf, hungrily watching a feeble bird.

Craig came home from Alaska. Twig and I photographed and put together another series of filmstrips, this time on endangered species and on human efforts to save them from extinction. Luke was in the White Mountains of California, studying Rocky Mountain sheep for the Forest Service.

I was ready to start a new book.

"Crows?" I asked myself. "Is it time to delve into the mystique and intelligence of those great communicating birds? Is it time to speak of vindictive crows who punish their own and who mourn their dead?" Yes, I answered.

I returned to Florida. Dad was in the hospital, weak and confused. Mother was thin and exhausted with tending him. As she and I inspected nursing homes, an awesome sadness tightened the muscles of my throat and neck.

Dad came home from the hospital.

"Jean," he said one day in a moment of clarity, "I want to show you something." He reached for his cane, picked up the machete he still kept and, taking a wide stance to balance himself, led me outside. I followed him across the parking lot to the damp wall of vines that wove themselves in and out of the forest edge. With a firm sweep of his arm he slashed a vine and I looked into a greenhouse of trees, ferns and airplants. A well-used trail led off into the blue-green jungle.

"Where did this trail come from?"

"I cut it. There's about a mile of it." I spun around to look at the frail old man with his wobbly knees and swollen ankles. A flame was in his eyes. He was seeing something, as clearly as I saw the wolf.

"Let's go back. You're tired."

He rose, tied to the forest by invisible threads of knowledge that were breaking. He fought to tie them back in place. Supporting himself, tree by tree, he led me through cascades of ferns to a huge cypress. He stopped and whacked down a Brazilian holly tree.

"Rotten plants," he said. "They're destroying Florida." As the tree fell, I saw we were in a moist grove of live oaks where orchids dripped from broad limbs, frogs piped and birds screamed. "This is the new lab," he said. "High school students will come here. They can study the changes that are taking place across the Florida landscape right here. It's all happening in this lab; falling water tables, saline seepage, foreign plants swarming into dry niches; armadillo and raccoon populations exploding, wood storks and tree snails becoming rare."

We circled back along the trail.

"I'm worried about the pills I am taking," he said. "I think they're poison."

I led Dad home, still not facing reality of his aging. He still made sense. He still remembered the scientific names of plants.

The lone wolf was eating the ptarmigan. His senses were tied to the cool wind that was coming up the valley bringing snow. The ravens announced the spot where the pack had made a kill, but this did not arouse him. A snowy owl, down from Barrow, floated to the limb of a spruce tree; he was white like a break in the shadows.

It is summer—Twig needs tending and confidence. She and I have planned a trip to Alaska, to the Katmai National Monument where the brown grizzly bears gather to catch salmon along the rollicking Brooks River that connects Brooks Lake with Lake Naknek. Luke, now an accomplished naturalist, is free to join us.

On a clear July day we set down on the cobalt water of Lake Naknek near the mouth of the Brooks River. No roads lead to this national monument, which includes the Valley of Ten Thousand Smokes—the first volcanic eruption to be studied by modern science. Around the lake the black and the white spruces of the north are like great pencils, gnawed by wind and ice. Above them rise the Aleutian Mountains, sharp, crystalline and snow-covered. Wind-curried clouds work themselves into the valleys and across their stone faces.

"This is the most beautiful place I've ever seen," says Twig as we splash ashore.

"Stop where you are," barks a lean park ranger. "I want to talk to you. The campground where you are going is in the midst of bear country."

"I'm scared stiff of them," she replies, and is still.

"Bears will be passing around you on their way to Brooks Falls. The salmon are running. They stack up at the falls before leaping up it. The bears congregate to catch the fish. But they have a cosmopolitan appetite. They like all the tastes we like.

"Put all your food, garbage, lipstick, chewing gum in that cache there." He points to a small log cabin on twenty-foot poles in the center of the primitive campground consisting of many tents, several lean-tos, two outhouses and one water faucet.

"You get to the cache by climbing that ladder on the ground. Take it down when you're done. Big grizzlies can't climb, little ones can. And they're not so little, three hundred pounds."

The water laps softly on the shore. A bald eagle soars into view. Out in the lake, just beyond the ranger's head, a grizzly brown bear swims, snorkeling for the salmon that are crossing the lake to the Brooks River.

"Pay attention," the ranger admonishes me. "This is important. If you meet a bear on the trail and he says 'woof,' don't say 'woof' back, although it sounds cute. The bear is challenging you. If you 'woof' back you are accepting his challenge. He'll charge.

"And don't turn and run. That's a signal for the bear to chase you. When you meet a bear on the trail, back up. Put your head down low against your shoulder, thus." He demonstrates. "That means you're a submissive bear; a lowly, humble bear.

"And leave no garbage." He glances from one of us to the other, then strides off through the woods to his bear-proof cabin, leaving us to the darkness.

Twig and I lie wide awake in our mountain tent, listening for the shuffle of grizzly feet along the bear trail not too far from our tent. I hear Luke tossing in his sleeping bag and wonder what he is thinking.

"Terrible endings for bear books," Luke explains the next morning.

Around 5:00 A.M., Twig and I crawl out into the mists of dawn and build a crackling fire. The flames shoot high, burning holes in the gauze, telling the bears—we hope—to stay back in the taiga. We wash in the icy lake, fill the pot for coffee and take into ourselves the smell and the beauty of Alaska.

Out of the fog comes a huge brown bear.

We back up, tuck our heads to our shoulders, and zip backward to the fire.

The Katmai bears are not fishing the Brooks River in as great numbers as we had anticipated. But we go on seeing them. They plod through a camp run by the airlines. They crash through the woods, swim the river and lakes, romp the river bank and belly-flop into salmon pools.

In an opening in the aspens we watch a female and her cub shoulder-deep in a clear pool of Margot River as she leaps, pounces and catches a salmon.

At Brooks Falls, where Luke is fishing I watch as he puts an artificial salmon egg on his hook.

"Why a salmon egg? Why one of his kind?" I ask.

"The individual," he tells me, "is not interested in saving his species. He is only interested in his own genes. The salmon strikes at the eggs of any other salmon to make room for his own offspring.

"And that," he tells me, "explains just about everything, except altruism and the Golden Rule." He casts his line. "Or maybe it explains those, too, if you think about it hard enough."

The black wolf is still lying under the twisted spruce where he has slept for three days. His nose is covered by the tip of his full tail. He lifts his head and then curls tight.

I returned to Florida for Christmas. As I looked across the table, I knew this would be my last Christmas at home with Dad.

John and Mother had put him in the nursing home before I came down for her ninetieth birthday. He found the home "very interesting. There are some unusual animals here," he said. "There's a grasshopper; and one I'll have to have identified."

I left Florida for Knab, Utah, where Frank and Es were vacationing in the bright warmth of the canyonlands. Esther had lung cancer, and no operation or chemotherapy could help. Each day I sat and talked to her until she fell asleep; then Frank and I walked across the countryside. Not far from Knab ran the Colorado River, along which Luke and I had rafted through the Grand Canyon. The land around it, like the canyon itself, humbled even death.

"I have often wondered," I said one day, "if when the chips are down, we Craigheads would really find a peace of mind in nature."

He said, "The answer is yes."

I went on: "These rocks under my feet, the sage and creosote bush, the distant cliffs, have let me accept Esther's death. The pain inside me has stopped."

The wolf awakes and gets to his feet. He is lean, his once loose and lustrous fur is clumped in dull bunches. The yellow eyes are cloudy. The old alpha limps stiffly as he walks deeper into the forest, following the trail of a snowshoe hare. He passes the animal by and trots to the top of the ridge. He blinks at the blue-gray sky, then, circling to the right, to the left, he stamps out a cup in the snow and lies down again.

An assignment from Andy took me to Ely, Minnesota, where David Mech was in charge of research on the wolf for the Fish and Wildlife Service's Endangered Species Bureau, using radio-tracking techniques. On the second day at Ely, I flew over wolf country in a Piper Cub with earphones on my head. A small black box in my lap tuned me in to the beeps from the radios worn by the wolves. The pilot had located the alpha male wolf of a lake land pack. He pointed, and I looked down on a trotting figure coming home to his family. Three pups ran out to greet him with leaps and chin kisses. The alpha female hung back among the spruce trees. From the air the wolves seemed tied by invisible but unmistakable threads to the cliff, lake, birds, deer and beaver. They were one with the earth below and with me.

That evening, sitting on the river dock Mech pointed to a spruce-filled area, a wolf no-man's-land or corridor, where a young female crouched. She was waiting to be invited into a pack. The greenery bristled with suspense.

"How do old wolves die?" I suddenly asked.

"They sleep more and more, curl tighter and tighter until they expire."

The black wolf on the ridge above Sanctuary River vanishes into the snow, giving nourishment to the ravens and jays and foxes. I cannot see him anymore.

I returned to my typewriter.

Craig came home from Alaska to live and work on a neighboring farm while he talked to a therapist, hoping to find what he wanted to do with his life. On a breezy spring day he walked into the house and sat down in the bentwood rocker. Sensing a crisis, I pushed back the typewriter table and joined him.

"I need your help," he said, and I heard again his voice on the phone from Miami. I stuffed my hands in my pockets and sat down on the couch.

242

"I'll have to move back home to get started." The pale chipmunk dived into his maternal den. "It'll take time to make money at it; so I'll chop and sell firewood like I did last winter."

"Yes?"

"I want to be a writer."

I bit my lip. "It's okay to come home," I said.

"It's not Oedipal. It's education and economics."

The ridge where the old wolf had lain faded from my mind and in its place I discovered the meadows at Craigheads where I had written poetry, the newspaper offices, the red pencil marks on manuscripts, the voices of the critics and the supporters, the successes and failures; the hill going upward all the way. I sat in silence.

"Will you help?" Skunks and raccoons ran up a wooded hill while Charlie, Otus and New York flew overhead. I scrambled up it to the den of the wolves, to the snowfields of the mountain goat. For Twig, Craig, Luke, my father, my mother, the uphill journey was the same.

"Will you?"

"Yes," I answered at last. "I will."

Although the children are gone again I awoke last night at 2:00 A.M., paused in the upstairs hall listening, then came downstairs and curled up on the couch. I closed my eyes and hugged my knees and was back in the house at Craigheads.

I am twelve years old and in the Victorian living room hugging my knees with my eyes closed. The house is deserted but for my cousin Sam and myself. He and I have stayed home from the farmers' market to play our string game.

"When the clock strikes ten," he instructs, "follow the string to the end." He places one end of the cord in my hand and steals off.

The clock strikes ten. I open my eyes, jump to the floor and begin to wind in the cord shivering with excitement. This can be a funny or frightening game; the string can lead you anywhere.

I am led three times around the newel post in the foyer, out the front door, around the maple to the falcon sitting on his perch. He calls plaintively. I climb through the kitchen window and go down the cellar steps. I run because the cellar is dangerous. We are warned not to come here. Homemade beer is stored on the shelves and occasionally a bottle explodes and shatters glasslike shrapnel. I dash up the cellar steps that lead to the yard and crawl through the hollyhocks.

"Not the briars, Sam," I plead. He is at the boat landing fishing and watching me out of the corner of his eye.

I manage the briars with a few scratches, then cross the lawn to the apple tree. I climb it to a limb, and balancing as I walk, I go down it, and into the house through the parlor window.

A note on the string says, "Feed the owl." I am led into a pantry where I find a disemboweled mouse on a string. I feed the owl.

Winding swiftly I run toward the creek. Suddenly I am embarrassed. I am too old for this. But I cannot stop. I wind around the sycamore tree, climb up the swinging rope to a limb and come down on the board steps nailed to the tree.

I am back in the kitchen and the ball has grown large. I am nearing the end of the game and these games have to end with a surprise, usually scary; at the beehive, in the bullpen with the bull, on the roof.

The string leads to the front door and I am surprised. It goes through the keyhole. The rules are that you have to stay with the string.

Now what do I do?

The telephone rang at that point and I jumped from the couch to answer it. Luke was calling from the University of New Mexico where he is getting his master's degree to tell me about a headstand beetle that shoots hot chemicals at its enemies.

It rang again. Kathy called to remind me of our talk-fest luncheon date with Gretchen at noon. The phone rang again. Mother asked me to purchase blank cards so she could begin making her annual hand-painted Christmas cards. Bob called asking me to check out the flashlights for a canoe trip we have planned. And so it wasn't until after I fed the black-billed cuckoo that was recovering from an injury that I finally asked myself.

"Just how did I solve that string game?"

But the sun was up and I walked outside to admire the flaming autumn leaves.